THE ENCYCLOPEDIA OF THE
Environment

CONSULTANT

Stephen R. Kellert, Ph.D.
School of Forestry and Environmental Studies
Yale University

GENERAL EDITOR

Matthew Black, M.E.S.
Director of School Programs
New Canaan Nature Center

ADVISORS

Marilee Foglesong, M.L.S.
Former Young Adult Coordinator
New York Public Library

John T. Tanacredi, Ph.D.
Supervisory Ecologist
U.S. Department of the Interior
National Park Service

THE ENCYCLOPEDIA OF THE
Environment

Consultant

Stephen R. Kellert, Ph.D.
School of Forestry and Environmental Studies
Yale University

General Editor

Matthew Black, M.E.S.
Director of School Programs
New Canaan Nature Center

Franklin Watts
A Division of Grolier Publishing
New York London Hong Kong Sydney
Danbury, Connecticut

DEVELOPED, DESIGNED, AND PRODUCED BY
BOOK BUILDERS INCORPORATED

Photographs ©: The National Audubon Society Collection/Photo Researchers, Inc.: Tom & Pat Leeson, cover (tr1), 99, 120; Jan Halaska, cover (tr2); Mark Newman, cover (br1); Douglas Faulkner, cover (br2), 75, 80; Tom McHugh, cover (ct), 88; Charles V. Angelo, cover (cm); Eric Haucke (cb), 29, 74; Tim Davis, 9, 62, 78, 103, 134; Rod Planck, 12, 32; Dan Guravich, 14; Michael Giannechini, 17 (b), 137; Alan & Sandy Carey, 24; Kenneth Edward, 34; Renee Lynn, 38, 113; Joyce Photographic, 42; Lee F. Snyder, 44; Bruce Brander, 47; Alan D. Carey, 48; Ronny Jaques, 50 (t); Jacques Jangoux, 51; Dean Krakel II, 55; Joe Rychetnik, 56; Jeff Greenberg, 59; Jerry L. Ferrara, 61, 135; David R. Frazier, 81; Jeff Lepore, 82, 90, 95, 107, 131, 148; Gary Retherford, 84 (t); Kjell B. Sandved, 84 (b); Jim Steinberg, 87; Jim Haswell, 91; Raven/Explorer, 96; Wesley Bocxe, 97; Craig K. Lorenz, 102, 104; Darwin Dale, 108 (t); Dr. Paul A. Zahl, 108 (b); Richard Parker, 110; Stephen Dalton, 114; Bill Bachman, 115; Gregory G. Dimijian, 117; Andrew G. Wood, 121; M.H. Sharp, 128; John & Maria Kaprielian, 139; Francois Gohier, 146; Dan Sudia, 149. **The Science Source/Photo Researchers, Inc.:** John Wells, cover (c); Andrew Syred, 17 (t); Don Getsug, 50 (b); Lowell Georgia, 70; Phil Farnes, 77; Francois Gohier, 140. **U.S. Fish & Wildlife Service:** Dave Clendenen, cover (bl), 27. Cover design by Ann Antoshak for BBI. Illustrations by Tilman Reitzle and Sherry Williams for BBI.

Every endeavor has been made to obtain permission to use copyrighted material. The publishers would appreciate errors or omissions being brought to their attention.

Visit Franklin Watts on the Internet at
http://publishing.grolier.com

Library of Congress Cataloging-in-Publication Data

The encyclopedia of the environment / edited by Stephen R. Kellert
and Matthew Black.
     p. cm.
     Includes bibliographical references and index.
     Summary: Provides basic information about such topics in the
environmental sciences as rain forests, savannas, sewage and sewage treatment, topography, troposphere, and more.
     ISBN 0–531–11709–X
     1. Environmental sciences Encyclopedias, Juvenile.
[1. Environmental sciences Encyclopedias.]   I. Kellert. Stephen R.
II. Black, Matthew, naturalist.
GE 10.E533   1999
333.7'03—dc21
                                99–25843
                                  CIP

GROLIER
EDUCATIONAL   1 2 3 4 5 6 7 8 9 10 R 08 07 06 05 04 03 02 01 00 99

Contents

Preface

THE SCIENCE FICTION WRITER H. G. Wells once wrote: "Human history becomes more and more a race between education and catastrophe." My experiences in the study of the environment have led me to similar conclusions. The history of the environment, especially in the last few decades, has been a story of tragedies versus the human desire to achieve greatness. To put it another way, the more I learn as a student of environment, the more dramatic news I hear—both good and bad.

I always prefer to hear the bad news first. The bad news about the environment is that never in history has the natural world been under such pressure from so many threats. As our population passes 5.5 billion and keeps on growing, we are doing more damage to other forms of life—as well as to the air, water, and earth we depend on for our survival and well-being—than ever before. Forests, deserts, and prairies shrink and disappear as we take huge amounts of space, energy, and resources for ourselves, leaving less for other creatures. Oceans, lakes, and the air we breathe become degraded as the waste products of our economies continue to pollute our atmosphere.

Worst of all, the many living things with whom we share our planet are disappearing rapidly, perhaps as quickly as three species per hour. We mourned the death of the last, lonely passenger pigeon, a female named Martha, at the Cincinnati Zoo in 1914. We also have seen the last of three subspecies of tiger, the huge moa from New Zealand, and the heath hen from Martha's Vineyard. Can the right whale, or African elephant, or harpy eagle, or giant panda be far behind? How will we feel when the last cheetah disappears? It's harder for us to grasp the extinction of the thousands of species we have never heard about, some of which may not even have been discovered or named yet—the insects, amphibians, fungi, corals, fish, plants, and other living things that disappear each year. These are the species that we may miss most in the future, especially if their loss changes the earth in ways we cannot yet imagine. Pollution can be cleaned up and forests can grow back, but extinction is forever.

The stories of many of these species, both the well-known and the unknown, are chronicled in this encyclopedia. Ultimately, it's our story, too. Will the loss of species continue until whole ecosystems collapse, or will we figure out a way to keep so many animals and plants from disappearing? Because the mass extinction we are living through now is arguably the biggest environmental problem we face, and because most people know very little about it, it receives a great deal of attention in the *Encyclopedia of the Environment*.

This brings us to the good news. We can turn it around. What I have learned as I've studied the environment is that people can do incredible things. People such as John Muir, Aldo Leopold, Jane Goodall, and Jacques Cousteau show how much people can achieve if they work hard to protect and conserve life on the earth. In the United States, the peregrine falcon has almost recovered from near-extinction since Rachel Carson's book *Silent Spring* (1962) led to a ban on the use of the chemical pesticide DDT in the United States in 1972. The hard work of people around the world has helped many other species, from American alligators and black-footed ferrets to white rhinoceroses and gray whales, to recover at least partially. Even as natural habitat is destroyed, other areas are being protected through the efforts of numerous communities and conservation organizations. As chemical pollution damages the atmosphere, thousands of people are working worldwide to clean up our air and water.

There are many more individuals out there with the potential to make a difference. As an environmental educator, I teach students almost every day, and all of them know more about wildlife and the environment than I did when I was their age. This, to me, is the best news of all. For every one of the heroes and heroines in environmental history mentioned above, there are hundreds or thousands of young people with the knowledge, interest, and commitment to carry on their good work. This book is intended to help these young people start to gather the knowledge they'll need along the way. If the history of the environment teaches us anything, it teaches us that people can do great things. As the anthropologist Margaret Mead said, "Never doubt that a small group of thoughtful, committed citizens can change the world; indeed, it's the only thing that ever has."

ACKNOWLEDGMENTS

I would like to thank the many people associated with Book Builders Incorporated, including the writers, editors, and artists who did such an excellent job on this project. I'm particularly grateful to Elizabeth Dooher, BBI's editorial director, and Lauren Fedorko, the president of BBI, for all the hard work that made this encyclopedia possible. I would especially like to thank the people in my family who have always helped me: my parents, Henry and Hallie Black, who cultivated my passion for the natural world, my interest in science, and my balanced view of the world; and my wife Becky Bleifeld Black, who time and time again supports my desire to continue to do what I always wanted to do. Most of all, I'd like to thank the two people who most inspired this book: Steve Kellert, my mentor and friend, to whom I credit my understanding of our place as humans in the natural world; and my younger sister, Dana Black, who is the reason why I have so much faith in young people.

MATTHEW BLACK

How to Use This Book

The Encyclopedia of the Environment contains basic and timely information on more than 300 entries on a variety of environmental topics, arranged from A to Z. Many entries contain cross-references, indicated by small capital letters. Located within the text and at the end of each entry, the cross-references direct readers to related topics in other entries. The encyclopedia also contains a number of "blind entries," which identify another entry in which a topic is fully discussed.

Scattered throughout the encyclopedia are more than 100 colorful photographs and illustrations—including maps, graphs, and charts—with some accompanied by a caption. At the end of the encyclopedia are a selected bibliography of other books and a list of organizations and sources of information on environmental issues.

The Encyclopedia contains four types of features, each of which is identified by a distinguishing icon, or design symbol, that appears at the top of the feature as well as within the related portion of the entry text.

☑ **Keywords**

Global warming. A general increase in temperatures worldwide.

Microorganism. A living thing so small it can only be seen with a microscope.

☑ **"Keywords"** contains important vocabulary words and their definitions. Marked keywords are defined in a feature box someplace within each chapter, or letter of the alphabet.

※ **"Fast Facts"** highlights particularly interesting facts and data.

See also

WHALES

Many species of whale have the ability to leap far out of the water.

grows almost eight feet (2.4 m) straight out from its head, and the beluga, a white whale with a large rounded forehead. Belugas that live in the St. Lawrence region of eastern Canada have been found to have high levels of toxic chemicals in their bodies, and scientists believe that OCEAN POLLUTION has harmed many of these whales. Toothed whales actively hunt fish, squid, and other prey. The familiar black-and-white killer whales, also called orcas, hunt animals as big as sea lions and penguins.

There are about ten species of baleen whales. Although they feed only on relatively small organisms, some baleen whales grow quite large, such as the endangered blue whale. The baleen plates are made up of a material called keratin—the same substance that is in human hair and fingernails and a RHINOCEROS's horn. These flexible baleen plates hang down from the inside of the whales' upper lip, filtering plankton as the whales swim slowly through the water with their mouth open.

Whales are found in all the world's oceans and even in a few rivers. The pink river dolphin, for example, lives in the Amazon and other rivers of South America. Many whales live and migrate in well-organized social groups, called pods. Some species, such as the gray whale, migrate thousands of miles each year from feeding grounds in the Northern Hemisphere to breeding and calving grounds in the Southern

🐾 **Endangered Species**

Blue Whale. The largest species of whale and the largest creature ever to inhabit the earth, the blue whale can grow to 100 feet (30 m) in length and weight as much as 300,000 pounds (136,000 kg). Blue whales live in all the earth's oceans. Most populations of blue whales migrate from the tropics in the winter to the edges of ice in the northern and southern hemispheres in the summer. Blue whales were nearly hunted to extinction for their oil, meat, and other products. Although protected by law, they are still a threatened species.

※ **Fast Facts**

In the humpback whales, the color patterns on the undersides of the tails are unique to each individual. Each pattern is like a person's fingerprint; no two are exactly alike. Scientists studying humpback whales photograph the undersides of the tails and use the photos to identify the individual animals in a group.

Hemisphere. Whales have excellent hearing, and they can produce sounds underwater. ※ Humpback whales produce sounds in a certain order, much like a song, which they repeat. These "songs" can last 20 minutes, and they are usually sung in the winter mating grounds. All of the whales in a migrating group sing almost the same song, which changes progressively from year to year.

Humans have hunted whales for centuries. In the 1800s, a huge whaling industry killed whales to provide oil for lamps and spermaceti, a thick liquid that was used to make fine candles. Though most large whales are now scarce and many species are protected by law, whales are still killed for their meat by Native Americans and by several nations.

WILDERNESS

An area where the earth and its ECOSYSTEMS are undisturbed by man. It is difficult to find a place that has not been changed in some way by humans. Even the barren ICE of the ARCTIC and ANTARCTICA bears evidence of humans. Today, there probably is no true wilderness left anywhere on the planet.

Wilderness areas provide HABITATS for wild animals and plants and protect the country's natural resources, such as water and soil. Henry David Thoreau's famous words, "in wildness is the preservation of the world," express the tremendous emotional, intellectual, and spiritual value of wild lands.

WILDLIFE MANAGEMENT

Managing and protecting the health, population, and environment of wild animals and their ECOSYSTEMS. In the United States, the U.S. FISH AND WILDLIFE SERVICE and similar state agencies govern wildlife management. These agencies enforce national, state, and local laws that concern wildlife.

During the 1960s, CONSERVATION an important focus of wildlife management. In 1964, the U.S. Congress passed two laws—the Wilderness Act and the Water Conservation Fund Act—to protect the forest lands where many wild animals and plants live. The Endangered Species Act, passed in 1973, was also aimed at stopping the rapid loss of plant and animal life. In addition to government agencies, many other organizations help to manage the nation's wildlife by teaching about wildlife issues, threats to particular animals or areas of wilderness, and how they can live in harmony with wildlife. [*See also* WILDLIFE REFUGES .]

WILDLIFE REFUGES

Areas of land set aside for the protection and preservation of wild animals. In 1908 President Theodore Roosevelt realized the importance of protecting wildlife and set up the nation's system of NATIONAL PARKS, NATIONAL FORESTS, and WILDLIFE REFUGES or reserves. Though

🐾 **Profile: Robert Marshall**

A founder of the Wilderness Society, Robert Marshall (1901–1939) was a research forester with the U.S. Forest Service in Montana from 1925 to 1928. During the mid-1930s, Marshall conducted a personal inventory of the largest remaining roadless areas in the country. He found 48 forested areas of more than 300,000 acres (121, 000 ha) and 29 desert areas larger than 500,000 acres (202, 000 ha). His purpose was to draw attention to the vanishing wilderness and to encourage efforts to preserve the largest remaining places. The Bob Marshall Wilderness Area in Montana, named after Robert Marshall, covers nearly 1.1 million acres (445, 000 ha) of mountain wilderness. It is usually called "The Bob."

Cross-Reference

🐾 **"Endangered Species"** provides a look at animals and plants that are considered endangered or threatened.

Feature icon

🐾 **"Profile"** offers short biographies of people in environmental and related fields.

A

ACID RAIN

Rain that mixes with SULFUR DIOXIDE and NITROGEN oxide in the atmosphere. Sulfur dioxide is released into the atmosphere when power plants and furnaces burn FOSSIL FUELS that contain sulfur, such as coal and oil. Nitrogen oxides come mainly from the exhausts of motor vehicles. These substances combine with water in the atmosphere to form strong acids. Rain is normally slightly acidic (like lemon juice or vinegar), but when it becomes too acidic, it becomes harmful. Acid rain can be harmful to forests, soil, crops, drinking water, and fish. It can even damage buildings and statues, causing the stone in them to dissolve. All forms of PRECIPITATION can be acidic, including snow, sleet, and fog as well as rain.

Acid rain is not limited to areas with heavy industry. Acid-producing pollutants can be carried hundreds of miles by the wind. That means that damage from acid rain can occur far from the source of the pollution. Since most acid rain comes from the activities of humans, there are also ways humans can control it. These include reducing the amount of nitrogen oxides emitted from smokestacks, burning low-sulfur oil and coal, and adding special devices called catalytic converters to automobile exhausts to reduce pollutants. Another way to reduce acid rain is through ENERGY CONSERVATION. [*See also* AIR POLLUTION.]

ADAPTATION

The ability of an organism to adapt, or adjust, to its environment. All living things must be able to adapt to a particular environment and adjust to environmental changes in order to survive. For example, they must be able to find food, shelter, and water, and defend themselves against other animals. Human beings are able to live in many different climates. If people move from one climate to another, they adapt to the new conditions. FISH must live in water. Yet within that environment there are variations in temperature, plant life, and salinity (saltiness). To survive, fish must adapt to these various environments as well. Organisms that make the necessary adaptations are the ones most likely to survive and have offspring that also are fit to survive. Organisms that do not adapt may die out. [*See also* BIOLOGICAL DIVERSITY; EVOLUTION; EXTINCTION; MASS EXTINCTION; SPECIES LOSS.]

AEROSOLS

(*See* CHLOROFLUOROCARBONS, CFCs)

AFRICA

The second largest continent on earth, making up about one-fifth of the planet's total landmass. Africa is a very diverse land covered by DESERTS, FORESTS, and GRASSLANDS. Deserts cover about two-fifths of the continent. One, the Sahara, is the largest desert in the world. Two other large deserts are the Namib and the Kalahari.

South of the Sahara lie large areas of grasslands (called savannas). Africa's savannas are covered with tall grasses, scattered trees, and

 Endangered Species: Slender-Horned Gazelle

The slender-horned gazelle inhabits dry regions and grasslands in northern Africa, from Egypt to Algeria. Both the adult males and females have long, slightly curved horns. These graceful antelope have been hunted excessively by humans and face competition for habitat from domestic livestock, farmers, and development.

The elephant is the largest animal species in Africa.

shrubs. Forests cover about one-fifth of Africa. They are mostly tropical RAIN FORESTS.

Plant and animal life in Africa is diverse, with thousands of different species of MAMMALS, BIRDS, REPTILES, INSECTS, and others. Huge herds of grazing animals, including giraffes, antelopes, ELEPHANTS, and zebras, feed on the savannas. These herds attract large CARNIVORES, such as LIONS and hyenas. Among the animals that live along Africa's tropical rivers and swamps are the crocodile and the hippopotamus, as well as many large and colorful birds.

Many of Africa's animals are ENDANGERED SPECIES. Some have been overhunted by humans. The spread of farms and cities has also destroyed much of the natural environment of many species. [*See also* BIOLOGICAL DIVERSITY; BIOME; HABITAT LOSS AND CONSERVATION.]

AGRICULTURAL POLLUTION

Wastes caused by chemicals and soil RUNOFF in farming activities. Agricultural pollution is caused mainly by excess PESTICIDES and HERBICIDES getting into soil and water. Large farms use a lot of chemicals to control pests and stimulate the growth of crops. When it rains, the water carries these chemicals in runoff to nearby streams and rivers. These pollutants can damage AQUATIC HABITATS and cause serious problems with SURFACE WATER waterways and with GROUND WATER supplies. [*See also* FACTORY FARMS; SOIL CONSERVATION.]

AIR POLLUTION

The act of making the air dirty with pollutants, such as vehicle exhaust, smoke, and chemicals. There are many harmful effects from polluted air. It can affect the health of people or animals. It can harm plants and even damage the outsides of buildings. Monuments and statues that stood for thousands of years have been ruined by a type of air pollution called ACID RAIN.

Most air pollution comes from the burning of FOSSIL FUELS, such as coal and oil. Emissions from vehicles, heating furnaces, and industrial burning contribute to air pollution. Some businesses discharge dangerous chemicals, such as lead and mercury, into the air as part of the process of manufacturing. Burning

A

solid waste, such as garbage, grass clippings, and leaves, also adds to air pollution as do chemical sprays.

SMOG is a common kind of air pollution. It develops when sunlight acts on exhausts from vehicles and factories, and there is not enough wind to disperse, or scatter, it into the air. Chemicals in the smog may cause headaches, burning eyes, and respiratory problems. If the smog is very bad, it can even kill people, animals, and plants. A weather condition called a thermal inversion results when a layer of warm air is over a layer of cooler air near the ground. (The word "thermal" means "heated.") The warm air traps pollutants, keeping them from rising and being blown away.

Other causes of air pollution include natural sources. Cattle, for example, produce and release METHANE, an odorless gas. Smoke from volcanic eruptions and forest fires send particulates into the air, where winds can carry them halfway around the world.

International, national, state, and local government efforts are necessary to reduce air pollution. Local governments limit or ban the burning of leaves and garbage. States set up long-range plans to reduce the use of gasoline-powered vehicles or pass laws requiring cleaner emissions from vehicles.

National governments pass clean air laws. In the United States, the Clean Air Act of 1972 set initial limits on the amount of pollutants that could be released by vehicles and industries. The ENVIRONMENTAL PROTECTION AGENCY (EPA) carries out such laws, working with state and local governments to reduce pollution.

International efforts to reduce pollution started with the recognition that what affects one part of the world affects the whole planet. In 1970, many nations signed a treaty called the Montreal Protocol, in which they agreed to reduce the production of chemical compounds called CHLOROFLUOROCARBONS. [See also ALTERNATIVE ENERGY SOURCES; GLOBAL CLIMATE CHANGE; OZONE LAYER; WASTE, SOLID.]

ALGAE

Simple plantlike organisms that live in freshwater or saltwater and other damp environments. There are over 20,000 SPECIES of algae found all over the world. Algae may float along the surface of the water or cling to rocks and shells.

Some algae grow on the backs of turtles and other animals, while other varieties grow in the intestines of MAMMALS, including humans. Seaweeds are a form of algae.

Algae contain *chlorophyll*, a natural green pigment that helps plants produce food through the process of PHOTOSYNTHESIS. Sometimes the green chlorophyll is masked by other colored pigments, which cause the algae to display different colors.

There are four main types of algae, which are grouped according to their color: blue-green, green, red, and brown. Blue-green algae, the simplest form of the plant, form slimy growths on lakes and ponds, fish tanks, or the sides and bottoms of swimming pools. Brown algae make up the largest algae plants, a type of seaweed known as kelp. Kelp and other seaweeds are the most complex forms of algae.

Either directly or indirectly, algae are the only source of food for water animals and fishes. Certain varieties of algae, mostly seaweeds, are eaten by humans. Algae is used in the production of a number of useful products, such as fertilizer and ice cream.

Overgrowth of algae can occur when pollutants enter the water. Such overgrowth can crowd out other plant species and upset the ecological balance of an entire BIOLOGICAL COMMUNITY.

ALTERNATIVE ENERGY SOURCES

Various ways to produce energy without burning FOSSIL FUELS such as oil or coal. Since the 1970s, AIR POLLUTION has become a growing problem throughout the world. As a result, many people have become more and more interested in discovering alternative ways to produce energy that do not require oil or coal. These alternative energy sources range from natural gas to windmills.

Some alternative sources of energy, such as ethanol or natural gas, are also fuels that burn. However, these fuels produce fewer pollutants than oil or coal. Other alternative energy sources may not burn at all. For example, SOLAR ENERGY uses the power of the sun. Windmills capture the energy of the wind. Other alternative energy sources include GEOTHERMAL ENERGY, which comes from heat deep inside the earth, and hydropower, which is generated by the force of moving water.

Alternative energy sources are often more expensive than the burning of oil or other fossil fuels. That is because these energy sources are still much rarer than oil. As more people switch to alternative energy, its price will drop. In an effort to reduce air pollution, the governments of the United States and many other countries are trying to encourage more people to use alternative energy. [*See also* ENERGY CONSERVATION; HYDROELECTRIC POWER; NUCLEAR POWER; OZONE POLLUTION.]

AMERICAN ALLIGATOR

☑ Large **carnivorous** reptiles belonging to a group called crocodilians. Alligators have short muscular legs and long bodies covered with thick scales. Though they may look quite awkward, they are actually very good swimmers and are well adapted for life in the water. Alligators have large lungs, so they can stay underwater for long periods of time. Webbed feet and a strong tail help them swim. An alligator's eyes, ears, and nostrils are all on top of its head, so that it can submerge itself almost entirely under the water while watching and waiting for prey to swim by. Alligators are excellent hunters and eat almost any kind of animal that ventures near water.

The American alligator, a species common in parts of the southern United States, can grow up to 20 feet (6.1 m) long. They have been hunted for their skins for many years. Earlier in this century, the alligator population declined dramatically and was placed on the list of ENDANGERED SPECIES. Since then, the American alligator has recovered.

AMPHIBIANS

A VERTEBRATE that, in most cases, lives part of its life in water and part on land. All amphibians go through two very different stages during their lifetime—an immature stage and an adult stage. They also share a trait which allows water to pass through their skin. The three main kinds of amphibians are salamanders, frogs and toads, and blind, wormlike creatures called caecilians. There are about 4,000 different species, which live in a wide variety of HABITATS. Of the three main groups, frogs are the most widespread.

Frog   *Newt*

Amphibians are likely indicators of the health of a habitat. Changes in land use and the introduction of TOXINS into the environment by humans may be responsible for the disappearance of or strange mutations (see MUTATIONS) in some amphibian populations.

Endangered Species: Golden Coqui

The golden coqui is a small frog that makes its home in forests in a small area on the island of Puerto Rico. Much of its habitat has been cut down for growing crops, such as coffee, and for grazing livestock. This species of frog lives almost entirely in the middle of plants called bromeliads, which grow high in the trees and collect rainwater. A golden coqui spends much of the day sitting in the plant, facing outward to catch insects, and at night ventures out onto the leaves of the same plant.

ANAEROBES

BACTERIA that do not need OXYGEN for obtaining energy. Anaerobic bacteria use oxygen, when it is available, but they can also survive without it. They can often use NITROGEN in place of oxygen for their chemical cycles. Because they can survive in environments without oxygen, anaerobes play a useful role in breaking down certain wastes found in places not in direct contact with air, such as the bottom of lakes and rivers or deep within LANDFILLS. Anaerobic bacteria are often used in sewage treatment plants to help break down wastes found in sewage water. In addition to bacteria, anaerobes include some species of ALGAE and FUNGI. [*See also* BIODEGRADABLE MATERIAL; DECOMPOSITION.]

A

ANIMAL RIGHTS

A movement whose members believe that animals share similar rights as humans. The ways that humans have interacted with animals have changed throughout history. Over the years, people have developed new relationships with animals, other than looking at them as simply sources of food and labor. At the same time, more people keep animals as pets. As a result, people have begun to realize that animals and people have more in common than they once believed. This belief led to the rise of the animal rights movement. Many people in the movement believe that animals should not be used for human purposes such as food, HUNTING, transportation, clothing, experimentation, or entertainment.

Animal rights groups grew in the 1970s and 1980s. These groups work to prevent people from exploiting animals and to provide animals with safe and humane treatment. In the United States the two largest groups are the People for the Ethical Treatment of Animals (PETA) and the Humane Society.

ANTARCTICA

The world's fifth largest continent, centered on the geographic south pole and surrounded by the southern Atlantic, Pacific, and Indian oceans. Antarctica is a barren, windswept land of constant ice and bitter cold.

The few species of wildlife that call Antarctica home live around the edges of the continent, where the climate is most moderate. Most of Antarctica's animals are tied to the sea. Native animals include several species of FISH, squid, WHALES, seals, and BIRDS. Seven species of penguins make up 80 percent of Antarctica's bird species. [*See also* GLACIERS.]

AQUACULTURE

(*See* HYDROPONICS)

Antarctica has several snow-covered mountain ranges.

AQUARIUMS

(*See* ZOOS AND AQUARIUMS)

AQUATIC HABITATS

Any watery setting that supports life. Oceans, LAKES, rivers, MARSHES, and SWAMPS support a wide variety of life-forms that live all or part of their lives in, on, or near water. There are two basic types of aquatic habitats: saltwater habitats, which include oceans, salt lakes, and salt marshes; and freshwater habitats, such as lakes, rivers, streams, and ponds.

Among the animals that live in saltwater habitats are MAMMALS, such as whales and dolphins; FISH; CRUSTACEANS, such as lobsters, clams, and snails; and various sponges, coral, and organisms so small that they can only be viewed under a microscope. A variety of birds, such as seagulls and pelicans, depend on saltwater fish for food. Plants that grow in saltwater include ALGAE and seaweed.

Aquatic habitats support many species of plants, fish, and water fowl.

Ducks, fish, frogs, snakes, snails, and INSECTS are a few of the animal species that live in freshwater habitats. Examples of freshwater plant life include algae, cattails, and water lilies. Swamps and WETLANDS are home to ALLIGATORS, crocodiles, and long-legged wading birds, such as egrets and cranes.

Some aquatic habitats have a mix of freshwater and saltwater. These are generally places where rivers flow into the ocean or where the ocean flows into swamps and marshes. These habitats support a mixture of both freshwater and saltwater animals and plants. [*See also* CORAL REEFS; ESTUARIES; MARINE ECOSYSTEMS; MARINE MAMMALS; MARSHES; SEAS AND SEASHORES; WETLANDS.]

AQUIFER

(*See* GROUNDWATER)

ARBOREAL HABITATS

A type of HABITAT in which the animals live in trees. Arboreal habitats may consist of an entire forest or just one tree. One tree may provide a home for several species at a time, such as INSECTS, BIRDS, and small MAMMALS.

Some animals that occupy arboreal habitats have become ENDANGERED SPECIES. Their habitats are being destroyed by DEFORESTATION as people cut down forests for timber, land development, and agriculture. Endangered arboreal animals, such as the orangutan—whose natural habitats on the Indonesian islands of Borneo and Sumatra are quickly diminishing—may one day end up surviving only in zoos.

ARCTIC

Earth's northernmost region, centered on the geographic north pole. The Arctic is often defined as the area within the Arctic Circle, an imaginary line at about 66 degrees latitude. Most of the area within the Arctic Circle is occupied by the ARCTIC OCEAN. Unlike ANTARCTICA, the Arctic is mostly free of ice and snow in the summer.

Much of the Arctic's land is TUNDRA, a treeless plain of tiny plants. The ground is permafrost—permanently frozen SOIL that thaws slightly at the surface only in summer. Although winters are long and cold, the Arctic has a diverse wildlife that is adapted to harsh conditions. It includes caribou, reindeer, polar bears, wolves, walruses, seals, and several types of

A

FISH. Many species of migratory BIRDS spend the summer in the Arctic. The Arctic has a small human population, which includes Native Americans called the Inuit in NORTH AMERICA and the Lapps of northern EUROPE. [*See also* GLACIERS.]

The polar bear spends much of its time roaming Arctic ice sheets.

ARCTIC OCEAN

Body of water surrounding the North Pole. The Arctic Ocean is the smallest and shallowest of the earth's five oceans.

Scientists are concerned about evidence of contamination of the Arctic Ocean. Radioactivity from a nuclear processing plant in the United Kingdom has spread through the Arctic Ocean into waters as far away as Northern Canada. A scientific study has revealed that rivers from Siberia in Russia have been flushing toxic chemicals into the Arctic Ocean. This contamination will undoubtedly harm walruses, seals, porpoises, WHALES, gulls, sea eagles, foxes, and polar bears who inhabit the region.

Arctic scientists are also trying to find out why there has been climatic change over the Arctic Ocean. The ocean has warmed up by at least 2.7° Fahrenheit (1.5° Celsius) since the late 1980s. Scientists are using aircraft, submarines, and buoys to gather data to determine if this temperature change is a result of **global warming**. [*See also* GLOBAL CLIMATE CHANGE; MARINE ECOSYSTEMS.]

ARTHROPODS

Group of INVERTEBRATES (animals lacking a backbone) with external skeletons and jointed limbs. With more than one million known species, the largest of any animal group, arthropods live in all HABITATS on earth. They are found in saltwater and freshwater, and many are able to fly through the air. Their habitats range from sandy sea bottoms to soil crevices, tree bark, rotting logs, rivers, streams, oceans, tropical forests, leaves, and the tops of trees. Arthropods include crustaceans—crabs, lobsters, spiders—and INSECTS—among them butterflies, bees, beetles, and cockroaches.

Arthropods generally have a three-sectioned body, including the head, thorax (midsection), and abdomen. Each section may have more than one segment. The external skeleton, called an exoskeleton, protects the animal and allows it to move easily through its many joints. When arthropods grow, they shed their old, outgrown exoskeleton and grow a new one. This process is called molting.

ASIA

The largest continent in the world, both in land area and population. The continent of Asia covers one-third of the land area of the earth. It is home to 3.4 billion people, or about 60 percent of the world's population.

Asia has six major land regions: Southwest Asia is dry, with DESERTS, MOUNTAINS, and plateaus. The world's highest mountain range, the Himalayas, forms the northern border of South Asia. Fertile soil lies at the base of these mountains. North Asia is covered with FORESTS. Because of the cold climate of that region, the ground remains frozen almost all

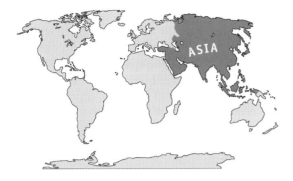

☑ Keywords

Carnivorous. Flesh-eating.

Global warming. A general increase in temperatures worldwide.

Radiation. Particles or waves of energy, including light, heat, and X-rays, given off by an object.

A

year. Southeast Asia and East Asia have fertile farmland, forests, and plentiful NATURAL RESOURCES. Central Asia has very poor, rocky soil and is mostly desert.

The growing numbers of people in Asia are crowding out some species of rare animals that live there, such as the GIANT PANDA bear. Many animals in northern Asia, such as ermines, otters and sables, are hunted for their fur. TIGERS, leopards, orangutans, Komodo dragons, tropical BIRDS, ELEPHANTS and RHINOCEROSES are among other ENDANGERED SPECIES native to Asia.

Endangered Species: Przewalski's Horse

The only truly wild horse that exists today is Przewalski's horse, named after Russian explorer Nikolai M. Przewalski, who first identified the species. The horse stands only about 53 inches (134 cm) tall at the shoulder. Some people think it looks more like a donkey than a horse. The few remaining wild Przewslski's horses live in their natural habitat in the deserts of Mongolia.

ATLANTIC OCEAN

The second largest body of water in the world. The Atlantic Ocean covers about one-fifth of the earth's surface. It connects with the ARCTIC OCEAN in the North and the Antarctic Ocean in the south. A great underwater mountain range lies in the middle of the Atlantic Ocean. Known as the Mid-Atlantic Ridge, it rises above the surface in some places to form islands, such as the Azores. There is a deep, narrow valley along the crest of the Mid-Atlantic Ridge. Scientists believe this valley marks the division between two of the huge blocks of earth called tectonic plates upon which the continents sit. When the tectonic plates move, cracks form on the ocean floor and fill with molten rock from the mantle, the portion of the earth beneath the crust. This movement of plates causes the Atlantic Ocean to widen by about an inch every year. This is part of a process know as CONTINENTAL DRIFT. [*See also* EARTHQUAKES; MARINE ECOSYSTEMS.]

ATMOSPHERE

The mixture of gases that surrounds earth and other planets. The gases that make up earth's atmosphere are mainly NITROGEN and OXYGEN, along with small amounts of argon and other gases. These gases are held in place around the planet by the force of gravity.

All living plants and animals need the air of the atmosphere to survive. The atmosphere also protects the earth and the living things on it. It blocks harmful **radiation** from the sun and helps keep the planet from getting too hot or too cold. Moisture in the atmosphere forms clouds, and the PRECIPITATION that falls from them brings earth the water that all life-forms need to survive.

Earth's atmosphere has five main layers. The higher each layer is above earth, the thinner the atmosphere is in that layer. The layer of atmosphere closest to earth is the TROPOSPHERE. Most of the planet's weather conditions happen in this layer. The layer above the troposphere is the STRATOSPHERE. The stratosphere contains an OZONE LAYER with gases that help block the sun's radiation. The other layers of the atmosphere are the mesosphere,

A

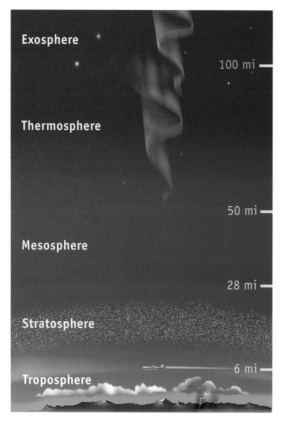

Exosphere

100 mi

Thermosphere

50 mi

Mesosphere

28 mi

Stratosphere

6 mi

Troposphere

thermosphere, and exosphere. The exosphere extends toward outer space and eventually merges with the atmosphere of the sun.

Although the earth's atmosphere covers the entire planet, the quality of air may vary from place to place. What people do on earth can affect the atmosphere. For example, the ozone layer in the stratosphere absorbs ULTRA-VIOLET RADIATION from the sun, which can be very harmful to living things on earth. Certain chemical compounds produced on earth, called CHLOROFLUOROCARBONS (CFCs), have destroyed parts of the ozone layer. Industrialized nations have cooperated to help prevent such harmful chemicals from affecting the earth's atmosphere.

AUSTRALIA

The world's smallest continent, located in the Southern Hemisphere between the Pacific and Indian Oceans. Its location has served to isolate Australia from other landmasses for millions of years, resulting in the development of many strange and unique species of plants and animals.

 Fast Facts

The native people of Australia are called Aborigines, meaning "from the beginning." It is believed that the Aborigines migrated to Australia from southeast Asia more than 40,000 years ago.

Australia has a diverse environment that includes dry sandy DESERTS, tropical RAIN FORESTS, GRASSLANDS, MOUNTAINS, and woodlands. The Western Plateau, an area covering nearly half of Australia, is mostly desert and is called the "Outback" because of its remoteness. Just off the northeast coast of Australia lies the Great Barrier Reef, the largest area of CORAL REEFS in the world.

Australia is home to a number of animals found nowhere else in the world. Many of these animals are marsupials—animals that carry their young in pouches. The best-known Australian marsupial is the kangaroo; Australia has many species of kangaroo. Another distinctive marsupial is the koala bear. One of the strangest animals of Australia is the platypus, an egg-laying, web-footed mammal with a beak like a duck, which lives in and near water. Among the unique bird species of Australia are the emu, a large flightless bird, and the kookaburra, which has a distinctive call that sounds like laughter. Australia is also home to many ENDANGERED SPECIES including the ghost bat, western swamp turtle, swamp orchid, paradise parrot, and wombat.

Endangered Species: Barred Bandicoot

Before Europeans settled in Australia, the barred bandicoot lived in dunes and dry areas in much of the south of the country. Today, it survives only on a few islands in Australia's Shark Bay because of both habitat destruction and the introduction of predators such as foxes and domestic cats. This small long-nosed marsupial is nocturnal and eats mostly insects.

B

BACTERIA

Bacteria are typically visible only under a powerful microscope.

Tiny one-celled organisms that grow on and inside other organisms. One of the most prolific life forms on earth, bacteria are organisms lacking a nucleus. There are two major kinds of bacteria: the eubacteria and archaebacteria. Archaebacterias, which include cells that produce METHANE, are adapted for living in extreme conditions, such as very high temperatures, very high salt concentrations, or zero-oxygen environments. The eubacteria, which are usually just called bacteria, are highly diverse. Found in every kind of environment, they may be round, spiral-shaped, or long and thin, and they range from several thousandths of an inch long to several hundredths of an inch long.

Despite their small size, bacteria are very efficient at meeting all their needs for life—finding CARBON, OXYGEN, hydrogen, NITROGEN, and PHOSPHORUS. They live on every kind of organism; for example, more than 600 million bacteria live on human skin.

Bacteria play a very important role in the environment, in virtually every kind of natural cycle. There are bacteria that carry out PHOTOSYNTHESIS with and without oxygen. They transform inorganic compounds in natural cycles affecting air, water, and soil. Bacteria are also responsible for many diseases, for some kinds of food poisoning, for food digestion, and for the DECOMPOSITION of wastes and pollutants. [*See also* ANAEROBES; BIODEGRADABLE MATERIAL; COMPOSTING; NUTRIENT CYCLE.]

BALD EAGLE

Powerful flesh-eating bird. One of the largest BIRDS in NORTH AMERICA, bald eagles can reach a wingspan of more than 7 feet (2.4 m). The bald eagle is not really bald. An adult has a dark brown body and wings with white feathers covering its head and on its neck and tail (the bird was named at a time when "bald" meant "white" or "streaked with white").

Bald eagles are a type of RAPTOR, or bird of prey, that catch small animals and FISH by swooping down on them from the sky. After carrying the prey to their nests, the eagles tear them to pieces with their strong beaks and eat the flesh.

Bald eagles generally build large nests, called aeries, at the tops of tall trees or on rocky ledges near LAKES, streams, or other bodies of freshwater. The eagles often use the same nests year after year. Bald eagles were once found throughout North America, but their populations have declined drastically in most areas of the continent because of hunting, loss of HABITATS, and exposure to PESTICIDES and other toxins, or poisonous, substances released by humans into the environment.

In some areas of the United States, bald eagles are considered endangered or threatened because of their small numbers. Since the 1970s the government has passed laws to protect eagles by making it illegal to hunt them or to bother the birds or their nests. As a result, their numbers are slowly increasing in some places. [*See also* ENDANGERED SPECIES.]

The bald eagle is considered the national symbol of the United States.

B

BARRIER ISLAND

(*See* ISLANDS)

BEACHES

(*See* EROSION; SEAS AND SEASHORES)

BIOACCUMULATION

The natural biological process by which certain substances collect in the tissues of people, plants, and animals. Bioaccumulation of toxic substances can be a serious hazard to the health of living organisms and to the environment. Bioaccumulation affects the FOOD WEB of all life and has been found in all parts of the world.

Harmful synthetic or organic compounds can get into the environment in different ways. Toxic chemicals used in manufacturing may end up in industrial waste, which is often dumped into the ocean near industrial sites. Toxic substances may also be released into the environment at nuclear plants and mining sites. Huge oil spills from ships have contaminated wide areas of the ocean and miles of coastline, killing wildlife and contributing to bioaccumulation in the surviving animals. Even AIR POLLUTION can contribute to bioaccumulation by mixing with PRECIPITATION, as in ACID RAIN, and contaminating lakes and soils.

Among the natural elements accumulated in living tissue are mercury and cadmium, which are toxic in large amounts. Other dangerous chemical compounds accumulated in organisms are identified by letter names, such as PCBs. Some harmless chemical substances may combine with each other when released into the environment to form compounds known as environmental estrogens. These compounds can mimic, or copy, natural processes that reduce the fertility of humans and wildlife.

Animals that have a high percentage of fat tend to accumulate more of such compounds in their tissues than other animals. Also, the substances are concentrated in fatty tissues. Toxic substances have been found in the fat of bears living in Arctic regions. Scientists have found bioaccumulation in FISH, turtles and **crustaceans**. Bioaccumulation of toxic substances has been found in the liver, brain, and kidney tissues of sea otters. Some children living in old buildings suffer from the effects of bioaccumulation of lead.

Scientists are studying patterns of environmental contamination and linking these to human bioaccumulation. They have found higher incidence of cancer and other diseases in people who live near contaminated sites.

BIOCHEMICAL CYCLE

The movement of chemicals through ECOSYSTEMS and organisms. Biochemical cycles can include how chemicals and drugs affect humans and how chemicals moving through air, land, and water can affect entire ecosystems. Biochemical cycles include the interactions of manufactured chemicals, such as PESTICIDES in the environment, and the movements of naturally occurring chemicals such as hormones in the body.

BIODEGRADABLE MATERIAL

Any material that can decompose or break down into simpler substances because of the action of BACTERIA or sunlight. With the spread of environmental awareness, many people have chosen to buy goods packaged in biodegradable materials instead of materials that do not break down easily (such as most plastics and many synthetic materials). A consumer, for example, might choose biodegradable paper trash bags over heavier plastic bags. Because they decompose, biodegradable materials pose less of a threat to the environment than nonbiodegradable ones. However, many LANDFILLS are packed tightly in layers of waste and SOIL. Under these conditions, even biodegradable materials will not break down quickly. [*See also* COMPOST; DECOMPOSITION.]

BIODIVERSITY

(*See* BIOLOGICAL DIVERSITY)

BIOLOGICAL COMMUNITY

All the plants, animals, and MICROORGANISMS living in the same natural place. There can be

Dry desert communities are home to many plant and animal species.

many biological communities within a single HABITAT. A biological community may take up a wide area or occupy only a small space. It may be a simple community with only a few members, or a complex one with many members. Camels and cacti are among the members of some large desert communities. Ponds are habitats for complex biological communities of turtles, lilies, FISH, frogs, and ALGAE. A single tree can provide a home for communities of squirrels and several species of BIRDS and INSECTS.

Sometimes humans create artificial habitats for biological communities. In 1997, for example, army helicopters placed specially manufactured giant concrete balls with holes in them in a bay off the coast of Long Island in New York State to create artificial reefs for fish that were becoming scarce in the area. Barnacles and algae will attach themselves to these artificial reefs and a FOOD WEB will be formed to support the new biological community. [*See also* ECOSYSTEM.]

BIOLOGICAL DIVERSITY

The multitude of different species of living organisms on earth, as well as the great variety within any single species. Biological diversity, or biodiversity, is an important feature of earth's various ECOSYSTEMS.

Life-forms have an amazing ability to adapt to almost every environment on earth. Plants and animals live in extremes of heat and cold. They live in dry and wet regions, in high mountain altitudes, and in the deepest parts of the oceans. As a result of ADAPTATION, specialized organisms living in a particular HABITAT or BIO-

LOGICAL COMMUNITY cannot exist in a different one. For example, a frog with a perpetually moist skin living in a tropical environment could not survive in a DESERT, nor would a cactus be able to survive in the RAIN FOREST.

Scientists are unsure about how many species of plants and animals exist on earth. Estimates range from one million to more than seven million. It is difficult for scientists to isolate, identify, count, and classify the world's species, because biological diversity also includes tiny MICROORGANISMS that are not visible to the human eye. Today's amazing biological diversity represents only about one percent of all species that have ever lived on earth during the billions of years that it has existed.

Biological diversity also refers to differences among species themselves. Variations within a species are caused by the random distribution of **chromosomes** from the species' parents, resulting in wide variations in offspring from the same parents. Biological diversity also includes differences in the ways in which species interact with each other, and their ability to adapt to changing environments.

EXTINCTION brings about the loss of biological diversity. Many species of plants and animals have become extinct during earth's long history. This has happened for a number of reasons. Scientists theorize, for example, that an abrupt change in the environment, such as a giant meteor hitting the earth or volcanic eruptions, may have led to the extinction of dinosaurs because they did not have time to adapt to the changes caused by these natural events. Species also may have become extinct because of gradual changes in the environment caused by the CONTINENTAL DRIFT or GLOBAL CLIMATE CHANGE. Today, virtually all drastic changes in the environment are caused by people. Because adaptation takes millions of years, when people destroy biological communities through DEFORESTATION, pollution, HUNT-

☑ Keywords

Chromosomes. Threadlike substances in the nucleus of cells that carry genetic information.

Crustaceans. A class of animals, such as lobsters and crabs, whose bodies are covered with a hard shell.

B

ING, MINING, and other actions, the species living in those habitats have no time to move to new environments or adjust to changed surroundings. They may become ENDANGERED SPECIES or extinct.

By allowing the loss of plant and animal species, people are harming themselves. For example, biological diversity allows farmers to develop new crops by crossbreeding different varieties of plants. Little known species of tropical plants have provided many new helpful drugs and medicines. Biological diversity allows a natural balance of nature, which includes pest control by natural PREDATORS. Plants are pollinated by specialized species, like bees and butterflies, enabling the very existence of the food chain. Without plant POLLINATION AND SEED DISPERSAL, people could not survive.

All the species of plants and animals in the earth's many environments function together as a whole, maintaining the delicate balance of life. The destruction of biological diversity can disrupt this balance, leading to the extinction of many different life forms. [*See also* BIOLOGICAL RESTORATION; HABITAT LOSS AND DESTRUCTION.]

BIOLOGICAL RESTORATION

A process to return animals and/or plants to an area. Biological restoration is often necessary because of damage to the environment caused by such activities as construction, waste disposal, mining or chemical waste dumping. Sometimes it is necessary because of human use of natural resources, such as cutting forests for timber or to create farmland.

The restoration process involves the analysis and decision making by citizens, environmentalists, scientists and local and federal governments. These groups decide what needs to be done to make an area livable, how to repair the damage, and what plant or animal life should be reintroduced.

Some controversy exists over the process of biological restoration. Some scientists suggest that it is often not possible to restore an area to its natural or original condition because sometimes no one knows what the condition was before the area was damaged. The best that can be done in such cases is to restore the area to a close approximation of its condition prior to disturbance.

Nevertheless, biological restoration is desirable. The reintroduction of plants, for example, helps to prevent EROSION. Restoration of animal life helps keep plant life from overrunning an area. Biological restoration helps to create stable biological communities and healthy ECOSYSTEMS. [*See also* BIOLOGICAL COMMUNITY.]

BIOMASS

The sum of the weight or volume of all living matter in a given area. Biomass is a measure of the quantity of life a particular ECOSYSTEM can support. It includes all plant and animal life, both above and below ground. But because of the difficulty of measuring underground life, scientists usually refer to only above ground vegetation in calculations of biomass. High volumes of biomass indicate an area with favorable environmental conditions. For example, warm, damp environments, such as tropical RAIN FORESTS, have more biomass than the cold, dry regions of the TUNDRA. [*See also* ECOSYSTEM.]

BIOME

A large geographical area in which conditions are generally the same throughout. These conditions include climate, vegetation, and animals. The major land biomes are TUNDRA, temperate FOREST, tropical RAIN FOREST, GRASSLAND, and DESERT. Some ecologists break these biomes down into other categories. For example, the temperate forest can be subdivided into coniferous (evergreen) forest and deciduous forest, which contains trees that lose their leaves for part of the year.

Any one type of biome can be found in different parts of the world. For example, the desert biome is found in NORTH AMERICA, SOUTH AMERICA, AFRICA, ASIA, and AUSTRALIA. While not exactly alike in all places, the biomes in different locations shares certain characteristics. For example, no matter where it is located, a desert biome is very dry, and vegetation is sparse. ADAPTATION allows the plant and animal life of the desert to find ways to survive. For example, plants or shrubs that grow in a desert biome have small leaves to conserve water. Cacti have fleshy stems in which they store water. Animal life exists, but it is usually

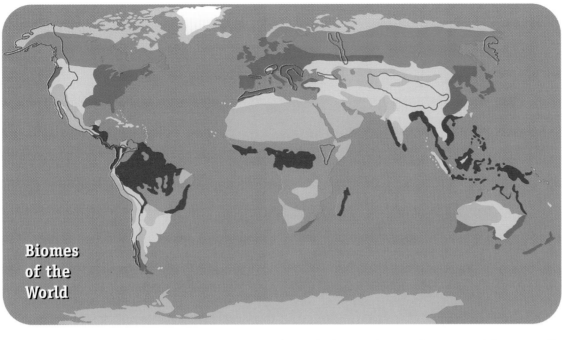

Biomes of the World

	Tundra		Scrubland
	Taiga		Savanna
	Tropical rain forest		Desert
	Temperate forest		Mountains
	Temperate grasslands		

the smaller animals, such as lizards, snakes, and small rodents, that do not require large quantities of water.

Climate is the principal factor in determining where a biome begins and ends. Any major change in climate changes those boundaries. Such changes usually happen gradually. However, since human activities can affect climate, there is reason for concern about such issues as AIR POLLUTION, GLOBAL CLIMATE CHANGE, DESERTIFICATION, and depletion of the OZONE LAYER. [*See also* BIOREGION; BIOSPHERE; OZONE HOLE.]

BIOREGION

An area of earth with a large, intact, and continuous ECOSYSTEM that supports a community of interacting plant and animal life. A bioregion may include a variety of CLIMATES and WEATHER, topography, water, SOIL, plant and animal life. Bioregions are very large ecosystems such as DESERTS, tropics, TUNDRA,

and the marine environment. They usually contain a number of different BIOMES. A biome is generally defined by the plant and animal communities it contains. A bioregion, on the other hand, is defined primarily by its geography, its location on earth, and its relation to other bioregions. The study of a bioregion includes looking not only at plants and animals, but also at the physical and chemical cycles that make the ecosystem work.

BIOSPHERE

The portion of earth that can support life. Earth's biosphere reaches five to six miles (8 to 10 km) above the planet's surface into the ATMOSPHERE. It also extends below the planet's surface and deep beneath the oceans. Earth's biosphere contains all living organisms on the planet. The biosphere can be divided into BIOMES—regions with distinct climates and organisms. Each biome contains several ECOSYSTEMS, in which various plant and animal species live and interact. Living things can go beyond the biosphere, but to remain alive they must depend on artificial support systems. For example, airplanes and spacecraft can carry humans beyond the biosphere for short periods of time. Space stations can support life far beyond the earth's biosphere as long as food and OXYGEN are available.

BIRDS

VERTEBRATES whose bodies are covered with feathers and who lay eggs to reproduce. While all birds have wings, not all birds can fly. The ostrich, for example, only walks and runs. Some birds can also swim.

There are more than 9,000 species of birds. They are very widespread, living in various types of HABITATS in all regions of the earth. Many birds have complex ADAPATATIONS to their environments. Most species of birds also engage in seasonal migrations, moving to different habitats in winter and summer.

Birds play an important role in their ECOSYSTEMS as both PREDATORS and as prey. By eating certain INSECTS and pests, birds help farmers by lessening infestations of species that can harm crops. Birds also play an important role in plant reproduction, helping with POLLINATION AND SEED DISPERSAL.

Over the past several hundred years, a number of bird species have become extinct. Some were hunted to EXTINCTION; others died out because of destruction of their habitats. Some birds today are considered endangered species. [See also BALD EAGLE; EVERGLADE KITE; OWL, NORTHERN SPOTTED; STORK, WOOD; WOODPECKER, RED-COCKADED.]

BIRDS OF PREY

(See RAPTORS)

BISON

Large, hoofed animals with short horns. Bison, also known as buffalo, belong to the same family as cows and oxen. They have thick growths of hair on their heads, necks, shoulders, and front legs. They also have a hump of fat on their shoulders. Bison are the largest land mammal in NORTH AMERICA.

NORTH AMERICA once had a bison population of between 30 million and 60 million on its central plains and PRAIRIES. They were an important animal to Plains Indian tribes, which used the animal for food, clothing, and the walls of tepees that provided shelter. But European settlers crossing the continent hunted the animals almost to EXTINCTION during the nine-

teenth century. By the 1880s, fewer than 1,000 bison were left.

The Buffalo Protection Act was enacted in 1894 to protect the surviving herds. It was the first federal legislation in the United States to protect an ENDANGERED SPECIES. The bison population has made a comeback since then. There are now thousands of bison living in North American NATIONAL PARKS and WILDLIFE REFUGES. [See also GRASSLANDS; MAMMALS; HUNTING.]

BUREAU OF LAND MANAGEMENT (BLM)

An agency of the U.S. government responsible for managing 264 million acres (107 million hectares) of PUBLIC LANDS, constituting about 11 percent of the nation's land surface. These public lands include FORESTS and grazing lands. The BLM also manages millions of acres of underground natural resources, including coal, natural gas, petroleum, gold, silver, and other minerals. Wildlife populations, including herds of wild horses and burros living on government lands, are also managed by the BLM.

Many BLM public lands are used for fishing, hiking, and camping by the public. There are also thousands of miles of BLM-administered recreational trails. Private industry also has the right to mine, graze cattle, and cut timber on public lands in exchange for minimal fees set by the government. Most BLM lands are in the western part of the United States The Bureau of Land Management is part of the U.S. Department of the Interior. [See also GRAZING; SOIL CONSERVATION; WILDLIFE MANAGEMENT.]

C

CAPTIVE BREEDING

(*See* ZOOS AND AQUARIUMS)

CARBON DIOXIDE

A colorless, odorless gas, found in the earth's atmosphere. As animals convert food into energy and tissue, they release carbon dioxide as they breathe out. Carbon dioxide is also released when any material that contains carbon burns or decays. Green plants take carbon dioxide from the atmosphere and give off OXYGEN, which animals take in during respiration—the process in which animals take in oxygen and give off carbon dioxide. This cycle helps maintain a balance between the supply of oxygen and carbon dioxide.

Carbon dioxide helps regulate the earth's temperature. It absorbs some of the sun's heat, keeping it near the surface of the planet. Otherwise, it would escape into space, and the earth would be very cold. In recent years the amount of carbon dioxide in the atmosphere has been increasing as a result of human activities and natural processes. Some scientists are concerned that this is contributing to global warming. [*See also* GLOBAL CLIMATE CHANGE.]

CARCINOGEN

Any substance that causes the disease of cancer in people or animals. Some carcinogens occur naturally, but many of them have been introduced into the environment by humans.

Smoke from cigarettes is one of the more common and most dangerous carcinogens. Many household items and products, such as aerosol-spray cans that release vinyl chloride gas, have also been found to contain carcinogens. Other carcinogens are found in PESTICIDES, such as DDT. Certain drugs given to humans have also been found to be carcinogens. Some

naturally occurring elements are carcinogenic, such as the building material asbestos and cadmium, a substance used in making some paints. Overexposure to the ULTRAVIOLET RADIATION of sunlight may cause skin cancer.

Carcinogens can be spread by air or by pathways such as rivers that flow near factories where carcinogenic chemicals are produced.

CARNIVORES

Animals that feed on the meat of other animals. Carnivores include a wide variety of animal species, including wolves, dogs, eagles, snakes, sharks, and LIONS and other cats. A few species of plants, including the Venus's-flytraps, are also carnivores. Animal carnivores generally have sharp claws and teeth that help them capture and kill their prey.

Carnivores can be divided into two groups. PREDATORS are carnivores that survive by hunting and killing other animals. Lions and TIGERS are predators. Humans are also predators. The other type of carnivores are SCAVENGERS. Scavengers eat animals that have been killed by other

Endangered Species: Snow Leopard

The snow leopard is one of the most beautiful of the large cats. It has a very soft, thick spotted coat and a long fluffy tail, which it wraps around itself to keep warm during the winter. It has long been hunted for its fur. Snow leopards range in Central Asia from Russia to Pakistan and Afghanistan, inhabiting forested ares and bare cliffs between 6,000 and 20,000 feet (1,830 and 6,100 m). They hunt native goats, sheep, deer, and rodents. Only about 5,000 animals still remain in the wild, and zoos around the world have a breeding program for this mammal; more than 250 snow leopards are in North American zoos.

C

animals or that are dying for some other reason. Scavengers include vultures and hyenas. [*See also* WILDLIFE MANAGEMENT.]

CAVE

Underground hollow space in the earth carved from the action of wind, water, or movement of rocks over thousands or millions of years. Caves range in size from small spaces with only enough room for a single animal to large spaces thousands of yards deep and wide. Caves provide unique HABITATS for many animals, such as bats, spiders, certain types of FISH, and bears. Caves often contain water, which may continue to carve them deeper and wider.

Some caves contain stalactites and stalagmites. These are icicle-like formations of minerals made by mineral-rich water dripping from a cave's ceiling for hundreds or thousands of years. Stalactites hang down from the ceiling, while stalagmites are built up from the cave's floor, climbing as the stalactites drip on them. [*See also* EROSION.]

CHEETAH

A large cat that lives on the GRASSLANDS of AFRICA. The fastest land animal on earth, the cheetah grows to a height of about 30 inches (76 cm) at the shoulder, has a distinctive

The cheetah is the fastest land animal, capable of running up to 60 miles (96 km) per hour.

spotted coat, sharp knifelike teeth, a slender streamlined shape, and a long tail.

Mainly solitary, cheetahs are excellent PREDATORS, who hunt at night or early in the morning. They remain hidden in the grasses as long as possible, and then at the last minute they break into a run for the remaining short distance to their prey.

Cheetahs, like other large cats, such as LIONS and TIGERS, are highly ENDANGERED SPECIES because of increasing destruction of their HABITATS.

CHEMICAL SPILLS

(*See* HAZARDOUS SUBSTANCES)

CHLOROFLUOROCARBONS (CFCs)

A group of chemical compounds containing chlorine atoms, long used in refrigeration and aerosol cans. Chlorofluorocarbon, or CFCs, by themselves are not harmful to humans and other organisms on earth. But, when these chemicals are released during manufacture or from refrigerator leaks, they rise into the ATMOSPHERE, accumulate there, and break apart when the sun's RADIATION strikes them. Once broken apart, the chlorine atoms that are a part of their structure react with ozone molecules that make up the OZONE LAYER of the atmosphere, changing their structure. In the 1970s, scientists noticed that the ozone layer was developing a large hole. They soon discovered that chlorofluorocarbons were the culprit because of their effect on atmosphere ozone.

In order to prevent further destruction of the ozone layer, the United States banned the use of CFCs in aerosol cans in 1978. Growing concern also caused many countries to sign an international agreement in 1987 calling for an end to CFC production. This agreement is known as the Montreal

Protocol. [*See also* OZONE HOLE; OZONE POLLUTION.]

CITIES

(*See* URBAN PLANNING)

CLEAR-CUTTING

A timber-harvesting technique in which all the trees in a forest are chopped down at the same time. Clear-cutting as a method of harvesting timber causes severe environmental problems. Many BIOLOGICAL COMMUNITIES occupy a forest. When a forest is clear-cut, entire ECOSYSTEMS disappear and the BIOLOGICAL DIVERSITY of the area is lost. Smaller plants and wildlife are destroyed along with the trees. In some cases, certain animal species are threatened with EXTINCTION because their HABITATS are destroyed.

Clear-cutting has other adverse effects as well. The few animals that survive are driven to populated regions where they may become nuisances, or even a danger to humans. Clear-cutting also leaves an area more susceptible to flooding and EROSION. When trees grow old and rot or burn, they produce nutrients that replenish the soil. Clear-cutting can lead to impoverished soils by eliminating sources of nutrients. DEFORESTATION caused by clear-cutting also contributes to GLOBAL CLIMATE CHANGE because it contributes to increased levels of CARBON DIOXIDE in the ATMOSPHERE.

The clear-cutting of ancient forests—old growth forests as they are called—is especially destructive. Forests that have taken thousands of years to grow can never be replaced. Replanting ancient trees with seedlings is not adequate because new trees do not provide the same type of habitats for the species who lived in the ancient forests. Once an ancient forest is clear- cut, the activities of humans who occupy the area change the ecosystem forever.

Conservationists have not been completely successful in stopping clear-cutting. This method of harvesting timber produces lumber and wood pulp for industries that provide jobs for many people. Sometimes the forestland is on private property. The owners of these forests may want to clear the land for profit. [*See also* CONSERVATION; HABITAT LOSS; CONSERVATION.]

CLIMATE AND WEATHER

The day-to-day state of the ATMOSPHERE in terms of temperature, moisture in the air, wind, and clouds. Climate is the overall weather conditions that are typical in one place over a long period of time. A climate zone is an area of the earth that has the same climate throughout. Climate does not change suddenly, though it can change over time. Weather, on the other hand, is continually changing.

Climate. The sun has the most influence on the kind of climate an area has. Areas that are near the equator have a hot climate because they get more of the sun's direct rays. Areas farther from the equator get more indirect rays from the sun, contributing to colder climates. The areas between the equator and the poles have more temperate, less extreme climates.

Climatologists, the scientists who study climate, divide the earth into different climatic zones. There are roughly five types of zones: arctic or polar, which is very cold; subarctic, which has cold winters; temperate, with milder winters; desert, which is very dry; and tropical, which is warm and rainy.

Winds have an important effect on climate. Winds are caused by the sun's uneven heating of the atmosphere. The air in some places is warmer than in others. Warm air rises. As it does, it is replaced by air from cooler areas. This movement of air is what creates wind. Winds may carry either rain or dry air, which has a lot to do with whether a climate is wet or dry.

Other factors involved in climate are altitude and distance from the ocean. Mountains can slow the passage of air masses. This means the climate can be different on either side of the mountains. The windward side of a mountain—the side from which the wind is blowing—will get more rain than the leeward, or protected, side.

Areas near the sea or any large body of water will have different climates than nearby inland areas. That is because the air over large bodies of water heats up and cools off differently from air over land. That difference affects wind and humidity—the amount of moisture in the air.

Weather. Weather is caused by large air masses that constantly move across the planet's surface. That is why weather is always changing. Because of the uneven heating of earth's atmosphere, some air masses are cold and some are warm. The place where air masses of different temperatures meet is called a front. A cold front occurs when a cold air mass pushes up behind a warm air mass. A warm front occurs when warm air pushes up behind a cold front. These meetings usually produce some kind of PRECIPITATION. Temperature and other factors that affect climate—such as winds, mountains, and large bodies of water—may also influence the weather.

CLIMATE CHANGE

(*See* GLOBAL CLIMATE CHANGE)

CLONING

(*See* GENETICS AND GENETIC ENGINEERING)

CLOUDS

Visible masses of water droplets, ice crystals, or dust particles in the ATMOSPHERE. Clouds help both to warm and cool the earth. They can also indicate differences in weather conditions and the presence of AIR POLLUTION.

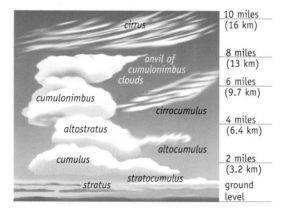

There are three main types of clouds: cirrus clouds, cumulus clouds, and stratus clouds. Feathery-looking cirrus clouds are formed high in the atmosphere. They are made up of ice crystals. Fluffy, white cumulus clouds are fair-weather clouds. When they darken and grow extremely large, they become storm clouds known as cumulonimbus clouds. Stratus clouds are low, flat sheets of grayish-colored clouds that often become rain clouds.

Clouds are formed when water droplets collect around tiny particles of dust. Snow forms in clouds when the air temperature drops below freezing and the water droplets form ice crystals. Places where there is air pollution often have heavy layers of brilliantly colored clouds, especially at sunset. These are actually clouds of smoke and particles that may stay in the atmosphere for long periods of time.

Scientists are discovering that clouds are more complicated that they had realized. Clouds over water affect the earth differently than clouds over land. They reflect sunlight in different ways, depending upon which zone of the earth they are in. Some biologists believe that clouds may carry BACTERIA, ALGAE, and other MICROORGANISMS across the world.

COMPOSTING

Process by which organic matter is broken down into nutrients. Compost is a nutrient-rich, dark soil often used for growing food crops and plants or as a natural FERTILIZER. To create compost, organic matter such as fallen leaves, grass clippings, and food scraps are collected and allowed to decompose in SOIL. During decomposition, bacteria and other tiny microorganisms break down the organic matter into fine particles.

People concerned about the harm chemical fertilizers do to the land and food grown on it support composting as part of a healthful lifestyle. Composting is also considered a method of waste reduction. It is estimated that as much as 20 percent of all waste material is organic matter. Removing some of that waste and recycling it into the soil through composting reduces the amount of garbage placed in landfills, where most garbage disposal takes place. [*See also* BIODEGRADABLE MATERIAL, ORGANIC AND NONORGANIC WASTES; WASTE DISPOSAL.]

CONDOR, CALIFORNIA

The largest flying bird in North America. A type of vulture, the California condor has a wingspan of nearly 10 feet (3 m). By the early 1980s, the birds had almost become extinct.

California condors began to disappear when settlers built farms near the condors' HABITAT. In the 1940s, farmers began using a

The California condor has begun to recover from the brink of extinction.

PESTICIDE called DDT. This chemical accumulated in the condor's bodies and prevented their eggs from hatching. California condors were also shot for sport. As vultures, California condors do not hunt and kill prey for food but rather eat animals that are already dead. Many condors were poisoned by swallowing lead bullets in the carcasses of animals shot by hunters. By 1985 only nine birds were alive in the wild. Five more lived in zoos. It was decided that all remaining California condors would be captured and placed in zoos. Condors do not breed until they are six or seven years old, and they lay only one egg during the breeding season. While the birds were in captivity, scientists removed eggs from the parents' nests to encourage a second or third egg to be laid. By 1992 the number of birds increased so that there were 52 condors

It has not been easy to release California condors into the wild. They do not adapt well to living near humans. When 13 birds were released in the early 1990s in Los Padres, California, five of them died. Five others had to be recaptured because they were landing on houses, flying near power lines and walking across roads. Now young condors scheduled to be released into the wild are trained to stay away from manufactured structures. They receive electric shocks when they land on wires in their pens to discourage them from going near power lines. As of 1994 there were 88 California condors, with all but three in captivity.

CONSERVATION

☙ The preservation, protection, and careful management of NATURAL RESOURCES. As world population increases, people use more and more of the world's resources. Many of these resources cannot be replaced once they are used up. The goal of conservation and conservationists is to protect both our RENEWABLE AND NONRENEWABLE RESOURCES and to manage them in a way that finds a balance between current and future needs.

Yellowstone National Park, the first national park, was established in 1872. Theodore Roosevelt, the twenty-sixth president of the United States, was a strong supporter of conservation. During his presidency, national land policy made a definite shift toward conservation, and the federal government took permanent control of certain lands.

Today conservation efforts are aimed at preserving ECOSYSTEMS and species of plant and animal life, conserving soil, water, mineral, and energy resources. One goal of conservationists is protecting fertile soil from EROSION, the carrying away of soil by rain and wind. Erosion is often due to human misuse of the land, such as CLEAR-CUTTING forests.

Another concern of conservationists is preserving the amount and quality of fresh water and preventing WATER POLLUTION. The federal government has set limits on industries to reduce the pollutants that are released into lakes and streams.

Conservationists also work to limit the overgrazing of GRASSLANDS by livestock. Overgrazing may kill the grasses, which are then often replaced with less desirable plants. Overgrazing can also cause soil erosion. Another issue of concern is the protection of wildlife. Conservation is also concerned with the depletion of mineral resources. RECYCLING efforts have extended the life of some minerals. But the use of FOSSIL FUELS remains a problem.

Profile: John Muir

John Muir immigrated to the U.S. from Scotland in 1849. Because of an interest in forests, he became a proponent of the need to preserve nature and defend species and wilderness areas from devastation by humans. A leader in the movement to preserve the sequoias in California, his efforts led to the establishment of Yosemite and Sequoia national parks. In 1892 Muir helped found the Sierra Club, an organization dedicated to the exploration and preservation of American wildlife and wilderness. Many natural sites have been named in his honor.

CONSERVATION ORGANIZATIONS

Groups of people working towards environmental protection. Conservation organizations vary widely in size, philosophy, the issues they work on, and approach. But they are all dedicated to the protection of NATURAL RESOURCES, such as land, water, air, and wildlife.

There are many conservation organizations in the United States. One of the oldest is the Sierra Club, which was founded in 1892. The Sierra Club, with other organizations like the Wilderness Society and Defenders of Wildlife, work to preserve open spaces, wildlife HABITATS, and ENDANGERED SPECIES. Other organizations, such as the Environmental Defense Fund and the Natural Resources Defense Council, focus on environmental research and laws. Some organizations, such as Greenpeace, have been called "direct action" organizations because they often try to effect change through dramatic actions such as holding demonstrations and protests or blocking anti-environmental activities.

Still other organizations—such as zoos, the World Wildlife Fund, Wildlife Conservation Society, and Conservation International—focus on scientific research and protecting habitats. Yet another group of conservation organizations focus on particular issues, such as the Rainforest Action Network, which works to protect RAIN FORESTS throughout the world.

Although some conservation organizations are quite old, many have been formed since the first Earth Day in 1970. The environmental movement has grown tremendously since then, and so have the number and size of environmental groups. [*See also* ENVIRONMENTAL PROTECTION AGENCY; UNEP.]

CONSUMER

Anyone who buys and uses either raw materials or finished goods. Consumer activists have affected the way business and industry operate. Lawsuits and bad publicity convinced many companies to make better, safer products. Environmental concerns also affect the way industries produce and label their goods. As attention was drawn to products that were dangerous to the environment, more industries began to produce goods that identified themselves as safe.

CONTINENTAL DRIFT

The gradual movement of the earth's continents. The continents are part of enormous sections of the earth's crust called tectonic plates. These plates float on the surface of the earth above semisolid material called magma, deep below the planet's surface. The movement of these plates is part of a process known as plate tectonics. As a result of plate tectonics and continental drift, the continents move about eight-tenths of an inch per year.

If you look at a map of the earth, you can see that certain continents appear to fit together like pieces of a puzzle. This is most evident with the continents of Africa and South America. About 225 million years ago, these separate continents formed a single giant landmass that covered more than a third of the earth's surface. The scientist Alfred Lothar Wegener called this original continent Pangaea. Over time, Pangaea broke up into separate continents, which slowly drifted apart. Scientists have found fossils of tropical plants and animals in extremely cold regions, proving that the continents have moved from one climatic zone to another.

North America
North America
Asia
PANGAEA
South America
Africa
India
Antarctica
Australia

About 200 million years ago

North America
LAURASIA
Asia
South America
Africa
India
GONDWANALAND
Antarctica
Australia

About 135 million years ago

The process of continental drift is largely responsible for the formation of VOLCANOES and MOUNTAINS. When the tectonic plates rub against each other, EARTHQUAKES occur, pushing up land masses and creating deep fissures in the earth. Volcanoes often form at the boundaries of tectonic plates, where the presence of cracks and fissures allows magma to rise to the surface. The process of continental drift is still going on, slowing changing the face of our planet.

CONTINENTAL SHELF

The submerged edge of the continent extending from the continental coastline to a steep drop-off to the deep ocean floor. In most places the continental shelf extends in a gentle slope outward from the shore. On average, the continental shelf is about 43 miles (70 km) wide, but varies from place to place. In some places it is narrower than 10 miles (17 km) wide, while in others it extends for hundreds of miles outward from the coast. Off the coast of the United States, the continental shelf is wide along much of the Atlantic and Gulf coasts. In these areas, flat coastal plains continue underwater for several miles. Off the Pacific coast of the United States, on the other hand, the continental shelf is very narrow. Some MOUNTAINS along the Pacific coast plunge almost directly into the ocean.

At its outer edge, the continental shelf meets the continental slope, an area that drops steeply to the bottom of the ocean floor. The edge of the continental shelf ranges from 0.6 to 6 miles (1 to 10 km) above the ocean floor below, making the drop-offs the highest cliffs on earth.

The world's continental shelves produce important resources, including petroleum and natural gas, as well as building and beach replenishment materials such as sand and gravel. [*See also* NATURAL RESOURCE; SEAFLOOR.]

CONTINENTS

(*See* AFRICA; ANTARCTICA; ASIA; AUSTRALIA; EUROPE; NORTH AMERICA; SOUTH AMERICA)

CORAL REEF

An underwater ridge or mound found mainly in warm, shallow seas. Coral reefs are usually at or slightly below sea level. Coral itself is a kind of limestone made by tiny animals called coral polyps. These animals build limestone shells around themselves for protection. Because some coral polyps live in colonies, or groups,

Coral reefs are found primarily in tropical regions.

they can form the thick ridges, or mounds, called reefs. Other living organisms, such as PLANKTON and ALGE, contribute to the formation of the reef by serving as food for the coral polyps. Waves may throw up bits of sand and coral that over time build up on top of the reef. If this happens, the reef may eventually become a coral island.

Coral reefs serve as HABITATS for marine animals, especially FISH. The fish feed on algae and other life-forms around the reef. Some types of fish feed on the living coral itself. One fascinating kind of reef fish is the cleaner fish. These are small fish that remove PARASITES from the skin, gills, and mouth of other reef fish. The cleaner fish's "clients" actually wait for their turn to be cleaned.

There are three kinds of coral reefs: fringing reefs, which are located close to shore; barrier reefs, which lie farther offshore; and atolls, which are found far offshore. Atolls are usually ring-shaped, with a circular body of water in the middle. The Great Barrier Reef, off the northeast coast of Australia, contains the largest deposits of coral in the world.

DAMS AND DIKES

Structures made by people to hold back and control bodies of water. People have built dams and dikes for thousands of years to help shape their environment for needs such as irrigation and flood control.

Dams generally block the flow of water in rivers or streams. They are built by placing dirt, concrete, metal, or other materials across a river or stream. The earliest dams were built to conserve water during dry seasons, for use in irrigation. Modern dams are constructed to create water reservoirs for drinking supplies, control FLOODING, divert water for navigation, and provide general electric power.

By slowing the speed of water downstream, dams can provide refuges for FISH and water BIRDS and cut down on EROSION. But dams can create problems, too. By slowing the flow of water, dams change the natural HABITATS along rivers. Valleys behind the dam are flooded, destroying habitats, and forcing the animals in them to leave. Although dams provide refuge for fish, they also prevent fish from migrating freely along rivers. This has been especially damaging to various species of SALMON in the Pacific Northwest.

Dikes are small dams that usually hold back water along rivers or seacoasts, protecting surrounding lowland areas from flooding. They are often just earthen embankments. Dikes are very common in the Netherlands, where they have been used for hundreds of years to hold back the North Sea and create more land for agriculture and living space.

In the United States, a type of dike known as a levee is used along certain rivers, such as the Mississippi, to help prevent flooding. Like dams, dikes and levees alter the environment around them. While they have a useful purpose in controlling flooding, they can also damage natural HABITATS. Moreover, if dikes or levees break, the flooding that results can be very destructive. [*See also* HYDROELECTRIC POWER; RIVER SYSTEMS.]

DDT

An insecticide widely used on crops for PEST CONTROL. DDT is a chemical compound developed in 1939. The letters "DDT" stand for the initial letters of its chemical name, dichloro-diphenyl-trichloroethane. DDT kills INSECTS very effectively. But it remains in the environment for a long time before decaying. Meanwhile, it is absorbed by plants and animals that eat plants sprayed with DDT. Humans who eat the plants and animals also absorb the PESTICIDE. In addition to killing harmful insects, DDT also kills useful insects, such as bees, which pollinate plants and produce honey.

Because of its danger to the food chain, DDT has been banned in the United States since 1972. However, it is still in use in other countries.

Calls for a ban on DDT were part of a growing antipesticide movement that began in the 1960s when people became aware of the dangers of pesticides. Many activists were first made aware of the danger of DDT and other long-lasting pesti-

Dams have been built on many of the world's major rivers, altering their normal flow.

cides by the book *Silent Spring*, written by Rachel Carson. The title of the book refers to what the world would have if all songbirds died as a result of DDT poisoning. Before it was banned, DDT had already caused a dramatic decrease in the numbers of many species of BIRDS in the United States and elsewhere.

Profile: Rachel Carson

Probably no other person had as much influence on the banning of DDT as American marine biologist and science writer Rachel Carson (1907–1964). Carson wrote with great feeling about nature and human interaction with nature. In her book *Silent Spring*, published in 1962, she warned of the dangers of the widespread use of pesticides. She demonstrated how pesticides such as DDT not only killed birds and fish but also endangered human food supplies.

Born in Springdale, Pennsylvania, Carson graduated from Pennsylvania College for Women, received a master's degree from Johns Hopkins University, and worked as a writer for the U.S. Fish and Wildlife Service.

DECOMPOSITION

Chemical process in which a substance is broken down into more simple materials. Decomposition is nature's way of breaking down a substance or compound. The process is also sometimes called decay.

All things are composed of a variety of different elements or compounds, which can be chemically rearranged to form new compounds or elements. Heat often helps speeds decomposition, loosening the chemical connections between elements and allowing them to form new arrangements. Scientists use heat, as well as other chemical compounds, to purposefully break down compounds into other substances they need.

Light is a natural catalyst for decomposition, as are MICROORGANISMS such as BACTERIA. Microorganisms are tiny, living organisms that use biological material as food. As they consume what they need to survive, the chemical structure of the substance is rearranged into other forms. This process can be beneficial: decomposition of organic based materials caused petroleum to form deep in the earth.

Bacteria are also the reason that plants and animals eventually decompose into SOIL after they die. If organic compounds did not decompose, new plants would have no soil to grow in and animals would have no plants to eat. An important part of the cycle of life, decomposition allows chemical substances in the environment to be recycled and used over and over again.

Most bacteria break down dead organic matter using an enzyme—a substance that helps speed the process by destroying the protein in the organic material. The bacteria can then absorb the nutrients they need. There are so many kinds of bacteria that there is probably no natural organic substance that cannot be digested by at least one bacteria species.

Scientists have learned that decomposition can help to clean up environmental contamination in our soil, air, and water. For example, bacteria can sometimes be used to break down the same petroleum products that they helped to create. This process, called bioremediation, helps scientists to clean up petroleum-contaminated sites such as soil or water threatened by large oil spills. [*See also* BIODEGRADABLE MATERIAL; COMPOSTING; NUTRIENT CYCLE.]

DEFORESTATION

Destruction of large areas of TREES and other plant life in a forest by burning, bulldozing, sawing, or chopping. Some deforestation occurs naturally, such as during storms or when lightning starts forest fires. But most deforestation is caused by human activities.

Deforestation contributes to many serious environmental problems. The largest ORGANISMS in the forest, trees support many other forms of life in an ECOSYSTEM. Trees and other plants produce OXYGEN needed by all animals to survive. The destruction of vast areas of forest removes the oxygen producers and leads to a buildup of CARBON DIOXIDE in the ATMOSPHERE. This has contributed to GLOBAL CLI-

D

MATE CHANGE, which can have an adverse effect on all life on the earth.

When deforestation occurs, animals as well as many plants besides trees are destroyed. Forests not only support plant and animal life but also the lives of MICROORGANISMS, FUNGI, and other organisms that break down the earth's waste. Deforestation also contributes to flooding and EROSION of soil.

Deforestation has occurred in all areas of the world, affecting various types of forests. The rain forests of South America, Africa, and Asia have been especially hard hit. Since 1950, one-fourth of Africa's rain forests have disappeared. In the late 1990s, an area equal to the size of seven football fields was destroyed every minute in the Brazilian rain forest.

People concerned with CONSERVATION are taking steps to stop deforestation. They are asking banks not to loan money to businesses for projects that destroy forests. Some forest areas have been set aside as WILDLIFE REFUGES. More trees are being planted, and RECYCLING programs help to save trees. People in the food industry are finding new places to raise inexpensive beef cattle so that forests are not cut to create land for GRAZING. Some people also choose to become vegetarians as a result of their knowledge of deforestation. [*See also* CLEAR-CUTTING.]

Deserts support various species of cactus, including the giant saguaro.

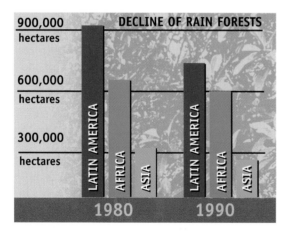

DECLINE OF RAIN FORESTS					
900,000 hectares	LATIN AMERICA				
600,000 hectares		AFRICA		LATIN AMERICA	
300,000 hectares			ASIA		AFRICA
					ASIA
	1980			1990	

DESERT

A dry region with less than normal vegetation. There are different kinds of deserts, but they all have one thing in common—very little rainfall. Deserts typically receive fewer than 10 inches (25 cm) of rainfall per year. Deserts are not nec-essarily flat and empty places. A single desert may have a variety of landscapes. Also, there is life in the desert. The plants and animals found in the desert have adapted to life in that particular type of environment.

Most people think of deserts as hot and sandy. Yet not all deserts are hot. In some deserts, it is so cold that whatever moisture there is freezes. Deserts cover about one-fifth of the planet's land area on earth. The largest desert in the world is the Sahara in Africa. It is about the same size as the United States. The Sahara is more typical of what most people think of as a desert. It is hot desert, with about one-third of it covered with sand and sand dunes. Other parts of the Sahara have a surface of gravel, stones, or bare rock. Scattered throughout parts of the Sahara are oases, areas of vegetation fed by underground water sources.

In some parts of the world, deserts are spreading in a process called DESERTIFICATION. This happens when winds blow sand from the desert onto nearby land. Drought and poor farming methods also contribute to desertification by reducing vegetation that holds soil in place. Without a good cover of vegetation, soil can be blown away by winds, allowing desert areas to expand.

DESERTIFICATION

A process by which an area is transformed into a DESERT, generally because of either climate change or human activities. Desertification has occurred in several areas of AFRICA and ASIA. Parts of AUSTRALIA and SOUTH AMERICA are also prone to desertification. The midwestern United States is an area that could be susceptible to desertification as well.

In some dry, semiarid areas, changes in land use or climate can have a significant effect on the natural BIOME to create desert conditions. For example, overgrazing of rangeland can destroy plants that help to retain moisture in the SOIL and hold the soil together. When the plants are gone, there is less moisture in the soil to support plant life, and the topsoil is also more vulnerable to EROSION. MINING and agricultural activities can also strip away soil and contribute to desertification. Long periods of drought create conditions that make regions susceptible to desertification. But desertification usually results when such climate changes are coupled with human activities that further damage the environment.

Desertification causes a reduction in BIO- LOGICAL DIVERSITY because it destroys the HABITATS of animal and plant species. It also reduces water reserves and places stress on rivers and GROUNDWATER supplies. Land that has become desertified can sometimes be restored through the process of BIOLOGICAL RESTORA- TION. But this is expensive and time-consuming, sometimes requiring many years to restore damaged areas. Efforts to reverse or prevent desertification also include human population control, reduction in livestock GRAZING, and the use of improved agricultural techniques, such as crop rotation. [*See also* GLOBAL CLIMATE CHANGE; HABITAT LOSS AND CONSERVATION; SOIL CONSERVATION; SPECIES LOSS.]

DIOXINS

Chemical compounds produced in the manufacturing of paper and PESTICIDES. Dioxins are dangerous to humans, even in quite small amounts. They are formed when chlorine is heated, or from the incomplete burning of gasoline or municipal wastes. Dioxins are also formed in chemical manufacturing; during the processes of making such substances as HERBICIDES, wood preservatives, and antibacterial agents; and during bleaching in the paper industry.

Dioxins have been associated with human diseases, primarily cancer, skin diseases, and problems affecting the nervous system. They are now tightly regulated by the ENVIRONMENTAL PROTECTION AGENCY (EPA), which monitors bodies of water near industrial plants for dioxin emissions. The EPA sets acceptable limits to the amount of dioxin allowed in water. If the dioxin level in rivers near manufacturing plants exceeds those limits, manufacturers may be fined.[*See also* HAZARDOUS SUBSTANCES; WATER POLLUTION.]

DNA

A substance found in cells that carries genetic information responsible for reproducing life. The nuclei of all living cells contain deoxyribonucleic acid, or DNA. The foundation of all life, DNA is a long, coiled molecule, or group of associated atoms, in the shape of a double helix—that is, like a twisted ladder. DNA is composed mainly of four kinds of molecules—adenine, thiamin, guanine, and cytosine (A, T, G, and C)—that are linked together in the rungs of the ladder. When chromosomes—substances in cells that carry genetic information—

D

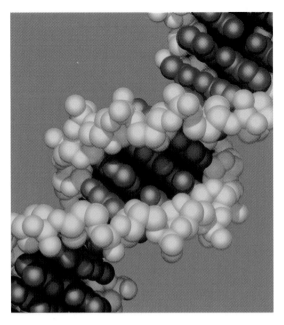

This model of a strand of DNA shows groups of atoms clustered together.

divide to make new cells, the two sides of the double helix split apart, and a single strand may move to a new cell where it can reproduce itself exactly. DNA therefore contains the instructions to make new cells and reproduce the organism.

A MUTATION, or mistake, in the DNA, can be the basis of genetic defects. When the DNA replicates itself, the mistake is passed along to the new cells, thus transmitting the defect into the next generation. This is why environmental conditions that increase the frequency of mutations—such as high exposure to chemicals or RADIATION—are potentially so dangerous to organisms. [*See also* GENES; GENETICS AND GENETIC ENGINEERING.]

DRINKING WATER

In its fresh, pure form, our most precious resource. Humans cannot live for more than a few days without it. Most drinking water in the United States comes from aboveground reservoirs or from underground systems called aquifers. Rainwater and melting snow refill aboveground reservoirs. Aquifers are replenished when rainwater seeps into them through the ground. Rivers, lakes, and wells also provide drinking water.

Chemicals, salts, organic matter and MICROORGANISMS can contaminate drinking water. In the United States, most of the drinking-water supply is highly regulated. It must meet strict standards set by federal, state , and local agencies. Water authorities test drinking water for 200 or more possible contaminants. If any are found, the water customers are notified immediately.

Contaminated drinking water causes many diseases, some of which are fatal. People in countries with contaminated drinking water and poor sanitation are susceptible to serious health problems. Improving drinking water in these countries is a major challenge. [*See also* GROUNDWATER; WATER QUALITY AND TREATMENT.]

DROUGHT

The result of an abnormal absence of PRECIPITATION in an area. There are four kinds of drought: unpredictable, permanent, seasonal, and invisible.

Unpredictable droughts are the ones with which people are most familiar. An unpredictable drought occurs when there is a temporary absence of precipitation in an area that usually receives adequate moisture. Unpredictable droughts usually occur in places with a humid or subhumid climate.

Permanent droughts occur in areas where precipitation is always scarce. These areas are DESERTS, which have a limited ability to support plants and animals. Irrigation is needed to support agriculture in permanent drought areas. The support of large cities in these dry areas requires the piping in of large amounts of water from hundreds of miles away.

Seasonal droughts occur predictably each year in places that have distinct wet and dry seasons. In such areas, several months of heavy rainfall are followed by a period of intense dryness. India and Southeast Asia are two regions with such seasonal wet and dry climates.

Invisible drought occurs during very hot summer weather. It causes high rates of evaporation of moisture from the earth's surface. There may be frequent rainfall, causing people to think that drought conditions do not exist. But the rainfall may not be adequate to replace the moisture lost during evaporation. [*See also* CLIMATE AND WEATHER; DESERTIFICATION.]

E

EARTHQUAKES

Strong, sharp movements along portions of earth's crust. Earthquakes can range from a minor shaking to devastating disasters. The intensity of earthquakes is measured by instruments called **seismographs** according to a scale of numbers called the Richter scale.

The earth's continents sit upon huge blocks of crust called tectonic plates. These plates drift over the molten rock within the planet's mantle, the part of the earth below its crust. Convection currents—movements in the mantle caused by the heat of the earth's core—cause the plates to rub and push against one another along their edges. When the tectonic plates make contact in this way, ripples called seismic waves radiate throughout the earth's crust. Small seismic waves are usually not noticed by humans, but they are picked up and recorded by seismographs.

Powerful earthquakes occur when the earth slips along fault lines, which are deep cracks that separate blocks of the earth's crust. They also occur when two plates come together rapidly, causing the earth to buckle. One tectonic plate may be driven under another, causing the second to rise up and form mountains. Earth-

MAJOR EARTHQUAKES IN HISTORY

YEAR	LOCATION	EST. DEATHS	MAGNITUDE
1556	Shaanxi, China	830,000	N.A.
1737	Calcutta, India	300,000	N.A.
1755	Lisbon, Portugal	60,000	8.7
1812	New Madrid, MO	unknown	8.7
1906	San Francisco, CA	700	8.3
1923	Yokohama, Japan	200,000	8.3
1950	Assam, India	1,530	8.7
1964	Alaska	131	8.4
1976	Tangshan China	242,000	8.2
1985	Mexico City	4,200	8.1
1989	San Francisco Bay Area	62	6.9
1994	Northridge, CA	61	6.8
1995	Kobe, Japan	5,477	7.2

quakes under the sea can create giant waves called tsunami that can devastate coastlines far from the earthquake itself.

Some scientists believe that animals may be able to predict earthquakes by sensing slight pre-quake movements that humans cannot feel. [*See also* CONTINENTAL DRIFT.]

ECOLOGY

The scientific study of the relationships between all living things and their environments. All living things, from the smallest to the most complex, depend in some way on other living and nonliving organisms. Living organisms need food, water, and air to survive. Any disturbance in the quality and quantity of these necessities in one area may affect all the plants and animals that live there. An area can also be affected by changes that occur far away, such as air pollution carried from one part of the world to another.

The knowledge gained by understanding ecology is helpful in the fields of CONSERVATION, WILDLIFE MANAGEMENT, FORESTRY, agriculture, and pollution control. Ecology itself brings together such fields of study as biology, physics, mathematics, oceanography, and EVOLUTION. Scientists study ecology by observing and analyzing three elements: population, community, and ECOSYSTEM.

Population. All the members of a species that live in one area are called a population. Ecologists are interested in knowing what affects the growth or decline of a population. The size of a population depends on such things as food supply, predators, competition with other organisms, climate, and disease. Sometimes natural events may cause changes that can affect the population. For example, certain populations may increase or decrease when the amount of rainfall changes. Human activities also bring about change, as when pollutants mix with moisture in the air and fall as ACID RAIN.

E

Community. A community is the group formed by all the animal and plant populations that live together in the same environment. Each species has a specific role in its community. Ecologists study that role. They may also study how the community changes and how that change effects the species that live in it. Sometimes the changes may be so great that the community is succeeded, or replaced, by a different kind of community. One example might be a GRASSLAND region that receives little rain. A change in weather pattern may result in DESERTIFICATION. Most of the organisms that lived in that community will be replaced by others more adaptable to the new conditions. Another name for a community of plants and animals in a large geographical area is BIOME.

Ecosystem. An ecosystem involves the complex interactions of a community and its physical nonliving environment. The physical environment includes energy, MINERALS, CLIMATE, SOIL, water, and air. One of the major goals of ecological research is to learn how organisms use and recycle the minerals within an ecosystem. For example, ecologists have studied how HERBIVORES, or plant-eating animals, speed the recycling of NITROGEN, PHOSPHORUS, and other minerals. They have observed that when a herbivore eats plants rich in minerals, the minerals are passed through the animal's system and returned to the soil *faster* than they would have been if the plants had not been eaten. Therefore, herbivores have an important function in returning nutrients to the soil. They are RECYCLING minerals.

Profile: Aldo Leopold

Aldo Leopold is often called the father of the conservation movement. Born in Iowa in 1887, he grew up at a time when the prairies and forests of the Midwest were rapidly disappearing. After graduating from college, he joined the U.S. Forest Service and was introduced to the idea of conserving wildlife, soils, and water in the nation's forests. After 1928, he devoted himself to wildlife research. In his book *A Sand Country Almanac* (1948), Leopold details the ideal that all persons must be stewards of the land and, rather than control the natural world, integrate themselves into it.

ECOSYSTEM

A natural system made up of the complex interactions of a community of organisms and its physical environment. A community is the group formed by all the animal and plant populations that live together in the same environment. The physical environment includes all nonliving elements, including energy, MINERALS, CLIMATE, SOIL, water, air, and nutrients.

When scientists study an ecosystem, one thing they are interested in is the cycling of materials. Each living and nonliving thing in an ecosystem has a NICHE, or role. There is the sun, which is the primary source of energy. There are PRODUCERS, such as plants and TREES. They use the sun's energy to make food, including seeds, nuts, fruits, and vegetables. The food is eaten by primary CONSUMERS, which include small animals such as BIRDS, mice, rabbits, and squirrels. Secondary consumers—such as hawks, crows, owls, or seagulls—eat the small animals. BACTERIA and FUNGI are decomposers, which speed up the decaying process by breaking down plant and animal remains. The remains have the nutrients that plants need. These nutrients are abiotic, or nonliving. Abiotics include water, carbon, hydrogen, NITROGEN, OXYGEN, PHOSPHORUS, and sulfur. The plants absorb these nutrients, and the process starts all over again. In other words, these materials are constantly cycling, or moving through the ecosystem again and again.

In an ecosystem that is working well, the amount of nutrients remains about the same. However, if the ecosystem is disturbed, it can lose some of its nutrients. This can affect the health and number of the plants, which in turn affects primary consumers, secondary consumers, and so on through the cycle. The disturbance can be caused by human activity, such as the CLEAR-CUTTING of forests and failure to replace the trees. EROSION can carry away many nutrients. Pollution from the use of PESTICIDES or chemical discharges can affect the air or the water of an ecosystem.

Ecosystems do change even without human disturbance. Such changes occur over a long period of time or suddenly, as when a fire burns through a forest. After a change, a new ecosystem may gradually replace the earlier one. This replacement is called SUCCESSION. A difference in any of the elements of an ecosystem can start the chain of events that causes a succession. It may be a change in climate. Or the soil may become too acid for the plants that have been living there, causing them to die and be replaced by other plants. Because their food source has changed, many of the consumers are replaced by other species. Some, though, are able to adapt to the new environment. Succession also occurs after a forest fire, beginning first with smaller plants, such as wildflowers and grasses. They are followed by shrubs and finally trees. Eventually, the ecosystem may again become a forest, though that forest may have different kinds of trees than before.

ECOTOURISM

An increasingly popular form of vacation in which visitors travel to remote places to learn about nature and ECOLOGY.

Most ecotourists are interested in vacations that are educational, adventurous, and spiritual rather than simply entertaining or relaxing. They accept and enjoy the fact that the environments they visit may be harsh. Ecotourists go to RAIN FORESTS, CAVES, MARSHES, MOUNTAINS, DESERTS or TUNDRA. They may study and photograph wildlife, collect fossils, hike in remote places, or go rafting down wild and dangerous streams. They may camp in snow-covered sites or stay in **aboriginal** settlements where they learn about the traditional life of native peoples. Ecotourists go bird-watching in Panama, view gorillas in Uganda, see cheetahs in Africa, and observe orangutans in Borneo. Others enjoy ecotourism closer to home by hiking on trails in state parks or taking boat trips to watch for WHALES.

Critics of ecotourism say that the presence of tourists in any environment disrupts natural HABITATS. For example, four-wheel-drive vehicles disturb wildlife and cause pollution. If people use soap in lakes and streams, it can cause the growth of ALGAE, which can harm INSECTS that provide food for FISH and BIRDS.

Others argue that when carefully managed, ecotourism can actually benefit habitat CONSERVATION. Money from ecotourism can help conservation efforts and encourage local residents to protect species.

Ecotourism can affect the future of thousands of rare species. Therefore, groups such as the Ecotourism Society in Vermont and the National Audubon Society have worked to have ecotour operators and participants adopt ethical practices. The main principles ecotourists must follow are "Do no harm, do not interfere, and leave no trace." The challenge of ecotourism is to enable visitors to experience remote places with the least amount of environmental impact.

EL NIÑO

A temperature abnormality on the surface of the eastern Pacific Ocean that occurs periodically, causing unusual air and sea currents that affect weather around the globe. In Spanish the term El Niño means "the child." It is called that because weather changes caused by the phenomenon usually start to happen around Christmastime. Weather events caused by El Niño generally occur every two to seven years, and they last from six months to a year. As a result of El Niño, weather conditions may be abnormally wet, dry, hot, or cold in different parts of the world.

Meteorologists do not fully understand all the events that cause El Niño. But they know that the phenomenon occurs when winds in the eastern Pacific are especially brisk. These winds force the surface water of the ocean toward the equator, causing the water to become unusually warm. Colder waters from the southern Pacific flow in to replace the moving surface water. This movement forms unusual ocean currents.

☑ Keywords

Aboriginal. Referring to the original, or native, inhabitants of an area.

Meteorologists. People who study weather and climate.

Seismographs. Scientific instruments that measure earthquakes and indicate their duration and intensity.

E

Humid air rises rapidly above the moving, warm surface water, setting up abnormal atmospheric temperatures and wind currents.

As a result of these changes in the sea and air, certain parts of the world experience unusual and sometimes severe weather conditions during El Niño. In 1998 for example, the California coast suffered extremely stormy and wet weather as a result of El Niño. At the same time, the northern Great Plains suffered unusual heat and drought, and the southern states had abnormally heavy rains and flooding.

The El Niño weather cycle has been repeated many times. Scientists now know enough about El Niño to be able to predict when it will happen. El Niño seems to be a regular part of the earth's climate. But some scientists are concerned that its effects may be intensifying as a result of GLOBAL CLIMATE CHANGE. [*See also* CLIMATE AND WEATHER.]

ELEPHANT

The largest land animal on earth. Elephants are descendants of mammoths and mastodons that roamed the earth more than 10,000 years ago. Today, elephants live naturally only on the continents of AFRICA and ASIA.

African elephants are larger than Asian elephants, weighing from 7,000 to 11,000 pounds (2,611 to 4,103 kg). They have large ears, as much as four feet across (1.2 m), which they flap to keep themselves cool. Asian elephants weigh between 6,000 and 10,000 pounds (2,724 and 4,540 kg). They have smaller ears than African elephants, perhaps because they have adapted to the cooler, shadier forest environment found in many places throughout Asia.

The number of African elephants has

African elephants are easily recognized by their large ears.

declined significantly over the last several decades. In the 1980s hunters killed about half of the total estimated 1.3 million African elephants for their ivory tusks. Asian elephants are even more endangered than their African relatives. Farmers have killed more than half of all Asian elephants, leaving only about 45,000 left in the wild. Another 16,000 Asian elephants are working elephants, carrying heavy loads or performing in circuses.

All elephants are HERBIVORES. In the wild, an elephant can eat up to 1,000 pounds (454 kg) of food a day. Elephants can live to be about 60 years old, but few of them live that long. Most are killed by hunters before they reach their natural life span. It has been predicted that in 50 years almost all elephants will live in zoos, circuses, and WILDLIFE REFUGES. [*See also* ENDANGERED SPECIES.]

ENDANGERED SPECIES

Animals and plants that are threatened with EXTINCTION. The number of endangered species increases every year. In 1993, more than 800 American plants and animals were listed as endangered, along with about 530 species in other countries. More plants than animals are endangered. Many additional plants and animals are considered "threatened species," whose future survival is uncertain.

A species is considered endangered when its members die faster than they can reproduce themselves. The minimum number of individuals needed to sustain a healthy population in a species is called the "threshold number." This number varies from one species to another.

During the last 300 years, most endangered species ended up that way because of the actions of humans. Humans destroy plant and animal HABITATS. They hunt animals for their meat, fur, tusks, hides, and horns or because they consider them to be pests. Some species, like the Great American BISON, have been hunted primarily for sport. Beautiful and unusual BIRDS and other animals become endangered when humans capture too many of them to put in zoos or sell as exotic pets. Sometimes domestic animals introduced by humans take over the habitats of wild animals, or become PREDATORS. EXOTIC SPECIES may also invade native habitats, crowding out NATIVE SPECIES, taking over their sources of food, and

sometimes preying upon them and their young. Some animals and birds have become endangered because their young never have a chance to grow and develop. For example, many birds' eggs, such as those of the California CONDOR, failed to hatch because they were poisoned by insecticides like DDT.

	ENDANGERED		THREATENED	
	U.S.	WORLD TOTAL	U.S.	WORLD TOTAL
Amphibians	6	14	4	9
Arachnids	4	4	0	0
Birds	57	210	8	25
Clams	50	52	6	12
Crustaceans	11	11	2	4
Fishes	60	71	32	70
Insects	16	20	9	18
Mammals	36	287	5	36
Plants	375	376	74	159
Reptiles	8	71	15	48
Snails	14	15	7	14
Total animals	262	755	88	236
TOTAL SPECIES	637	1,131	162	395

In 1973 the United States government passed the Endangered Species Act to protect endangered animals and help them survive. This law allows the federal government to take direct action to protect species that are threatened or endangered. An international law, the Convention on International Trade, bans the trade of furs of endangered species, such as TIGERS, CHEETAHS and leopards, and forbids the export or import of ivory tusks from ELEPHANTS.

Scientists have placed endangered species in ZOOS AND AQUARIUMS and other controlled environments in an effort to help them reproduce and grow under protected conditions. Some of their efforts have been successful, as with ALLIGATORS, BALD EAGLES, and peregrine falcons. Other species have not fared as well, including the giant PANDA of China and eastern Tibet. Scientists try to rescue endangered plants by gathering their seeds and growing them under special greenhouse conditions.

The habitats of endangered species must be protected if the species are to survive. Thus, National Parks have been established and grassroots efforts in small communities have helped to preserve open spaces. [*See also* BIOLOGICAL DIVERSITY; CLEAR-CUTTING; DEFORESTATION; FIRE ECOLOGY.]

ENERGY

(See ALTERNATIVE ENERGY SOURCES; GEO-THERMAL ENERGY; HYDROELECTRIC POWER; NUCLEAR POWER; SOLAR ENERGY; TIDAL ENERGY; WIND-GENERATED ENERGY)

ENERGY CONSERVATION

Saving and not wasting energy. The main sources of energy used by humans come from petroleum (from which oil and gasoline are extracted), coal, natural gas, water and NUCLEAR POWER. Different sources of energy can be used to create heat, to fuel vehicles, or to generate electricity. Scientists are trying to improve ALTERNATE ENERGY SOURCES, such as solar power and new fuels for cars. But these new sources are experimental, expensive, or impractical. Most of the sources of energy we use now are in limited supply on earth. Once they are gone, they cannot be replaced. Therefore, it is extremely important to conserve energy. Energy conservation also saves money and helps to preserve the environment.

☀ There are many ways to conserve energy. People can reduce the use of electric appliances by installing insulation, using high-efficiency lighting, turning down the heat a couple of degrees in winter, and using the air conditioner sparingly in summer. Some new appliances are designed to conserve energy, such as water-saving washing machines and energy-efficient televisions. Fuel can be conserved by carpooling and using mass transit, or just by riding a bicycle or walking.

By conserving energy, pollution can be reduced. For example, using rechargeable bat-

---

☀ Fast Facts

Even when a TV is turned off, it still uses about eight watts of electricity to maintain the remote control and quick-start functions.

The United States uses 24 percent of all the energy produced in the world. But the population of the U.S. makes up just over four percent of the earth's population.

---

teries cuts down on the number of disposable batteries containing contaminating chemicals that end up in LANDFILLS. Avoiding energy-consuming power tools, such as leaf blowers and weed whackers, cuts down on fumes released into the atmosphere that can contribute to AIR POLLUTION. Cutting back on the use of such tools can also reduce NOISE POLLUTION.

Reducing the huge amounts of garbage created by humans can help to conserve energy. Unnecessary packaging materials require paper made from trees, which must be chopped down. Packaging material made of plastic never deteriorates and remains in the environment indefinitely, sometimes harming animals or their HABITATS. Hauling, sorting, and finding places to dispose of garbage uses a great deal of energy.

By expending a little more human energy, we can conserve our precious, limited energy sources while at the same time creating a healthier environment.

ENERGY CYCLE

The transfer of energy from one organism to another. All living things need energy to survive. Sunlight is the primary source of energy in most ECOSYSTEMS. Plants convert this solar energy into chemical energy that they need for growth and development through a process called PHOTOSYNTHESIS. When animals eat plants, they take in the sun's energy indirectly.

Organisms that do not grow and develop through photosynthesis must go through cellular respiration to get the energy that they need. Cellular respiration is the process of breaking down food to get energy as a product. All animals use cellular respiration to get energy from food, and even some organisms that make their own food use cellular respiration to get energy from that food.

The energy cycle is affected by who eats what. Food chains and FOOD WEBS show the pattern of energy transfer from one organism to another. When PRODUCERS (plants) are eaten by CONSUMERS (animals), the energy is transferred from the plants to the animals. When animals die, they provide energy for decomposers (BACTERIA), which then recycle the chemicals back into the soil and atmosphere where plants can use them, allowing the energy cycle to continue.

ENVIRONMENTAL ETHICS

Exploration of moral questions about human impact on the environment. Environmental ethics examines how humans can live responsibly with other species on earth. One fundamental question of environmental ethics is whether other living things have value independent of their worth and usefulness to human beings.

People's relationship to animals and the planet has been an important issue for centuries. Modern environmental ethics has challenged traditional arguments on several grounds. For instance, traditional ethical systems have been based on "anthropocentrism," the idea that ethics is concerned only with the welfare of human beings. New philosophers ask: When does an animal have "moral weight"? Another aspect of modern ethics argues that not just people and animals but entire ECOSYSTEMS and biological processes should be covered by ethical systems. Such arguments may seem abstract, but they can have enormous practical significance. For instance, in a 1972 U.S. Supreme Court dissenting opinion, Justice William O. Douglas argued that the federal government should allow environmental lawsuits in the name of inanimate objects that will be harmed by human activity.

Since the 1600s, environmental ethics has been increasingly influenced by scientific findings. In recent years, the ability of chimpanzees to learn symbolic language and of parrots to display astonishing reasoning abilities has called into question the assumption that animals did not have "consciousness" in the same way that humans do. Modern environmental ethicists are struggling with philosophical systems that incorporate new moral obligations to animals. "Animal rightists," for instance, have called for the abolition of the use of animals in scientific experiments, for the dissolution of animal agriculture and the elimination of HUNTING. Others are arguing for a more biologically based ethical system, and still others for a return to limited "animism."

ENVIRONMENTAL LABELING

Information on products that explains their effects on the environment. Environmental labeling is most often used by environmentally friendly companies to point out the advantages of using their products. These labels point out such things as low environmental impact, use of recycled or organic materials, and approval by environmental groups.

Some kinds of environmental labeling are optional, where companies choose to highlight the positive environmental effects of their products. Other labels are required by law. For example, labels are required on lumber imported from other countries to tell consumers where it comes from. This policy is meant to minimize the import of lumber from tropical RAIN FORESTS.

In general, labeling is an extremely useful method of allowing consumers to educate themselves about products and make informed choices about the kinds of products they buy and the environmental impacts of buying or using them.

ENVIRONMENTAL PROTECTION AGENCY (EPA)

A federal agency established in 1970 to protect the environment. The primary mission of the Environmental Protection Agency is to protect human health and safeguard the natural environment of the United States. The agency regulates and enforces environmental laws, monitors environmental conditions, and works to solve pollution problems. The pollution caused by SOLID WASTES, PESTICIDES, toxic substances, noise, and RADIATION are a few of the issues the EPA works to solve. The EPA seeks to reduce environmental risks through scientific research and federal laws.

The EPA has many established programs for pollution control. Its goal is to provide research, education, and practical solutions aimed at improving the environment. Among major programs of the EPA are SUPERFUND, the Acid Rain Program, the National Estuary Program, the Non-point Source Pollution Program, the Office of Pesticide Program, and the Oil Spill program. The EPA is a large agency with regional offices to help coordinate pollution control efforts with state and federal governments. By providing different types of programs and services, the EPA tries to maintain diverse, sustainable, and productive ECOSYSTEMS so that the environment can be accessible for environmentalists, business people, and the general population.

EROSION

The wearing away of a surface by natural forces. Erosion may be caused by the action of water, wind, or the movement of ice. The process of erosion moves rocks, SOILS, and other materials, carrying them from one area of the earth's surface to another.

Erosion can create deep valleys such as this one in the American Southwest.

Not all erosion is harmful. Ice breaks up rocks. Rivers carry soils and deposit them farther downstream, producing rich farmland. Lakes, river valleys, and other geographical features were formed by the erosive forces of large moving masses of ice called GLACIERS. Human practices, however, have increased the amount of harmful erosion. For example, CLEAR-CUTTING a forest for firewood or lumber leaves the land bare of vegetation. Wind and rain may then carry away the unprotected topsoil. Heavy rains rushing down bare hillsides can create mud slides that destroy whatever is in their path. Erosion can also carry pollutants into water supplies, or it can clog streams and rivers with rocks or other debris.

Erosion can be reduced by replacing trees that have been cut down or planting certain crops to "cover" the soil. The roots of the trees and crops will help keep the soil in place. Clearcutting and building on certain hillsides can be limited. Farmers with fields on hillsides can plant in strips that alternate thicker crops with others. [*See also* SOIL CONSERVATION.]

ESTUARIES

The tidal mouths of rivers where freshwater mixes with seawater. Estuaries are important ECOSYSTEMS for many organisms. In shallow areas of estuaries, marsh grasses grow in the mud. Estuaries contain plenty of light and NUTRIENTS needed for plant PHOTOSYNTHESIS. Large populations of plants and PLANKTON are found in estuaries as well as INVERTEBRATES, such as oysters, barnacles, and clams that live on the bottom or in marsh grass. Estuaries serve as protected harbors for many organisms, nursery grounds for many ocean fish species, and a source of nutrients for ocean life. They also absorb the tremendous energies generated by storms, including hurricanes, and act as flood protection systems. Many large city ports have been built on estuaries, and sewage, RUNOFF of soil, PESTICIDES, and toxic wastes are polluting many of these areas. [*See also* MARSHES; WETLANDS.]

EUROPE

The second smallest continent, Europe is made up of 47 independent countries with a total population of 707,880,000. Although considered a separate continent, it is actually a huge peninsula attached to an enormous landmass sometimes called Eurasia.

Europe is divided roughly into three major land regions: the Northwest Highlands, the Great European Plain (also known as the Central Lowlands), and the Alpine Mountains. The Northwest Highlands is a region of rugged MOUNTAINS and plateaus that stretches

E

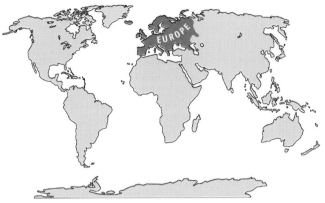

through Scandinavia and includes northern England and Wales. The Great European Plain includes southeast England, France, Belgium, the Netherlands, northern Germany, Poland, and Russia. The Alpine Mountains, which form a wall across southern Europe, consist of five mountain ranges: the Pyrenees, the Alps, the Apennines, the Carpathians, and the Balkans. Europe has a very irregular coastline with many peninsulas and good harbors. It also has many lakes and rivers.

Europe's climate ranges from the damp, cool marine climate of the lowlands of Holland and Belgium to the extremes of hot and cold in the dry steppe region of Russia and Ukraine to the bitterly cold climate of northern Scandinavia. However, most European countries have a mild climate because winds warmed by the OCEAN CURRENT known as the Gulf Stream keep temperatures moderate.

Large cities and industrial centers cause serious pollution in Europe. ACID RAIN caused by pollution from factories has killed plants and animals in forests in Germany, central Europe, and in more than a thousand lakes in Scandinavia. To help control AIR POLLUTION, the United Nations has drafted a resolution to limit poisonous sulfur dioxide and nitrogen oxide emissions into the ATMOSPHERE. Concerned Europeans have signed petitions to support these and other pollution controls.

Pollution of the Mediterranean Sea is another serious environmental problem in Europe. Industrial pollution of the water occurs because many cities along the coast dump sewage into the water. In 1976, seventeen European countries met to discuss ways of protecting this body of water. They established preserves to protect ENDANGERED SPECIES and agreed to prevent dumping of dangerous sub-

stances such as lead, DDT, mercury, and cadmium into the water.

The North Sea is also fragile. Giant oil rigs disrupt natural habitats of FISH and cause OIL SPILLS. Overfishing and whale hunting have imperiled certain species.

Since land is scarce in Europe, nondomesticated animals live only in a few remote areas or in protected WILDLIFE REFUGES, parks, and zoos. The European brown bear, one of the largest species of bear, lives in Russia and northern Scandinavia. Foxes, wolves, reindeer, boar, hedgehogs, and waterbirds such as egrets live in the wild. However, as Europeans continue to develop land areas, animal HABITATS shrink. Animals such as moose and foxes often wander into cities and towns in search of food.

EUTROPHICATION

A natural aging process that causes a lake to fill up with vegetation and soil. The process usually takes place over many thousands of years.

Lakes go through three stages in the eutrophication process. Young lakes are clear and open, with few nutrients to support plants. With few plants, animal life is also scarce. As a lake ages, nutrients such as phytoplankton, the foundation of water food chains, accumulate. These nutrients support various plants and animals, creating a more complex lake ECOSYSTEM. Old lakes are nutrient rich. Large numbers of plants grow around the lake, on its bottom, and in floating mats on its surface. The ecosystem of the lake is also very different than it was in its younger stages. Over time, SEDIMENTS build up in the lake, eventually turning it from open water into a grassy MARSH.

However, human activities have hastened the process of eutrophication in some lakes, with harmful effects on AQUATIC HABITATS. Nutrients added to lakes through the dumping of liquid wastes or FERTILIZER runoff from farm fields encourages more plant growth. The excess plants decrease the amount of oxygen in lake waters, which can affect the animal species living in the lake.

Although eutrophication is primarily associated with lakes, it can also occur in marine ESTUARIES along seacoasts. [See also NUTRIENT CYCLE.]

E

EVERGLADE KITE

The Everglade kite uses leaves and branches to build its nests.

A small, endangered RAPTOR. The Everglade kite is a slim bird with thick, fleshy feet. Much smaller than most eagles and hawks, the Everglade kite is a graceful flier and has a hooked beak that helps it eat its favorite food, the freshwater snail.

As its name suggests, the Everglade kite lives in the Everglades region of Florida. While the Everglades is its only habitat in the United States, it can also be found in Cuba, eastern Mexico, and in Central America. The bird is highly endangered due to destruction of its HABITATS and runoff of PESTICIDES into its environment. [*See also* ENDANGERED SPECIES.]

EVOLUTION

Idea that plant and animal species change gradually over time as a result of ADAPTATION to changes in the environment. Most scientists believe that evolution is responsible for the development of the millions of different plant and animal species that now inhabit the earth.

Though scientists had earlier discussed the idea of evolution, it was an English naturalist named Charles Darwin who fully developed the idea in the mid-1800s. Darwin's ideas became well known through his book, *The Origin of Species by Means of Natural Selection*, published in 1859. By natural selection, Darwin meant that some individuals in any species are better adapted than others to find food, survive disease, and escape PREDATORS. According to his reasoning, these are the individuals who are most likely to survive, mate with other survivors, and produce offspring. Those offspring would inherit the same survival characteristics. Meanwhile, the individuals who lack the ability to survive will die out.

Darwin gathered most of the evidence for his theory as a member of a scientific expedition aboard the HMS *Beagle*. This ship sailed along the coast of South America in the years 1831–36, stopping so that Darwin could collect specimens of plants and animals. The most interesting stops may have been on the Galapagos Islands in the Pacific Ocean off Ecuador. Darwin found that there were many differences between animal species on the islands and those on the mainland. Not only that, but there were differences among the same species on different islands within the Galapagos group. Eventually, he concluded that the differences were adaptations by individuals within each species to their environment. Since the islands were separated from the mainland and from each other, they evolved, or changed, in different ways.

The one thing Darwin could not explain was how the successful adaptations could be passed from one generation to the next. Scientists now know that these characteristics are passed from one generation to another by GENES. Genes are what determine the characteristics an individual is born with, such as eye, skin, and hair color in human beings. Genes can also pass on a number of hereditary diseases.

Profile: Charles Darwin

Born in 1809, British naturalist Charles Darwin traveled aboard the HMS *Beagle* on a scientific expedition around the world in 1831. Darwin observed geological formations of different continents and islands, as well as a huge variety of fossils and living organisms and became impressed with the effects that natural forces had on shaping the earth. Based on his experiences, Darwin laid the foundation for the theory of evolution and the idea of natural selection. His revolutionary theory was published in 1859 in the book, *On the Origin of Species by Means of Natural Selection*. Darwin also introduced the concept that all related organisms are descended from common ancestors.

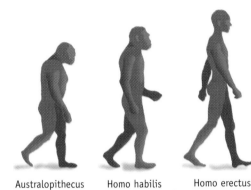

According to the theory of evolution, modern humans are descended from apelike ancestors.

Australopithecus   Homo habilis   Homo erectus

Although it is commonly referred to as the "theory" of evolution, support for the idea comes from many sources. One is the science of embryology. An embryo is an early form of an organism. According to Darwin's thinking, organisms that have evolved will retain some reminders of their past history. Such a reminder is called a vestigial feature—that is, it is structure that once had a function but no longer does because the organism has evolved. The embryos of all VERTEBRATES (animals with backbones) look very much alike in their early stages. For example, they all have a tail-like body part, though only in some species does it later develop as a tail. The other species lose the part as they develop. In some cases, the same body part may have been adapted for different uses. For example, a cat's paw, a bat's wing, a dolphin's flipper, or a human hand—all have a similar structure but are used in different ways.

Fossil records also support evolution. Evolution theory says that early species were more primitive, or simpler, than organisms that currently exist. Since fossils are found in layers in the earth's crust, the most primitive organisms should appear in the oldest layers. And that is true. The more complex organisms appear only in more recent layers.

One way species change is through MUTATION, a permanent change in an organism. The mutation is usually passed on to offspring. Some mutations are helpful in that they increase the animal's chances of surviving. Often, however, changes brought about by mutations are not helpful. Some mutations are caused by environmental factors such as chemicals or radiation.

EXOTIC SPECIES

Nonnative plants and animals that migrate into new ECOSYSTEMS. Almost 20 percent of the ENDANGERED SPECIES of plants and animals in the United States are endangered because of the introduction of exotic species.

Members of stable BIOLOGICAL COMMUNITIES compete with one another in order to preserve a natural balance in which one species does not gain dominance over another. Natural PREDATORS help to maintain this balance. But when nonnative species are introduced to a community, this balance can be upset. Exotic species may begin to monopolize available food sources. They may eventually crowd out NATIVE SPECIES, destroying their HABITATS. They may prey upon native species and introduce diseases. The affected native species may be forced into other ecosystems, where survival is not possible. It is difficult to tell which exotic species are harmful until after damage has been done.

Exotic species are often introduced intentionally. Starlings were brought to the United States from England. They multiplied rapidly, eventually crowding out the habitats of the eastern bluebird and other native bird species. Mongooses, mammals known for their ability to kill rats and poisonous snakes, were brought to the islands of Jamaica, Cuba, Puerto Rico, Hawaii, and other parts of the world to destroy large populations of rats. But in most areas the mongooses destroyed more native birds than rats.

Humans have planted new grasses to feed grazing cattle, and these grasses have crowded

Profile: Eugene Scheifflin

A wealthy British drug manufacturer named Eugene Scheifflin is responsible for introducing the starling, now considered a nuisance, to the United States. A lover of literature, Scheifflin believed that all of the birds mentioned in Shakespeare's plays should be seen in the New World. Because the starling was mentioned, Scheifflin released 40 pairs of the birds in New York City's Central Park in 1890. The birds spread quickly to other regions.

out native species, including valuable wheat grasses. The eucalyptus tree, introduced into Florida, has crowded out native plant species there. Humans have stocked rivers, lakes, and streams with fish to improve sport fishing. But in certain areas the fish carried viruses that infected native marine life. Farm animals brought into an area may consume native plants and destroy natural habitats.

Plants and animals have always migrated or extended their habitats, but humans have dramatically increased the rate of movement. Trade and transportation have enabled many species to migrate far from their original habitats. In Hawaii, for example, exotic species have reached epidemic proportions. During the past 50 years alone, an average of 18 new insect species have migrated there. Dangerous fire ants from Brazil have invaded areas of North America, killing off as much as 40 percent of all native plant and insect species in some areas. Outbreaks of the gypsy moth, a native of Europe, cost communities in the United States millions of dollars in crop losses and control costs.

Great damage can occur when exotic species interbreed with native species. This interbreeding can cause a species to lose its distinctiveness and create new, harmful species. For example, crop potatoes interbred with wild potatoes produced the Bolivian weed potato, which crowds out other crops. [*See also* DEFORESTATION; EXTINCTION.]

EXTINCTION

The disappearance of all members of a particular species. In the last 200 years, hundreds of species of animals have become extinct. Since 1901, it has been estimated that approximately 120 species of MAMMALS and 150 different types of BIRDS have disappeared. Some species of plants and animals become extinct because of a catastrophic change in their environment. Others die out from unknown natural

causes. Most of these extinctions, however, occurred because of the actions of humans.

Many species driven to extinction by humans have been rare plants and animals that lived only in small, specialized HABITATS. For example, the spread of Polynesian people during the past 1,000 to 4,000 years resulted in the extinction of around 2,000 bird species on the various islands of the Pacific Ocean.

In the last 50 years, a number of animals that once thrived, including TIGERS and ELEPHANTS, have become ENDANGERED SPECIES. Exploding human populations and expanding settlement destroy wildlife at a rate far exceeding the destruction of species in the past. Current extinction rates are between 100 and 1,000 times higher than during prehuman times.

DEFORESTATION, particularly in tropical RAIN FORESTS, has caused the mass extinction of hundreds of thousands of plant and animal species. Some species have been slaughtered to extinction, such as the dodo bird of the island of Mauritius in the Indian Ocean. These turkey-like birds have been extinct since 1680. European sailors killed them for food. Pigs and monkeys, brought to the island by Portuguese settlers in the sixteenth century, ate the eggs and the young of the dodo until none of the flightless birds remained.

Once a species is extinct, its loss affects all the other life-forms in its BIOLOGICAL COMMUNITY. Its unique beauty and ways of interacting with the rest of the world are gone forever. [*See also* BIOLOGICAL DIVERSITY; ENDANGERED SPECIES; EXOTIC SPECIES.]

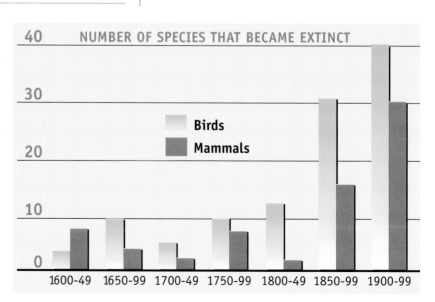

NUMBER OF SPECIES THAT BECAME EXTINCT

Birds
Mammals

1600-49 1650-99 1700-49 1750-99 1800-49 1850-99 1900-99

F

FACTORY FARMS

Animal farms that maintain large quantities of animals in small areas. Factory farms are very efficient in raising animals as a source of food, but they can also be unsanitary and environmentally unsound if not managed effectively. The enormous amounts of wastes produced at these farms, if released into the environment, can lead to polluted soils, rivers, and shorelines. Hog factory farms, for example, produce wastes that contain large amounts of NITROGEN and phosphorus. These NUTRIENTS can cause excess growth of ALGAE, rob water of oxygen, and kill fish. Ammonia nitrogen can also escape into the air from hog operations and contribute to AIR POLLUTION. Disposal of factory farm wastes onto land can also lead to contamination of GROUNDWATER. Certain metals from the animal wastes, such as zinc and copper, can accumulate in open-air pits, which can be toxic to plants and animals. The heavy metals accumulate for years in these pits, making it difficult to remove them safely. [*See also* AGRICULTURAL POLLUTION; ORGANIC AND INORGANIC WASTE.]

FECAL COLIFORM

(*See* WATER POLLUTION)

FERNS

Simple nonflowering plants that reproduces from specialized cells called spores instead of from seeds. The spores are located on lacy-appearing leaves called fronds. Ferns are vascular plants—that is, they have specialized tube-like tissues to conduct food, water, and other nutrients to the plant's cells. An ancient group of plants, they have existed on earth for more than 350 million years.

About 10,000 different kinds of ferns exist today. Most can be divided into three large groups based on their HABITATS. Many ferns are terrestrial, meaning that they live on land, often in damp, shady woodlands and along riverbanks. Another large group of ferns are acquatic. They live in watery environments, either floating on the surface of the water or growing from SOIL at the bottom of ponds or streams. A third large group of ferns live in the air high in trees, their roots anchored in tiny cracks in the tree bark. These ferns get moisture from rainwater that runs down tree branches.

Ferns are among the oldest surviving plant species on earth.

FERRET, BLACK-FOOTED

A short-legged, slender weasel with black mask, feet, and tip of tail. The black-footed ferret is considered the rarest MAMMAL in the United

F

Black-footed ferrets are curious and highly alert animals.

States. The species was once widely distributed in the Great Plains, from Alberta, Canada, south through the Rocky Mountains to the southwestern United States. By 1978, the black-footed ferret was feared extinct because of HABITAT destruction and massive HUNTING and poisoning campaigns by farmers and ranchers against the prairie dog, the ferret's main food. In 1981, a small ferret colony was discovered near Meeteetse, Wyoming, but many of these animals died from disease. Biologists captured 18 surviving ferrets and set up a breeding program. Today, black-footed ferrets are being bred at a U.S. government facility and at several North American zoos. In 1991, 49 captive-bred juvenile ferrets were released in Wyoming's Shirley Basin. Since then, ferrets have been released at sites in Montana, South Dakota, and Arizona, but none of these introduced populations is well established. The ferrets are threatened by habitat destruction, elimination of prairie dogs, predation by coyotes, and diseases. The search continues for wild black-footed ferrets, but the outlook is not good. Less than eight percent of the species' prairie habitat remains.

FERTILIZER

Any substance added to soil to help plants grow. Plants produce their own food through the process of photosynthesis. To carry out PHOTOSYNTHESIS, plants must draw certain nutrients from the soil. These nutrients include calcium, carbon, hydrogen, magnesium, NITROGEN, OXYGEN, PHOSPHORUS, potassium, sulfur, and other MINERALS. If the soil is missing any of those nutrients, the plants will not thrive. The addition of fertilizer to the soil ensures that plants will get the nutrients they need to live and be healthy.

Growers have always used "homemade" fertilizers—substances such as animal waste, wood ashes, and decaying plants. These are known as organic, or natural, fertilizers. Growers also use synthetic fertilizers, that is, substances that are not made from organic (once-living) materials. Many large-scale growers today use synthetic fertilizers. However, the use of organic fertilizers has been increasing.

Adding fertilizer to the soil has improved crop production greatly over the years, making it easier to feed the world's expanding population. However, the growing use of fertilizers has also created environmental problems. The use of too much fertilizer, for example, can lead to WATER POLLUTION. Rain may carry the fertilized soil into rivers and lakes, where the fertilizers encourage the growth of ALGAE. When the algae die, it is their decaying that pollutes the water. [*See also* COMPOSTING.]

FIRE ECOLOGY

The relationship between the existence of many species and fire. Certain BIOLOGICAL COMMUNITIES strongly depend on the changes in the environment produced by fires. For example, the seeds of some forest TREES, such as pitch pines, require the searing temperatures of undergrowth fires to **germinate** successfully. For years, people have tried to stop all forest fires as soon as they start. But now scientists are learning that fire plays an important part in the the balance of nature.

Some of the worst forest fires in recent years have been due to the successful efforts of humans to prevent and immediately extinguish all forest fires. When a fire finally does ignite, it quickly roars out of control because there are such large amounts of undergrowth to provide fuel for a major blaze. The undergrowth would have been burned away by smaller fires if those fires had not been suppressed.

By preventing all forest fires, humans have unknowingly caused some species of plants to become endangered and even extinct. For example, scientists have discovered that an endangered plant in Virginia called *Iliamna corei* needs fire so that its seeds can germinate. The plants almost died out completely until scientists discovered that none of the seeds sprouted because there had been no fires in its HABITAT for many years.

Some plants cannot grow well when too many shrubs cast heavy shadows on them. Controlled fires burn some of this shrubbery to allow in more sunlight. Fire ecology also encourages new plant growth. After an uncontrolled forest fire destroys large trees, new trees may be planted. These young trees are weak and do not have the shade of larger trees to protect them from too much wind and sun. Fire ecology saves many larger trees, which can then provide protection for the new ones.

FISH

Fish are an important source of food in many human societies.

Aquatic animals that breathe through gills. Almost all fish have fins, which they use to propel themselves through the water. All fish are VERTEBRATES. That means they have backbones. Most fish are cold-blooded animals—that is, their body temperature changes with the temperature of the water.

There are thousands of different species of fish, and they live in nearly every AQUATIC HABITAT on earth. They can be found in both freshwater and saltwater environments. Fish vary greatly in size, with the smallest being about 2/3 of an inch (1 cm) long and the largest 40 feet (12 m) long. Fish vary in shape, too. For example, some are flat, while others can puff themselves up like balloons. Many fish are brightly colored with a variety of patterns, ranging from stripes to polka dots.

Endangered Species: Giant Catfish

The Mekong giant catfish can reach 10 feet (3 m) in length and weigh more than 650 pounds (295 kg). It is the largest freshwater fish in the world and lives in the Mekong River in Southeast Asia. Every year, the catfish swim up the river to lay their eggs. Fishermen gather to catch them as they migrate upriver. One adult fish can be sold for as much as $3,000. The government of Thailand set up an artificial breeding program in 1983. Eggs are collected, and the young that are raised are sold or released into the river. These is no evidence that the fish have bred, and the program continues to rely on eggs taken from the wild.

FISH AND WILDLIFE SERVICE

Federal government agency charged with the CONSERVATION of the country's migratory birds, threatened and ENDANGERED SPECIES, certain MARINE MAMMALS, and sport fish. The U.S. Fish and Wildlife Service works with others to conserve, protect, and enhance FISH and wildlife and their HABITATS for the continuing benefit of the American people.

The Fish and Wildlife Service dates back to 1871, when Congress established the U.S. Fish Commission to study the decline in the nation's food fish. In 1903, the commission was placed under the Department of Commerce and renamed the Bureau of Fisheries. In 1885, Congress had created the Office of Economic Ornithology in the U.S. Department of Agriculture to study migratory birds; this office was eventually renamed the Bureau of Biological Survey. The Bureaus of Fisheries and Biological Survey were transferred to the Department of the Interior in 1939, and a year later, they were combined and named the Fish and Wildlife Service.

The Fish and Wildlife Service enforces such federal wildlife laws and international agreements as the Endangered Species Act, the Migratory Birds Treaty, and the Marine Mammal Protection Act. In 1987, the service established the National Fish and Wildlife Laboratory in Ashland, Oregon, to provide crime-lab support for wildlife enforcement investigations, such as DNA testing to identify species of spotted cat skins. The Fish and Wildlife Service manages the country's 500 NATIONAL WILDLIFE REFUGES.

FISHING

The harvesting of FISH, usually for human or animal consumption. There are two basic types of fishing: commercial and recreational. Com-

F

The fishing industry takes huge amounts of fish from the oceans each year.

mercial fishing provides an important source of food for people around the world. Certain fish by-products are also used in industry and in agriculture. Recreational fishing is a popular outdoor sport practiced in both freshwater lakes and rivers and in the oceans.

Modern commercial fishing places a great strain on fish populations, resulting in a dramatic decline in the numbers of some species of fish. Besides harvesting fish, the commercial fishing industry also catches crustaceans—such as shrimp, crabs, and lobsters. Certain MARINE MAMMALS, such as WHALES, have also been harvested from the oceans. But because of declining whale populations, whaling has been outlawed by many nations.

In some areas of the world the commercial fishing industry has collapsed because of a shortage of fish due to overfishing. Some countries have responded to this problem by restricting fishing areas in coastal waters and limiting the numbers of fish that can be harvested. Commercial fisheries have also been established for some fish species, such as SALMON, allowing the fish to be raised instead of harvested from the oceans.

Recreational fishing has had a much less dramatic impact on fish populations. Nevertheless, for centuries many societies have had laws restricting recreational fishing.

In the United States, for example, recreational fishermen must get fishing licenses each year that enable them to fish only during certain times of the year. States also have laws restricting the size, number, and species of fish that can be caught. [*See also* OVERHARVESTING; SPECIES LOSS.]

FLOOD

Any greater-than-normal supply of water that causes a river, LAKE, or other body of water to overflow its banks and spread into surrounding areas. Excess PRECIPITATION or high waves resulting from undersea disturbances or ocean storms can cause flooding.

Spring and flash floods are two common types of flooding. Spring floods occur as a result of heavy spring rains that melt winter snow cover. The water flows into streams and RIVER SYSTEMS, causing them to overflow their banks and spill into nearby towns and farm fields. Flash floods occur during short periods of time when precipitation is extremely heavy. The ground becomes saturated, and torrents of water spill into streams and rivers, causing them to rise and overflow their banks.

Sometimes flooding occurs near oceans. Tsunamis are a type of ocean wave caused by an undersea earthquake, landslide, or volcanic eruption. A tsunami races across the ocean as a

Floods can cause great damage to property, as well as loss of life.

wave that appears no different than any other. But as it nears shore, it rises into a huge wall of water that breaks upon the shoreline and rushes far inland. Tsunamis do not occur often, but they can strike coastal areas without warning. Hurricanes that occur at high tide can also push a huge wall of water onto the shore. This is called a storm surge.

Flooding is a serious problem today because many more people live on floodplains, the lowlands near rivers. Many people also live along coasts that can be swamped by tsunamis or storm surges. The National Weather Service issues flood watches and flood warnings to warn people about weather conditions that might cause flooding. This can give the public time to evacuate and move to higher ground.

Floodplains provide a natural outlet for flood waters.

FLOODPLAIN

A broad, flat section in the floor of a valley on either side of a river. Floodplains form when rivers flood and spill out of their channels, depositing SEDIMENTS of sand, gravel, and clay. Large rivers such as the Nile in Egypt, the Amazon in Brazil, and the Mississippi have extensive floodplains.

Rivers carry sediments from upstream down to the floodplain. When the water reaches the flatter regions of the floodplain, it slows and the sediments settle to the bottom. When FLOODING occurs, the sediments in a floodplain are picked up and redeposited, reshaping the floodplain by creating new sandbars and channels. The sediments that are deposited in some floodplains provide fertile SOIL for plants, particularly agricultural crops. People have long sought out these areas, creating great civilizations on the floodplains of the Nile River and the Yangtze in China, for example. In fact, most of the world's human population can be found on lands that are subject to flooding. Floodplains also attract wildlife, such as migratory waterfowl that rest there and feed on the abundant grasses.

Floodplains serve as safety valves, allowing floodwaters to spread out over a large area and slowing their flow. When people try to control flooding rivers with DAMS AND DIKES, levees, and other manufactured structures, they alter natural processes, often causing faster and more damaging flood events. When the river flow is artificially slowed upstream, the flooding river deposits the sediments above the dam and little reaches the floodplain area below, reducing the deposit of nutrients on the floodplain. [*See also* RIVER SYSTEMS; WATERSHED.]

FLOWERING PLANTS

Plants that produce flowers, fruits, and seeds. Flowering plants, or angiosperms, are the dominant forms of plant life on earth, and they occupy almost every ECOSYSTEM. The more than 200,000 known flowering plants include most shrubs and herbs, the majority of trees except pines and other conifers, the succulents (fleshy plants such as cacti), and other specialized plant forms.

There are two types of flowering plants: the monocots and the dicots. Monocots are plants that have a single cotyledon, the leaf produced by the embryo. Dicots have two cotyledons. The cotyledons store the plant's food reserves for germination. Monocots are primarily tropical plants, including floating water plants such as duckweed, water hyacinths, and grasses. Orchids and other epiphytes—plants that grow on the surfaces of trees and other plants—are monocots. Oaks, maples, roses, and tomatoes are all dicot plants.

The characteristic feature of angiosperms is the flower, which is responsible for the reproduction of the plant through the development of seeds. The flower is made up of four fundamental parts. The outer parts are the sepals, which are modified leaves and are usually green. The sepals act as protective covering for the inner flower bud. Continuing into the flower, next are the petals, which are also modified leaves but are usually more colorful. The petals make up what most people call the flower. Petals are usually consistent in number within a group of flowering plants; for example, there are five petals in roses. Third are the stamens, the male part of the plant which produces the pollen. Stamens are usually slender stalks that contain the pollen grains. The innermost part of the flower is the pistil, the female structure that produces the seeds. The pistil is the central part of the flower. The seeds of angiosperms develop in an ovary, located in the bulbous part of the pistil, which enlarges into a fruit as the fertilized seeds grow. [*See also* ENDANGERED SPECIES.]

Endangered Species: Hawaiian Gardenia (Na'u)

An evergreen shrub native to the Hawaiian Islands, the Hawaiian gardenia is also called the na'u. More treelike than shrub, the na'u has a tan trunk and small blossoms, with a more subtle fragrance than the average gardenia. Like many plants native to Hawaii, the na'u is endangered by habitat destruction and by the introduction of alien species that outcompete the native plants.

FOOD CHAINS

A series of connections in which nutrients and energy are transferred between organisms as they eat and are eaten by others. There are many different food chains, and they vary among ECOSYSTEMS. But they all contain PRODUCERS (primarily plants), CONSUMERS (most animals), and decomposers (such as BACTERIA). A series of interconnected food chains is called a FOOD WEB.

Food chains follow a pattern that, in general, goes from smaller to larger organisms. However, there are various levels of consumers, and some feed on animals larger than themselves. Each level of a food chain is known as a TROPHIC LEVEL. The higher levels of many food chains are usually occupied by CARNIVORES. But the highest level of any food chain consists of the decomposers, which get energy and nutrients by eating dead organisms. Most food chains contain only a few different types of organisms. [*See also* BIOACCUMULATION; ENERGY CYCLE.]

FOOD WEBS

Patterns of feeding and energy links among organisms in a BIOLOGICAL COMMUNITY. A food web links the different living parts of ECOSYSTEMS. The energy and nutrients in food webs flow from **producers** to **consumers** and finally to **decomposers**. Energy is transferred each time one organism eats another organism. Food webs can be very complex because they show all of the feeding relationships within a particular ecosystem.

Food webs are a series of interconnected food chains. Because many species do not eat only one kind of food, food webs show how a species may feed at different TROPHIC LEVELS. Food webs show the feeding relationships among species, with certain species playing important roles for the entire community. Although there may be various food chains within a food web, there are usually no more than five links from a plant to the top PREDATORS in an ecosystem.

Food webs may be affected by the loss or addition of a species, such as the loss and reintroduction of wolves in Yellowstone National Park. The number of prey—for example—rabbits, increased when wolves died out. But when wolves were reintroduced into the park, the number of prey evened out again. By understanding and studying food webs, scientists can see how much biological changes may affect a particular ecosystem.

Issues of biodiversity and environmental stability can be studied through food webs as well. An example of this would be the effect of whaling on the linkage of the organisms in the ecosystem of ANTARCTICA. When whales are hunted in Antarctic waters, the population of krill goes up. Krill are small, shrimplike crustaceans that are an important food source for many animals. When the number of whales decreases, the krill population increases, and the number of penguins, squids, and seals increase as a result. Thus, the food web changes completely, and the ecosystem has been reconstructed. [*See also* CARNIVORES; HERBIVORES; MARINE ECOSYSTEMS.]

FOREST SERVICE

 An agency of the U.S. Department of Agriculture (USDA) established in 1905. The Forest Service is responsible for managing public lands in NATIONAL FORESTS and NATIONAL GRASSLANDS. Gifford Pinchot, the first chief of the USDA Forest Service, helped establish the goals of the Forest Service, providing for the CONSERVATION and best use of the country's forest resources. Aldo Leopold, a conservationist and pioneer in the application of environmental principles to WILDLIFE MANAGEMENT, joined the Forest Service in the early 1900s. He soon recognized a need for the agency to do more than simply manage timber production. He introduced a sense of responsibility for the wildlife, SOILS, and WATERSHEDS in the nation's forests.

The USDA Forest Service conducts research in the use of forest products and management of rangeland. It also provides technical and financial assistance to state and private forestry agencies. The Forest Service is organized under a chief, who reports to the undersecretary for Natural Resources and Environment in the USDA. Each of the 155 national forests and 20 grasslands under its jurisdiction is overseen by a forest supervisor. Each forest is made up of ranger districts; there are more than 600 in the National Forest System. Each district ranger and the staff are responsible for trail construction and maintenance, operation of campgrounds, and management of vegetation and wildlife HABITATS.

The Forest Service issues permits for farmers and ranchers to graze livestock on public lands, and the rangers are responsible for monitoring these activities to guard against overgrazing. In addition, the Forest Service assists state and local governments and landowners with management of WATERSHEDS, or river channels. These areas encompass another 480 million acres (194 million hectares). Rangers plant ground cover on slopes, distribute plants, fight forest fires, and furnish information on tree pests and harvesting forest products.

The Forest Service also operates the Forest Products Laboratory, in Madison, Wisconsin, where researchers explore new ways to use wood and other forest products. [*See also* CONSERVATION; FORESTRY.]

FORESTRY

The science of caring for the growth and management of TREES. Forestry involves the management of FORESTS for human needs, such as providing timber for building homes or parks for recreation. Forestry involves making decisions about which trees to cut down and when to cut them, as well as which trees to leave standing. Forestry in the United States is managed by the U.S. FOREST SERVICE, which takes care of forests owned by the U.S. government. The Forest Service decides how forests can be used and what areas should be preserved. People who practice forestry are called foresters.

There are many techniques foresters use in the management of forests. These include the control of accidental forest fires and the use of controlled fires to open up areas so that new trees have more sunlight. They also include different ways of cutting down trees. CLEAR-CUTTING means removing entire areas of trees,

Profile: Gifford Pinchot

Born in 1865 and often considered the father of American conservation, Gifford Pinchot was the first forester in the United States and the chief of the U.S. Forest Service. He worked with Congress to provide the foundation for today's national forests and parks. Pinchot introduced the idea of sustainable-yield forestry and tripled the land area of forests under national management. He helped to found the Yale School of Forestry and Environmental Studies, where many of today's professional foresters are trained. He later became a two-term governor of Pennsylvania in the 1920s and 1930s.

F

which provides a lot of timber. The problem with clear-cutting is that it is very traumatic to the forest and to the wildlife living there. It also may lead to increased EROSION into nearby streams and rivers, since trees and tree roots are no longer there to hold the soil. Selective cutting requires more work on the part of the forester, because it requires choosing only certain trees and species to remove, and leaves others standing. Selective cutting leaves the forest better able to function.

The techniques foresters use depend on the services they want from the forest. Many forests are now managed for more than one purpose, such as timber. They are managed for MULTIPLE USES, which might include timber production, preservation of wildlife habitat, recreation, and so forth. Forestry also involves the planting or replanting of trees—also for multiple uses. Sometimes a certain species of tree is planted to provide habitat for an endangered animal or to provide future timber sources. [*See also* CONSERVATION; ECOLOGY; LOGGING; RAIN FORESTS; TAIGA.]

FORESTS

Large land areas with dense growths of TREES and underbrush. Different types of trees have adapted to live in different climates and regions of the world, and so there are a variety of forest types. The leaf shapes of trees are one of these ADAPTATIONS. Needle-shaped evergreen leaves are prevalent where the growing season is short and winter is cold or where the climate is hot and dry. The cone shape of needle-leafed trees, such as spruces, allows snow to fall off easily and not weigh down the branches. Needles have a waxy coating, which slows moisture loss in desert conditions. Broad-leafed trees do well with ample moisture and long growing seasons. Most broad-leafed trees are deciduous, which means they drop their leaves in winter.

Scientists classify forests into five categories: tropical RAIN FORESTS, tropical deciduous forests, temperate deciduous forests, temperate evergreen forests, and the TAIGA. Tropical rain forests occur near the equator, in such places as SOUTH AMERICA'S Amazon Basin, where the climate is warm and wet year-round. These forests contain a great variety of tree and other plant species, as many as 1,000 species per square mile (2.6 sq. km). The trees are mostly broad-leafed evergreen hardwoods that shed their leaves continuously throughout the year, not seasonally. The thick **canopy** may be 150 feet (52 m) above the forest floor. The ground below the trees is relatively free of undergrowth because plant debris decomposes quickly in the warm, humid environment. Vines and **epiphytes** grow on many of the trees; some may actually kill the host trees.

Tropical deciduous forests look much like rain forests and grow in tropical and subtropical regions. These forests, however, have distinct wet and dry seasons. Rainfall during the wet season is usually less than in rain forests. During the dry season, the trees lose their leaves. The canopy is not as high as in a rain forest, about 100 feet (30 meters), and the forest floor may be covered with thick stands of palms and bamboos.

Temperate deciduous forests are found in the regions of the Americas, ASIA, AFRICA,

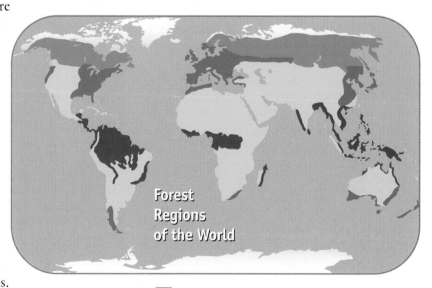

Forest Regions of the World

■ *Taiga (Boreal forest)*
■ *Temperate forest*
■ *Tropical rain forest*

and EUROPE where there are four distinct seasons. Most of the trees are broadleafs, and they shed their leaves in one season. Common deciduous hardwoods include beech, poplar, maple, oak, hickory, and sycamore. The undergrowth is made up of many species of herbs and woody shrubs.

Temperate evergreen forests occur in coastal areas that have heavy rainfall and cool, but not cold, winters. The Pacific Northwest of the United States is one example. There, rain and coastal fog promote the growth of large conifers such as Douglas fir, Sitka spruce, and western hemlock. The canopy tends to be dense, and trees grow tall.

Taigas, also called boreal (northern) forests, are found in regions with extremely cold winters and short summers. Spruce and fir are the dominant tree types in these conifer forests. Because the growing season is short, the tallest trees reach only about 75 feet (23 m) above a floor with abundant MOSSES and LICHENS.

Forests are important in their environment. They help prevent EROSION of topsoil, filter rainwater through soil, help reduce wind force over land, cool the earth, provide shelter for many animal and other plant species, and provide man with a variety of products. Environmentalists warn that humans are cutting down valuable forests at unsustainable rates all over the world. In 1990, for example, scientists found that 41 percent of Honduras was covered by forest. Five years later, the figure had dropped to 35 percent, and experts blame DEFORESTATION, for the mud slides and floods that devastated the country during Hurricane Mitch, which struck Central America in the fall of 1998. [See also CLEAR-CUTTING; FIRE ECOLOGY; FORESTRY.]

FORESTS, TROPICAL

(See RAIN FORESTS)

FOSSIL FUEL

Any material used to provide energy. Fossil fuels are coal, petroleum, and natural gas that were produced by natural processes from the remains of plants and animals that died millions of years ago. Fossil fuels provide most of the energy used in the world today.

Coal is mined from the surface of the earth, generally using large earth-moving machines.

Petroleum is the most commonly used fossil fuel. Most of it is used to produce transportation fuels, such as gasoline and diesel fuel. It is also used to make heating fuels. In its original form, petroleum is a liquid called crude oil, which is generally found deep in the earth. Before it can be used, crude oil must be refined, or purified.

Coal is another important fossil fuel. A solid fuel mined from deposits in the earth, it is used mainly to produce steam, which in turn generates electricity or operates steam engines. Coal is also used in the manufacture of steel. Though coal was once used to heat many homes and buildings in the United States, by 1950 it had gradually been replaced as a heating

Offshore oil wells produce large amounts of petroleum.

fuel by oil. However, it is still in common use in Europe and Asia. One reason for the decline in popularity of coal as a heating fuel is the problem of AIR POLLUTION. Coal releases sulfur and other chemical substances into the air when it is burned. Laws in the United States and other countries have required large factories that burn coal to install special devices that limit the release of pollutants.

Like coal and crude oil, natural gas also comes from underground deposits. This fossil fuel is a cleaner source of energy. Once removed from underground, natural gas does not need further refining. It can also be changed into a liquid. While coal and petroleum must be transported like other heavy goods, natural gas can be carried through long pipelines.

Concern about future shortages of fossil fuels and the effects they have on the environment has led to more research on ALTERNATIVE ENERGY SOURCES, such as SOLAR ENERGY, HYDROELECTRIC POWER, and WIND-GENERATED ENERGY.

FREON

(*See* CHLOROFLUOROCARBONS, CFCS)

FUNGI

A group of organisms that include mushrooms, molds, yeasts, LICHENS, and mildew. Fungi were once considered plants, but now they are classified in a kingdom of their own. Unlike plants, which use PHOTOSYNTHESIS to make their own food, fungi get their NUTRIENTS through absorption from the environment around them. Many are PARASITES that grow and live on other organisms.

Fungi have many cells, but their cells are different from those of plants and animals because they have no cell walls. Their cytoplasm—the fluid and tiny organs inside a cell—is continuous and often has more than one nucleus in each compartment. Fungi reproduce both sexually and asexually. Certain fungi release reproduction cells called spores into the air, and these travel by wind to find other fungi with which to reproduce. Other types of fungi produce spores inside their bodies.

Fungi play an important role in ecosystems, decomposing dead plants and animals and recycling their nutrients back into the environment. They are both harmful and helpful to humans. Molds and mildews cause millions of dollars of damage through plant diseases, and both the chestnut blight and Dutch elm disease have killed off these trees to near extinction. They also cause human diseases, such as athlete's foot. On the other hand, many cheeses are made with the aid of molds, antibiotics—such as penicillin—are derived from molds, and yeasts are used in the fermentation of bread, beer, and wine. [*See also* DECOMPOSITION.]

☀ Fast Facts

The invention of the steam engine was key to the development of the Industrial Revolution, which began in the eighteenth century. The first steam engines were fueled by wood. By 1890, though, coal had replaced wood as the chief fuel for driving steam engines. What brought about the change? Oddly enough, it was the steam engines themselves. They made it cheaper to pump water out of coal mines. With coal easier to mine, it became more affordable.

G

GARBAGE

(*See* SOLID WASTE)

GENES

The part of an organism's cells that carries a specific charactersistic of the organism and passes it on from one generation to the next. Genes are the basis of heredity—what causes children to look like their parents. For example, there is a gene for blue eyes, for brown eyes, and for green eyes. When cells from both parents combine to form a new offspring, genes mix in different ways so that the offspring will get some traits that look more like its mother, some more like its father, and some a mixture.

Genes are found on chromosomes in the nucleus of living cells. Chromosomes are long, threadlike strings of DNA and proteins. Genes are made up of strings of DNA. The hereditary information in the genes, such as eye color, is carried in the sequence of molecules in the DNA. When DNA from two parents combines to make a new organism, genetic information from both parents is combined. Most organisms have pairs of chromosomes. Humans have 23 pairs of chromosomes, and approximately 100,000 different genes. [*See also* GENETICS AND GENETIC ENGINEERING.]

GENETICS AND GENETIC ENGINEERING

An area of biology that sudies genetic variation and how traits are passed on from parent to offspring. Genetics helps to explain how GENES work, how they are passed on from one generation to another, and how genetic traits are expressed. Through genetics, scientists can discover how the differences in organisms occur and what factors are involved in maintaining BIOLOGICAL DIVERSITY.

Genetic engineering refers to various methods of transferring genes from one organism to another organism. For example, if one type of plant is immune to a certain disease, scientists may try to add the gene for this disease resistance to other plants, including farm crops. Genetic engineering is proving to be a very useful technique. It allows scientists to research and study genes that may cause diseases. It has been used in agriculture to make bigger and tastier vegetables that grow better under difficult conditions. It has been used for **cloning** organisms. Genetic engineering also has led to the use of DNA in solving crimes.

Geneticists, the scientists who study genetics, use genetic engineering to prepare recombinant DNA—DNA whose segments are from different sources. This genetic technology allows scientists to isolate specific genes, recombine genes from different organisms, and transfer this recombinant DNA into **host cells**. In the cells, the recombinant DNA can be replicated, providing multiple copies of the genes for study. Recombinant DNA can also be used to produce proteins such as insulin that can be helpful for people with diabetes. A technique of genetic engineering is gene-splicing, a process by which DNA from one organism is incorporated into the DNA strand of another organism, producing recombinant DNA. Enzymes, protein or part protein molecules, catalyze the reactions for DNA recombination to occur.

Genetic engineering may have a huge impact in the medical field in the near future. Through various methods of genetic engineering, doctors may be able to determine genetic defects or diseases in babies before they are

---

☑ Keywords

Cloning. Process of making many copies of a DNA molecule.

Host cells. Cells that contain recombined genes from different organisms.

57

G

even born. They may also be able to change the genes of future generations, determining the traits children will have.

While genetic engineering has many benefits, it may also have negative consequences. Many people, for example, wonder if the genetic engineering of crops might pose some dangers to human health. Moreover, uses of genetic engineering raise many ethical questions. Should humans determine the genetic characteristics of other organisms? Which human disorders should be treated with genetic engineering? Although genetics is an amazing field of biology that leads to the understanding of life, scientists must make careful decisions about how to use the new technologies associated with it.

GEOLOGY

The study of the earth, including its structure, processes, composition, and natural history. People who study geology are called geologists. Geologists study many topics relating to the earth, including chemistry, minerals, fossils, landforms, physics, oceans, and rocks.

One important topic in geology is the structure of the earth's different layers. Geologists can drill deep into the earth to remove core samples showing the composition of SOIL and rock hundreds of feet deep. But there is only so far they can drill down. Since they cannot see deep inside of the earth directly, geologists study it by observing how quickly sound waves travel through the earth. This tells them how thick the various layers are and what kind of material they are made from.

Geologists have discovered that the earth has three major layers—the crust, the mantle, and the core. The crust is only about 20 miles thick (32 km), but it is where all life exists. The deepest people have ever dug into the crust is about 9 miles (14.5 km). The earth's crust is made up mostly of OXYGEN, silicon, aluminum, iron, calcium, magnesium, and sodium. The mantle consists of both molten and solid rock. The upper part of the mantle holds the huge blocks of earth, called tectonic plates, that cause the continents to move about in what is called CONTINENTAL DRIFT. The earth's core, the innermost part of the planet, is made largely of iron. Part of it is liquid rock and is thought to be thousands of degrees Fahrenheit (Celsius).

Many geologists study the formation, history, composition, and movement of rocks, which are made up of various MINERALS and crystals. There are three major types of rocks, divided into categories by the way they form. Igneous rocks are formed by the cooling of molten rock, like that from VOLCANOES. Sedimentary rocks are formed from the hardening of layers of SEDIMENTS formed when older rocks break apart. These older rocks are broken down by EROSION, through the actions of wind, water, ICE, chemicals, and so on, forming smaller and smaller particles of material. These particles resettle, often at the bottom of oceans, and become hardened into new rock over the course of millions of years. Metamorphic rocks are igneous and sedimentary rocks that have been changed by heat and pressure. They can also be formed from other metamorphic rock. The oldest rocks discovered on earth are more than four billion years old and are the oldest known objects on the planet.

Geology is very important to the study of environmental issues. Geologists drill cores into the earth and ocean floor in search of oil, which has many potential environmental impacts. The geology of an area also greatly determines the kind of soil that has formed on top of it, which in turn affects the plant and animal life in an ECOSYSTEM. Geology also plays a part in determining the impact of environmental factors such as EROSION. [*See also* LITHOSPHERE; MOUNTAINS.]

GEOTHERMAL ENERGY

Energy produced by using naturally heated steam and water under the earth's surface. Far beneath the planet's surface, molten rock called magma heats reservoirs of underground water. In some places, this heated water rises to the surface as hot springs and geysers, which are fountains of boiling water and steam. Geothermal power is produced by drilling into these underground reservoirs and piping hot water and steam to electric power plants on the surface.

In geothermal power plants, steam from underground turns turbines that generate electricity. In some places, however, it is used directly for heating. In Iceland, for example, steam and hot water are pumped from underground and sent directly through pipes that heat buildings.

Geysers are found in only a few places on earth.

Geothermal energy is a nonpolluting energy source, but it is not inexhaustible. Once the hot water reservoir is emptied, it cannot be refilled. Each geothermal energy field has many wells. Each one generally lasts for between 10 and 15 years. Additional wells must be continually activated to keep up the production of power. But the geothermal field is eventually exhausted.

Although geothermal energy does not provide a large percentage of the world's energy, it is important in some areas. The United States, Mexico, Italy, Indonesia, the Philippines, and New Zealand all have local areas in which geothermal energy is an important part of the production of electric power. In the United States, geothermal energy development is concentrated in a few western states such as California and Nevada. [*See also* ALTERNATIVE ENERGY SOURCES.]

GLACIERS

Huge masses of slowly moving ICE that develop in the colder regions of the earth. Formed over thousands of years by compacted snow and ice, glaciers can be miles (kilometers) thick and wide. During long periods of cold climate known as ice ages, the last of which ended about 10,000 years ago, glaciers covered thousands of square miles (kilometers) of land. As they receded when temperatures warmed, they carved huge grooves into the earth. Today these scars in the land form ridges, valleys, cliffs, and other land features.

Many glaciers can still be seen in places such as the regions around the North and South Poles and even in certain parts of the United States. Glacier National Park in Mon-

tana is home to a number of glaciers, which continue to become smaller as global temperatures rise. Because they shrink when overall temperatures rise, scientists use the rate of glacier shrinkage as a useful indicator of GLOBAL WARMING. [*See also* ANTARCTICA; ARCTIC; GLOBAL CLIMATE CHANGE.]

Some glaciers look like huge rivers of ice.

GLOBAL CLIMATE CHANGE

The effect on the earth's atmosphere due to human activities. The earth's atmosphere contains various gases that act as a blanket to trap heat from the sun and help keep the earth warm. The trapping of the sun's heat by these gases is called the greenhouse effect and the gases are called greenhouse gases.

The burning of FOSSIL FUELS to heat our homes, power our cars, and light up our cities produces CARBON DIOXIDE and other greenhouse gases. The increased amount of these gases in the atmosphere contributes to global

G

climate change. Computer simulations of the climate have shown that global temperatures will rise as atmospheric concentrations of carbon dioxide and these other gases increase. Although the earth's climate has steadily warmed over the course of thousands of years, the rate at which the temperature changes is what concerns scientists today. Continued warming of the atmosphere may change precipitation patterns, cause the sea level to rise, and alter the distribution of freshwater supplies. The emission of greenhouse gases as a result of human activity is estimated to be growing at about 1 percent per year, which may cause significant global warming.

Global warming speeds up the global water cycle, with higher temperatures causing more evaporation, so that SOILS dry out faster. An increased amount of water in the atmosphere will then lead to more rain or snow, and the growing seasons of different areas may be altered. Within the last century, glaciers have melted worldwide and glacial ice caps in the ARCTIC and ANTARCTIC have also begun to melt. This melting could damage ECOSYSTEMS and cause sea levels to rise.

Global climate changes are likely to have many negative effects on ecological systems, as well as on human health. Some human health problems could result from heat stress, SMOG, and other air-quality problems. Warmer climates may raise the populations of disease-carrying organisms, increasing the incidence of diseases such as malaria and yellow fever.

Rising sea levels would erode beaches and coastal WETLANDS and increase the risks of floods from storms and heavy rainfall. Global warming could also change forests and natural areas. The increase in carbon dioxide levels could negatively affect the growth of trees, and cause natural glaciers to recede at a faster rate. Predictions about global climate change show that the atmospheric concentrations of greenhouse gases will likely increase over the next 100 years. The higher latitude regions will warm more than areas nearer to the equator, and there will be less variation in temperature from night to day. [*See also* AIR POLLUTION; CLIMATE AND WEATHER; DESERTIFICATION.]

GORILLA

The largest of the primates and the group of MAMMALS most closely related to humans. Gorillas are great apes that live in the RAIN FORESTS of central and western AFRICA. Male gorillas weigh up to 400 pounds (181 kg), while females weigh about half as much. Gorillas live in groups called troops with one dominant male—called the silverback because of his gray hair—several females, juvenile males, and babies.

In popular culture, gorillas have developed a reputation for being fierce. In reality they are gentle and will not attack unless provoked. They rarely eat meat, preferring to munch on the rich vegetation of the rain forest. The silverback protects the troop from any outside attack, and if he feels threatened, will pound his chest in an effort to scare away intruders.

There are three subspecies of gorillas: the mountain gorilla, the eastern lowland gorilla, and the western lowland gorilla. They are only slightly different in appearance, with mountain gorillas having longer, thicker fur. Lowland gorillas are slightly larger than mountain gorillas. All three are highly ENDANGERED SPECIES

 Profile: Dian Fossey

Born in California in 1932, Dian Fossey had an interest in animals from a young age. During a trip to Africa in the early 1960s, she became interested in mountain gorillas. Fossey began observing gorillas in the wild in 1967 in Zaire (now the Democratic Republic of Congo). She later moved to Rwanda and started the Karisoke Research Center. Fossey lived there for nearly 18 years among the mountain gorillas. After a favorite gorilla was killed by poachers, she started a campaign against poaching. She was found dead in her cabin on December 26, 1985; her murder has never been solved.

Gorillas have a reputation for fierceness, but they are actually quite gentle unless provoked.

in their native HABITATS because of human HUNTING and habitat destruction. Scientists estimate that there are only about 600 mountain gorillas left in the wild. In North America, zoos and wildlife organizations are working hard to save the gorillas that are left by studying their behavior and working with Africans to establish protected areas for them. [*See also* HABITAT LOSS AND CONSERVATION.]

GRASSLANDS

Vast plains of land covered by grasses. Grasslands are ECOSYSTEMS that occur in temperate climates where rainfall is low. TREES do not grow well in grassland areas because there is not enough water. Grasses, however, can survive in the drier climates that characterize

G

grasslands. Many animals have adapted to grassland HABITATS, digging burrows underground or evolving camouflage colors. Prairie dogs and other kinds of rodents make grasslands their home, as do many kinds of antelope, which can run fast to escape PREDATORS on the open plains.

There are several different kinds of grasslands, including PRAIRIES and SAVANNAS. Savannas tend to be drier and bordered by DESERT and FOREST on either side. Animals such as LIONS, CHEETAHS, zebras, and giraffes are often found foraging for food in the great savanna grasslands of AFRICA, in places such as the Serengeti and Masai Mara.

GRAZING

Style of eating in which an animal spends most of its time consuming grasses. Animals such as cattle, goats, sheep, and other HERBIVORES are grazers. They eat various kinds of grasses and other plants that grow in the fields or on PRAIRIES.

Overgrazing is a significant environmental problem in many areas of the world. When too many animals are allowed to graze the same area for too long, they may eat everything in sight, leaving no plants in the area. When this happens, the land becomes damaged, and bare SOIL may lead to EROSION and DESERTIFICATION.

Another environmental problem occurs when farmers remove FORESTS to create new grazing land for their animals. The removal of forests also may lead to increased erosion, poorer soil quality, and desertification as well. Overgrazing is an important factor in the destruction of tropical RAIN FORESTS. [See also OVERHARVESTING.]

GREENHOUSE EFFECT

(See GLOBAL CLIMATE CHANGE)

GRIZZLY BEAR

The largest PREDATOR on land. Known for their huge size, grizzlies can grow to 10 feet tall (3 m) and weigh close to 1000 pounds (454 kg). Female grizzlies, which are often darker brown than males, only grow to about half the size of the males. Grizzly bears are basically OMNIVOROUS, which means that they will eat many different kinds of things, including fruits, berries, nuts, and animals they kill, such as deer or fish.

Grizzly bears generally avoid contact with humans.

Grizzlies are closely related to European brown bears and Kodiak bears, a species of bear found only on Kodiak Island and in Alaska. They live throughout wilderness areas

Frank and John Craighead are wildlife biologists who study grizzly bears, elk, and other large mammals. During the 1970s, the Craigheads helped manage grizzly bear populations in Yellowstone National Park. Frank is president and founder of the Craighead Environment Research Institute, which seeks to increase the understanding, appreciation, and protection of our natural environment, particularly wildlife populations and wild landscapes of the American West. The institute focuses its work on grizzlies and other large carnivores.

in the northwestern part of North America, and are found in NATIONAL PARKS such as Yellowstone and Glacier. Their range has been shrinking over the past 100 years due to human population expansion and loss of their natural HABITATS. Grizzlies are mainly solitary, except when a female has her cubs with her. In the winter, the bears enter a state of inactivity, living off their fat reserves in small CAVES lined with SOIL and leaves. Females give birth to 1–3 young in the middle of the winter. The cubs stay with their mother for about a year and a half.

Grizzly bears need very large ECOSYSTEMS to support their wandering lifestyles and their need for large quantities of food. They live in and near FORESTS, rivers, and MOUNTAINS. As humans have removed forests and fragmented what were once vast wilderness areas, grizzlies have less and less area in which to live. This loss of habitat has posed a real threat to the bears' survival. [*See also* MAMMALS; PREDATORS.]

GROUNDWATER

Water below the surface of the earth that feeds wells and natural springs. Groundwater comes from rain and melted snow that soak down into the ground. It may also come from rivers, LAKES, or ponds that leak water into the SOIL. Groundwater generally collects in areas with rocks, gravel, and sand. Large underground storage areas such as this are called aquifers.

Groundwater is a very important source of DRINKING WATER. But it can be polluted by industrial, agricultural, and residential sources. Sewers, septic tanks, amd chemical spills may leak into groundwater. Seepage from some LANDFILL is another source of groundwater pollution, as is water RUNOFF containing FERTILIZERS used on farms. [*See also* WATER POLLUTION; WATERSHED; WATER TABLE.]

GUAM RAIL

Closely related to cranes, a group of BIRDS that prefer walking to flying. The Guam rail and other rails are are found primarily on islands and in WETLAND areas. The Guam rail lives only on the island of Guam in the Pacific Ocean. Its population numbered around 80,000 in 1968, but the species faced EXTINCTION due to the accidental introduction of the brown tree snake to Guam sometime after World War II. By 1983, the brown tree snake had destroyed most of the Guam rail population. There were barely 100 of the birds left, making the species one of the most highly endangered birds in the world.

The Guam rail is large among rails, measuring about 1 foot (.3 m) tall. It has a dark brown head, back, tail, and bill; a gray throat, breast, and stripe; and striped black and white wings. Its preferred HABITATS are scrubby areas and mixed FORESTS. A flightless bird that builds its nest on the ground, the Guam rail eats flowers, seeds, fruit, crustaceans, nd worms, and will even feed on dead animals. Males will forcefully defend territories, and the birds spend time in family groups of two parents and young.

The fate of the Guam rail is an excellent example of the potential effects of introduced species. Since the brown tree snake, which can reach 8 feet (2.4 m) long, had no natural predators on Guam, its numbers rapidly increased, threatening the native rail on this relatively small island. Guam rails are held in captivity at several zoos worldwide and there are plans to reintroduce them on Guam once the tree snake's population is brought under control. [*See also* ENDANGERED SPECIES; EXOTIC SPECIES; NATIVE SPECIES.]

GULF STREAM

(*See* OCEAN CURRENTS)

H

HABITAT

The place where an animal lives and meets all its basic needs—including food, water, shelter, and space. A habitat is chiefly characterized by the kinds of vegetation that grow in any one place. Almost any place on earth can be a habitat for some kind of animal. Animals live in FORESTS and inside TREES, deep in the oceans, the DESERTS, on frozen ICE in the ARCTIC, and in tropical rain forests. AQUATIC HABITATS include a range of places, from deep in the ocean to small streams and ponds. Different animals live in saltwater, freshwater, moving water, and still water. Terrestrial habitats (those on land) range from the tops of MOUNTAINS to deep within CAVES.

Animals are adapted to live in a particular habitat, with characteristics that help them survive there. An animal that can live in saltwater, such as a crocodile, is highly adapted to deal with the salt in the water and would not be able to survive on top of a mountain. A bat adapted to live in a cold, dark cave would do poorly on the open GRASSLANDS. ADAPTATIONS to a habitat include the color, shape, size, and behavior of an animal. [*See also* BIOME; ECOSYSTEM; ESTUARIES; GRASSLANDS; MARINE ECOSYSTEMS; MARSHES; PRAIRIES; SAVANNAS; SWAMPS; WETLANDS.]

HABITAT LOSS AND CONSERVATION

Loss of living spaces for animals and plants and attempts to conserve them. As human population has expanded, especially in the past century, people have taken up increasing amounts of space for homes, agriculture, recreation, and other uses. This trend has led to a tremendous loss of animal and plant HABITATS. When animals can no longer meet their needs for food, water, and shelter because of habitat loss, they may face EXTINCTION.

Habitats can be lost in a number of ways. The destruction of FORESTS by LOGGING is one major cause of habitat loss. Many animals depend on forests for food and shelter. When the TREES are destroyed and removed, animals can no longer live there. Habitats are also destroyed by pollution. When factories discharge chemicals into nearby rivers, those chemicals can destroy the habitat of fish and other aquatic animals. Habitats may also be lost due to commercial development, drainage of WETLANDS, introduction of EXOTIC SPECIES, and many other factors.

Habitat loss is one of the major reasons that increasing numbers of animals and plants are becoming ENDANGERED SPECIES. Large animals that depend on a lot of space are especially endangered by habitat loss. These include animals such as ELEPHANTS, TIGERS, bears, and GORILLAS.

Habitats are being lost throughout the world. RAIN FORESTS, which hold more than 50 percent of the world's wildlife, are being destroyed at a rate of more than 100 acres (40.5 hectares) per minute. As habitats are lost, more animals will disappear.

Endangered Species: Quetzal

The quetzal, which lives in the rain forests of Central America, is often called one of the most beautiful birds in the world. It is the national bird of Guatemala. The head of the male quetzal is covered with a soft crest of feathers, and the birds can have a tail 32 inches long (81 cm). Males defend their territories by flying the perimeter and flashing their distinctive metallic-colored plumage, which can be seen from quite far away. Some people consider the quetzal's flight the most beautiful sight in the world.

Conservation organizations and some governments work hard to prevent habitat loss. Environmental protection laws now try to prevent excess pollution and set limits to how much logging can occur. The Endangered Species Act, for example, lists endangered animals and requires the government to come up with habitat conservation plans. These plans create protected areas for the animals where they will be safe. Other laws, such as the Clean Air Act and Clean Water Act, work to improve habitats that have been degraded by human activity. When the air and water are cleaner, animals can often return to their old habitats. As people become more aware of their overall impact on habitats, it will be important to be careful to preserve them for all animals. [*See also* AGRICULTURAL POLLUTION; BIOSPHERE RESERVE; CLEAR-CUTTING; DEFORESTATION; NATIONAL WILDLIFE REFUGES; SPECIES LOSS; WILDLIFE REFUGES.]

HAZARDOUS SUBSTANCES

Substances that can be harmful for humans and the environment. There are many types of hazardous substances. Homes often contain chemicals that are useful but dangerous. Ammonia, bleaches, toilet-bowl cleaners, disinfectants, furniture polish, paints, oils, and even old medicine are examples of potentially hazardous substances. If ingested or let loose in the environment, many of these substances can cause severe health problems. Hazardous chemicals tend to be poisonous, and if not properly used, stored, or disposed of, they can be deadly.

People use many hazardous substances daily without much thought to the dangers of such chemicals. However, some common substances such as pesticides—chemicals that are used in farming to get rid of bugs and rodents—can be extremely hazardous to human health and the environment. Such chemicals are often sprayed onto the foods people eat and they are found in drinking water due to RUNOFF from farms.

The presence of hazardous chemicals can also damage the environment. The nutrients in the soil may change, and these substances can contribute to a major WATER POLLUTION problem. The land may become unsuitable for certain crops to grow. Using pesticides causes

farmers other problems as well. For instance, many pests adapt to the pesticides and are unaffected by these chemicals, creating more of a problem for the farmers. Today, scientists are trying to create better methods to help rid themselves of pests and keep food healthy for consumers by using less hazardous or natural products. [*See also* HAZARDOUS WASTE; TOXICS RELEASE INVENTORY.]

HAZARDOUS WASTE

Solid, liquid, or gaseous materials that can be harmful to humans and the environment. Hazardous wastes have been classified by the ENVIRONMENTAL PROTECTION AGENCY, into specific categories, including reactive wastes, corrosive wastes, ignitable wastes, toxic wastes, radioactive wastes, and MEDICAL WASTES.

STATES WITH MOST NATIONAL PRIORITY LIST HAZARDOUS WASTE SITES, 1994			
State	**Nonfederal**	**Federal**	**Total**
California	73	23	96
Florida	52	5	57
Michigan	77	1	78
Minnesota	39	2	41
New Jersey	103	6	109
New York	81	4	85
Ohio	33	5	38
Pennsylvania	96	5	101
Washington	37	19	56
Wisconsin	40	0	40

Reactive wastes are those that can explode, such as gunpowder. Corrosive wastes are chemicals that can eat through many materials like steel. Battery acid and certain chemicals in drain-cleaning solutions are examples of corrosives. Transportation and storage of corrosive wastes are difficult because very few containers can hold these chemicals for a long time. Ignitable wastes are substances that can burst into flames at low temperatures. Paint thinners, oils, and some cleaning fluids are examples of ignitable wastes that cause toxic fumes, smoke, and fire. Toxic wastes are chemicals that are poisonous. Arsenic, cyanide, mercury and PESTICIDES are toxic wastes. Radioactive wastes give off radiation that can burn skin and destroy body cells and tissues.

Many experts believe that birth defects and cancer-related illnesses are related to exposure to hazardous wastes. The burying of hazardous wastes may result in their entering the water systems of different neighborhoods, leading to health risks. Many products people rely on daily, including plastics, electronics, solvents, and other materials in appliances and furniture, can also leave toxic **by-products** in the environment. Keeping these harmful chemicals away from food, water, and the environment can be done by disposing wastes safely and cautiously in areas that are not near homes and the HABITATS of other organisms. [*See also* HAZARDOUS SUBSTANCES; TOXICS RELEASE INVENTORY.]

HEAVY-METAL POLLUTION

Environmental pollution caused by the presence of certain metallic elements. Heavy metals are chemical elements that have high atomic masses, such as mercury, lead, cadmium, arsenic, nickel, and chromium. Heavy-metal pollution occurs when such metals enter GROUNDWATER and surface water, either by seeping into the dirt near the water or by direct disposal into the water. Large deposits of MINING wastes can lead to heavy-metal pollution. Rainwater LEACHING through these deposits carries the wastes into the groundwater and surface water. Industrial processes of making metals, paint, and plastics also produce BY-PRODUCTS of heavy-metals that go into the water systems.

Many health problems occur from heavy-metal ingestion. Heavy metals are poisonous

and can cause brain, liver, and kidney damage and, in some cases, may lead to coma and death. One of the best-known examples of heavy-metal poisoning occurred in the 1950s in Minamata Bay in Japan. Mercury released by industries around the bay contaminated the fish, and the people who ate the fish suffered terrible health problems. Industries can help maintain the safety of the environment and human health by being careful and responsible with the disposal of their waste products. [*See also* HAZARDOUS WASTES.]

HERBICIDES

Chemicals designed to kill unwanted plants. Herbicides are used mainly in commercial agriculture to eliminate weeds from crops grown for food. When herbicides were first developed, they were made of inorganic (nonliving) compounds, such as copper sulfate. In 1935, the first organic compounds were used. These compounds are able to kill weed plants, while allowing crop plants to remain growing.

Though herbicides allow commercial agriculture to produce larger crops, they can also cause a number of problems. When herbicides are applied, they remain on the plants that humans and animals will consume. They also enter the WATER CYCLE. If these chemicals are consumed by humans in significant quantities, they can cause cancer and other deadly diseases. Herbicides can also become part of chemical RUNOFF from farms, when excess rain carries the chemicals to rivers, oceans, or bays. There, it accumulates and can cause WATER POLLUTION and prove harmful to marine animals.

Widespread use of herbicides did not begin until shortly after World War II. Because they were viewed as miracle aids to farmers, they were used liberally before scientists really understood their potentially harmful effects. The potential dangers of too much chemical use was first brought to public attention by the publication in 1962 of *Silent Spring*, a book written by American biologist Rachel Carson. Most herbicides —along with PESTICIDES— are now tightly regulated by environmental laws in the United States. [*See also* AGRICULTURAL POLLUTION; EUTROPHICATION; LEACHING.]

HERBIVORES

Animals that eat only plants. A number of very common animal species are herbivores, including cows, goats, ELEPHANTS, deer, horses, sheep, rabbits, monkeys, and apes.

The teeth of herbivores are specially adapted for their diet. Some herbivores have sharp front incisors that allow them to nip off leaves or bite into tough nuts and seeds. Most of their teeth, however, are broad and flat, allowing them to mash and grind the grass and leaves they eat.

Herbivores are never PREDATORS—animals that hunt and kill other animals for food. But they are often the prey of meat-eating animals called CARNIVORES. In most parts of the world, INSECTS are the dominant herbivores. But plant-eating MAMMALS and BIRDS are among the more noticeable herbivores.

Endangered Species: Brown-antlered Deer

The brown-antlered deer, also called the thamin or Eld's deer, lives in swamps and wetlands of Asia. It grows antlers that can reach 3 feet (0.9 m) in length, and has long spreading hooves, which probably help it walk in swampy areas. Illegal hunting and habitat destruction by logging, farming, and livestock grazing have made it an endangered species.

Herbivores play an important role in FOOD CHAINS. When they eat plants, they store energy produced by the plants in their bodies. This energy becomes available to carnivores that feed on them. [*See also* OMNIVORES.]

HUMAN POPULATION GROWTH AND CONTROL

An increase in human population and the methods used to control population growth. Earth's human population has been increasing steadily for thousands of years. The most dramatic growth rates have occurred during the 1900s, when some areas of the world experienced a population explosion in which the population doubled or tripled in relatively short periods of time. This tremendous growth in population has resulted, in large part, from advances in medicine that have reduced death rates at childbirth and from disease.

Profile: Paul Ehrlich

A professor of Population Studies at Stanford University in California, Paul Ehrlich began his career in entomology (the study of insects). Ehrlich later turned to the study of human population growth. Through his book *The Population Bomb* and other works, Ehrlich has focused attention on the connection between human population growth and wildlife extinction, changes in the atmosphere, global warming, and other envrionmental problems.

Left unchecked, human population growth can have a very negative effect on the environment. The earth has a limited supply of resources needed by humans and other animal species to survive. If human population continues to expand at an uncontrolled rate, the population may one day exceed the ability of the environment to support humans and other species. Human population growth also threatens the environment in other ways. Human activities are responsible for various types of pollution, destruction of plant and animal HABITATS, and damage to ECOSYSTEMS. As human population grows, these threats become increasingly serious.

HUNTING

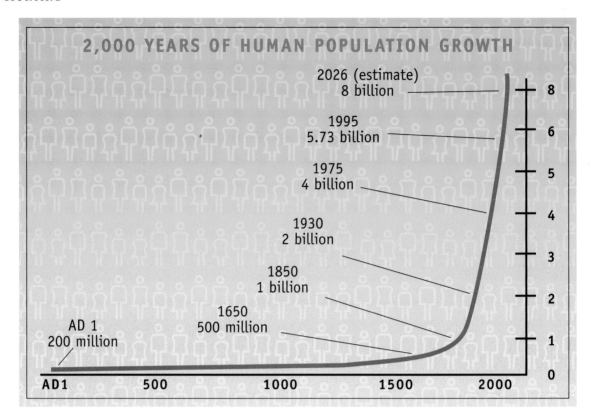

2,000 YEARS OF HUMAN POPULATION GROWTH

2026 (estimate)
8 billion

1995
5.73 billion

1975
4 billion

1930
2 billion

1850
1 billion

1650
500 million

AD 1
200 million

AD1   500   1000   1500   2000

In recent decades, population growth has declined naturally in some countries, largely a result of education and changes in societal attitudes toward child-rearing. Some nations with high population growth rates, such as China, have tried to limit growth by establishing guidelines and laws regarding such things as age of marriage and numbers of children a couple may have. Programs also exist that seek to promote the use of birth control methods and to educate people about family planning issues. [*See also* HABITAT LOSS AND CONSERVATION.]

HUNTING

Pursuing and/or killing animals for food, clothing, shelter, or recreation. Throughout history, humans have hunted for what they needed. In fact, some groups, such as **indigenous** cultures in AFRICA and SOUTH AMERICA, still meet their needs this way. In industrialized societies today, however, most food is now raised on farms. Most hunting in industrialized societies is sport hunting, people hunting animals for recreation. Hunters may hunt for the thrill of the chase, or to obtain food or trophies.

Hunting patterns vary throughout the world and within individual countries. In 1990, there were approximately 14 million hunters in the United States, a much larger number than in most **developed countries**. Most hunters in the United States are found in Texas, Pennsylvania, Michigan, Wisconsin, and New York. They hunt mostly deer, elk, and smaller animals such as squirrels, pheasants, and waterbirds.

Hunting can be both good and bad for the environment. The main difference between human hunters and animal PREDATORS is the fact that predators tend to kill weak and sick animals. Through NATURAL SELECTION, animals that survive predation pass on successful genes. Humans, by contrast, tend to kill strong, healthy animals, either because they want something big or hope to exhibit an exciting trophy. The loss of such animals weakens the species being killed because it eliminates the healthier animals that would tend to produce strong offspring. On the other hand, hunting organizations often manage natural areas to make sure they have enough animals for hunting. This means they often support habitat protection, and that benefits all species.

Illegal hunting, or "poaching," is a problem in some areas. Hunting laws now exist that limit what kind of animals and how many can be taken. Hunting and killing animals that are classified as ENDANGERED SPECIES in this country and others is not allowed. Yet it continues to occur in many places because people will pay a great deal of money to buy skins and other body parts of certain animals or to have them as pets. It is often difficult to enforce hunting ☑ laws, especially in **developing countries**, because there are few wildlife officials and it is easy to smuggle animals in and out.

HURRICANES

A rotating tropical storm, with winds at the center of more than 74 miles (119 km) per hour, which occurs in the western Atlantic and eastern Pacific Oceans. Similar storms that occur in the Indian Ocean are called tropical cyclones, and those in the northwest Pacific are called typhoons. Most hurricanes originate within the doldrums, a narrow belt of intermittent calms, light breezes, and squalls that lies on the equator between the northeast and southeast trade winds. These storms are capable of producing dangerous winds, torrential rains, and FLOODING, particularly along coastal areas. Hurricane Andrew, which struck southern Florida in 1992, was responsible for at least 50 deaths and more than $20 billion dollars in property damage.

Hurricanes are formed from simple thunderstorms over warm water, which provides the energy for the storm. The clouds and thunderstorms form an organized system with a defined circulation that is called a tropical depression. The high-velocity winds of a hurricane blow counterclockwise around the low-pressure center, termed the eye of the storm. Within the eye of the storm, the winds are calm and the sun may be shining. The Saffir-Simpson Hurricane Scale is a 1-5 rating based on the storm's intensity. A Category 1 storm, the mildest, has winds of at least 74 miles (119 km) per hour. A Category 5 hurricane has winds exceeding 155 miles (249 km) per hour. Category 5 storms are rare; Hurricane Mitch in October 1998 reached Category 5.

Powered by the heat from the ocean, hurricanes are steered by the easterly trade winds. In the Northern Hemisphere, hurricanes move in a northwesterly direction. Thus storms

After forming in the mid-Atlantic Ocean, hurricanes generally head westward toward Cuba and the United States.

spawned in the Atlantic move toward the West Indies and the Caribbean Sea. In the Southern Hemisphere, they first move southwesterly and then to the southeast. As they move on shore, hurricanes can spawn tornadoes.

U.S. military aircraft have been flying into hurricanes to measure wind speeds and directions, location and areas of the eye, and the pressure since the 1940s. In the 1950s, a coordinated system was devised in the United States to track Atlantic Ocean hurricanes from June 1 through October 30, considered the critical hurricane season. The hurricanes are given names starting with A for the first storm, B for the second storm, and so on through the alphabet. The hurricanes' paths are tracked closely by the National Hurricane Center in Florida. The names for hurricanes are recycled every six years, and every so often names are dropped and others are added. Timely warnings have greatly diminished fatalities in the United States. Still, hurricanes cause great property damage, particularly in areas where people have built along the shorelines. [*See also* CLIMATE AND WEATHER; METEOROLOGY.]

HYBRID

The product of a cross between two unlike individuals, usually members of different species. Hybrids occur in nature and serve to increase genetic variety. They are also produced artificially by breeders who combine sex cells from two different organisms. The closer the parental relationship, the more successful the hybrid. Animals of two different species usually produce sterile hybrids, animals that cannot reproduce. A mule, for example, is the sterile offspring of a female horse and a male donkey. In plants, hybrid offspring are also usually sterile, but they can be reproduced by cuttings or grafting.

Hybrids often are characterized by what is called hybrid vigor; that is, they manifest the best characteristics of each parent—the sum being greater than the parts. Mules are bred for their strength, which is superior to that of either parent. Nearly all the corn and tomatoes grown today are hybrids that bear much larger fruit than their parental stock.

Most hybrids are the result of human intervention. In nature, species normally do not hybridize because they have different breeding seasons or courtship patterns, or because they are separated by physical barriers such as oceans and MOUNTAINS. When cross-breeding does occur naturally between species, the number of different gene combinations is increased and if the hybrid is fertile, it can establish a new species, a process called SPECIATION. [*See also* GENES; GENETICS AND GENETIC ENGINEERING.]

HYDROELECTRIC POWER

Production of electricity from the energy of moving water. Hydroelectric power has many benefits for the environment. The use of moving water is nonpolluting, and it is less expensive than burning FOSSIL FUELS, such as coal and oil. Hydroelectric power can be created by building DAMS in areas where there are large bodies of water.

Dams are barriers that block the normal flow of rivers, thereby collecting water to use for generating electricity. Electricity is created when the water behind the dam is directed through the blades of **turbines**. The energy of the moving water turns these turbines, and the spinning turbines create energy that is transferred to coils of wire in **generators**. The coils then pass through a magnetic field, and electricity is produced.

Although hydroelectric power may be beneficial for the environment in many ways, it can also harm the environment. The use of dams alters water depth and flow, and this can affect plant and animal life. The blades of the turbines can be deadly for fishes, which may get caught in the blades. Dams also disturb the reproductive cycle of some fish species by making it difficult for them to swim upstream to spawning areas where they reproduce. Disturbance in FOOD WEBS, changes in water temperature, and FLOODING are other possible consequences of using dams.[*See also* ALTERNATIVE ENERGY SOURCES.]

H

Much of the energy used in the western U.S. comes from hydroelectric power.

HYDROPONICS

The study of plants that grow in nutrient-rich water instead of SOIL. Hydroponic agriculture has several benefits. It allows growers more control over a plant's environment, so they can eliminate diseases, pests, and weeds. It also requires less space and allows plants to grow more quickly. The water and nutrients can be recycled and reused.

In hydroponic agriculture, plant roots are submerged in water containing all the impor-

tant NUTRIENTS for growth and development, such as NITROGEN, PHOSPHORUS, potassium, calcium, sulfur, iron, zinc, and copper. Sometimes the water is sprayed over the plants in a fine mist. Plants are kept in a controlled environment where they can grow in the proper humidity, warmth, and light conditions. Plants are often placed in large plastic pipes or boxes, with gravel or sand to support the roots as they grow. The nutrient-filled water is pumped through one end of the system and collected back again for reuse at the other end.

Hydroponic agriculture has been around a long time, but the term was first used for commercial agriculture in 1936. During World War II, the U.S. Army used hydroponic farms to provide food for soldiers stationed on barren islands. Today, many plants grown in greenhouses are grown hydroponically, including tomatoes, peppers, and many herbs.

HYDROSPHERE

All the waters on, below, or above the earth's surface. The hydrosphere consists of surface waters, ice caps, GROUNDWATER, and water vapor in the ATMOSPHERE. Most of the water in the hydrosphere is found in the oceans, which cover three-fourths of the earth's surface. Water in underground reservoirs called AQUIFERS makes up about four percent of the hydrosphere. The earth's ice caps contain less than two percent of the water in the hydrosphere. Water vapor in the atmosphere accounts for less than one percent.

The hydrosphere makes earth unique among the planets of our solar system. No other planet has as much water as earth. The hydrosphere contains the water needed by all living things to survive.

The hydrosphere also makes life possible on the earth by moderating the CLIMATE AND WEATHER. For example, equatorial ocean currents carry warmth toward the poles. The currents raise the temperature of the colder waters, helping to create milder weather. The Gulf Stream is a warm current that flows from the waters of the Caribbean across the Atlantic Ocean to northwestern Europe. As a result of the Gulf Stream's warming influence on winds and weather, the climate of northwestern Europe is much milder than the climate at the same latitude in North America. [*See also* BIOSPHERE, WATER CYCLE.]

I-K

ICE

Water that has reached its freezing point of 32° ☀Fahrenheit (0° Centigrade). Ice, or frozen water, can appear in many forms. It can be flat and clear, such as ice that forms on a frozen pond in winter. It can be in balls or clumps, like hailstones in a storm. Snow is made up of finely patterned ice called crystals. Sleet is made of transparent ice pellets, or little globs. All are forms of frozen water. [*See also* GLACIERS; GLOBAL CLIMATE CHANGE.]

☀ Fast Facts

In the last ice age, about 10,000 years ago, ice covered close to 16 million square miles (41 million sq km) of the earth, including much of Canada and the northern United States. Today, polar ice and the remaining glaciers cover about 6 million square miles (15 million sq km).

ICE AGES

(*See* GLACIERS)

INCINERATION

The process of burning SOLID WASTES. Facilities that carry out the burning are called incinerators. Incinerators can help to eliminate wastes that would otherwise take up space in LAND-FILLS. They also produce steam that can be used in generating electricity. However, incinerators are often controversial. They produce ash that can be highly toxic, and the smoke from the burning process can contribute to AIR POLLUTION. Incineration is also an expensive method of waste disposal. [*See also* SOLID WASTE.]

INDIAN OCEAN

One of the world's great bodies of saltwater, stretching from the eastern coast of Africa, north to India, and east to Australia, New Zealand, and Indonesia. The Indian Ocean is the third largest ocean on earth—73,427,000 square miles (190,175,000 sq km) in area and containing 20.3 percent of the world's volume of water. The Indian Ocean provides some of the most spectacular and species-rich saltwater HABITATS in the world, such as the CORAL REEFS off the coasts surrounding the island of Madagascar. [*See also* AQUATIC HABITATS; MARINE ECOSYSTEMS.]

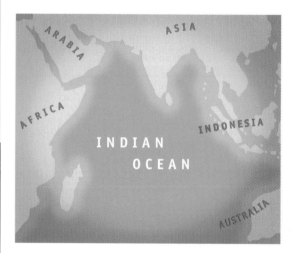

INSECTS

ARTHROPODS—INVERTEBRATES with exoskeletons—with six legs and segmented bodies. Insects make up the largest group of animals on earth. They live on land, in freshwater, and in the sea. Their ability to fly allows them to find food and protects them from PREDATORS.

There are nearly a million different species of known insects, and there may be nearly that many still undiscovered. All insects are recognizable by their three main body parts: the

Thread-waisted wasp

Alfalfa butterfly

Worker ant

head, thorax (midsection), and abdomen. The head of an insect has antennae, eyes, and mouths. The thorax usually has three segments, each with a pair of legs attached and often two pairs of wings as well. The abdomen has 9 to 11 segments, with the last one usually having a tail. All insects have a hard outer shell called an exoskeleton, which covers their soft inner body parts. This exoskeleton must be shed as an insect grows larger.

During their life cycle, most insects go through metamorphosis, a process of transforming from one form to another. One example of this process can be seen with butterflies, which start their lives as wingless caterpillars but eventually build cocoons and hatch out as beautifully winged flying insects.

Insects play an important role in almost every ECOSYSTEM. As larvae, they may help to loosen SOIL. As adults, they eat other insects and are themselves food for many animals such as BIRDS and small MAMMALS. Some insects,

like mosquitoes, spread diseases such as malaria. Others are very helpful to humans, helping to control other organisms considered pests. Still others do great damage to agriculture by eating crops. Pest insects are often eliminated by the use of chemical PESTICIDES, which can contribute greatly to AIR POLLUTION and WATER POLLUTION. [*See also* SWAMPS; WETLANDS.]

INTERIOR, DEPARTMENT OF THE

An executive department of the United States government. Established in 1849, the Department of the Interior is the custodian of the nation's NATURAL RESOURCES. The department is headed by a secretary appointed by the president with the approval of the Senate.

The department's major responsibilities are to protect and conserve the country's land, water, MINERALS, FISH, and wildlife; to promote the wise use of all these natural resources; to maintain NATIONAL PARKS and recreation areas; and to preserve historic places. The department constructs irrigation works, enforces mine-safety laws, makes geological surveys, conducts mineral research, and administers wild and scenic rivers as well as national and regional trails. It is in charge of the U.S. FISH AND WILDLIFE SERVICE, the NATIONAL PARKS SERVICE, the Geological Survey, the Bureau of Mines, and the Bureau of Indian Affairs, which provides for the welfare of Native American reservation communities.

INTRODUCED SPECIES

(*See* EXOTIC SPECIES)

INVERTEBRATES

Animals that lack a backbone, or vertebra. There are many different kinds of invertebrates, comprising over 95 percent of all known animal species. There are so many different invertebrates that they are divided into several major groups called phyla. Among these is a group that includes snails, oysters, scallops, octopuses, and squid. Another group contains such creatures as the jellyfish and Portuguese man-

Endangered Species: American Burying Beetle

The American burying beetle is a large shiny black beetle, with orange spots on the wings. It feeds on the flesh of dead animals. This beetle reproduces by burying the carcass of a small animal in an underground hole. The beetle lays its eggs in a tunnel off this chamber, and after they hatch, the larvae feed on the carcass. Scientists have introduced a population of this endangered beetle on Penikese Island, in Massachusetts, and they are studying another group that lives on Block Island in Rhode Island.

I J K

Many invertebrate species, such as this brown jellyfish, are found in aquatic habitats.

of-war, each of which has a stinging organ. One of the largest groups of invertebrates contains animals with an outer skeleton-like armor, such as INSECTS and spiders.

Invertebrates play important roles in the environment. They help pollinate plants, improve the texture of SOIL by burrowing within it, and provide a source of food for humans and other animals. [*See also* VERTEBRATES.]

IONOSPHERE

A sublayer of the thermosphere, which is the outer layer of the earth's ATMOSPHERE. The ionosphere layer is affected by energy from space in the form of solar radiation. This forms a layer of electrically charged particles —called ions and free electrons—beginning at about 50 miles (80 km) above the earth's surface. The

ionosphere benefits communications because the electrically charged particles in the layer reflect radio waves, allowing signals to be transmitted long distance on earth. Auroras— ribbonlike lights in the atmosphere—occur when charged particles in the atmosphere collide with atoms, giving off light. Auroras are brightest near the North and South Poles.

ISLANDS

Bodies of land surrounded by water. Islands are found in oceans, LAKES, and RIVER SYSTEMS. They can be oceanic or continental.

Oceanic islands rise from the ocean floor and project above the water's surface. Many oceanic islands are the tops of volcanoes that gradually increased in size as lava accumulated and hardened on their sides. The volcanoes eventually become tall enough to break through the ocean's surface. The islands of Hawaii are oceanic islands.

Continental islands are found within continents or in the oceans near them. Islands within

I
J
K

Islands provide sheltered, but often isolated, habitats for plant and animal species.

continents are areas of raised land within lakes and rivers. Islands adjacent to continents are often areas of raised land on the CONTINENTAL SHELF. For example, the Florida Keys are coral islands that formed on the continental shelf south of Florida. Some large islands are connected underwater to nearby continents. Greenland is such an island connected to NORTH AMERICA. The islands of the United Kingdom are connected to Europe. Some islands form long, curved chains called island arcs or archipelagoes. Many such islands are formed by chains of undersea volcanoes. The Aleutian Islands of Alaska and the Lesser Antilles of the Caribbean are island arcs. [*See also* CORAL REEF.]

Endangered Species: Komodo Monitor

The Komodo monitor is a large lizard that lives on several small islands in Indonesia. This reptile grows to nine feet (2.7 m) in length and weighs about 140 pounds (63 kg), making it the largest lizard in the world. It is often called the Komodo dragon. It hunts by lying along a trail, waiting for a deer, goat, or wild pig to walk by. The Komodo monitor is an endangered species because people poach the deer and other animals that this lizard depends on for food and because of habitat destruction. Several of the islands on which these lizards live have been declared the Komodo Island National Park, to protect the 3,500 resident lizards.

KEYSTONE SPECIES

An animal or plant that has a large effect on its natural community or ECOSYSTEM. The loss of the keystone species can significantly change the physical characteristics of the ecosystem and perhaps the numbers of other species in the community. As a result, conservationists place extra emphasis on protecting keystone species.

In AFRICA and ASIA, the ELEPHANT is considered a keystone species. While moving through an area and feeding, elephants pull up or push over TREES, creating gaps in the forest. These gaps create HABITATS for other smaller species and also let in more light, which stimulates the growth of other plant species. When a population of elephants is killed, the forest CANOPY may grow too dense to allow other species to survive. Similarly, ALLIGATORS and crocodiles play important roles in their environments. These REPTILES dig deep holes in the earth during dry seasons, creating small pools that provide water for other animals and plants. The giant saguaro CACTUS is an example of a plant keystone species. BIRDS depend on these tall cacti for roosting and nesting sites, and the saguaro flowers attract INSECTS, which, in turn, are fed upon by bats. [*See also* SPECIES AND SUBSPECIES.]

L

LAKES

An inland body of water surrounded by land. Most lakes contain freshwater, but some contain saltwater. Lakes can range from small bodies of water the size of large ponds to huge inland seas. The GREAT LAKES of NORTH AMERICA are the world's largest areas of freshwater, covering 95,000 square miles (245,000 sq. km). The largest of the Great Lakes, Lake Superior, is the world's biggest freshwater lake. Europe's Caspian Sea is larger, but it contains saltwater.

Lakes form in several ways. Most lake basins were formed by the action of GLACIERS that scoured out or deepened depressions in rock and SOIL. Some lakes were formed when water filled the craters of extinct VOLCANOES. Lakes have also formed in cracks or depressions formed by movements in the earth's crust.

Chemical pollution from industry and agriculture has degraded the WATER QUALITY of many lakes. This WATER POLLUTION is a problem because lakes supply DRINKING WATER for many communities. A large number of lakes also suffer from EUTROPHICATION, the enrichment of lakes with nutrients from agricultural and sewage RUNOFFS. The nutrients cause an explosive growth of plant life that depletes a lake's oxygen supply, harming some types of animal life. [*See also* AQUATIC HABITATS; BIOLOGICAL COMMUNITY; GROUNDWATER; WATER POLLUTION.]

LANDFILLS

A disposal site where SOLID WASTES are dumped and buried. In 1976, the U.S. Congress defined solid wastes as all garbage, refuse, and sludge products from agriculture, FORESTRY, MINING, and municipalities. Garbage dumps have existed for centuries to limit the dumping of garbage onto the city streets. In the early 1900s, some garbage that was collected was dumped into the oceans. Landfills were established to deal with the mounting garbage problem faced by communities and to prevent wastes from being washed up onto seashores from polluted oceans. Today, about 70 percent of the garbage people generate is disposed of in landfills.

The first open landfills were merely sites where truckloads of garbage could be dumped. Open landfills were gradually stopped because of the foul odors they produced and the number of rats, flies, cockroaches, and other unwanted organisms that lived in them. Open landfills also posed a problem because rain carried pollutants from the garbage into the soil, and LEACHING took the pollutants into GROUNDWATER systems, causing health problems for nearby communities.

Today, open landfills are illegal in most states. Instead, sanitary landfills are used. In such landfills, solid waste materials are spread out into different layers, deep in the ground. Garbage is added to the site until the waste material reaches a certain designated height. Sanitary landfills have alternating layers of soil and garbage so that the garbage breaks down in the soil more easily. All of the garbage is compacted by a bulldozer, and then the landfill is closed with a layer of soil about 24 inches (60 cm) thick. Then grass and trees can be planted and the site reserved for future use.

Sanitary landfills do have negative effects. The DECOMPOSITION of garbage in landfills produces METHANE, a gas that is highly flam-

☀ Fast Facts

Currently, many hazardous and solid wastes are exported from wealthier nations to poorer nations. In the United States it costs about $800 to $900 a barrel to dump toxic waste, while some African nations charge only $50 per barrel.

mable and explosive. Ventilation pipes are put into the ground to prevent the buildup of methane, allowing the gas to slowly escape from the landfill. Another problem with sanitary landfills is the leaching of toxic substances into the surrounding land and water. To prevent leaching of these substances, clay and plastic liners are used to seal the landfill area. [*See also* WATER POLLUTION.]

LANDSLIDES

Landslides along roads and highways can be dangerous to motorists.

Movements of masses of rock, earth, and debris down a slope. Landslides often result from a combination of human impact and weather. Land mismanagement, such as clearing vegetation and building houses on mountain slopes, is a leading cause of landslides. Such activities loosen soil and eliminate root systems that help hold the soil in place. Landslides can also be caused by various factors such as earthquakes, volcanic eruptions, and rainstorms as well as by fires, which can wear down the ground, making it unstable. In some areas, landslides continue to occur over a long period of time. Some warning signs of landslides include cracks on hill slopes, slow downhill movement of rock and soil, tilting of trees and other objects, and formation of sags and bumps on slopes. Planting trees and not building on slopes can help prevent landslides. [*See also* EROSION.]

LEACHING

Process by which rainwater moves through soil and removes or carries minerals and other chemicals into a deeper layer of soil. Leaching can be a beneficial process that allows different layers of soil to receive minerals needed for plant life. Leaching occurs most often in envi-ronments where there is plenty of rainfall. In desertlike areas, very little leaching occurs, and as a result, many plants cannot survive in the soils found there.

Leaching is not always beneficial. When hazardous chemicals leach into the soil, it can have a harmful effect on the environment or on plant and animal life. Toxic substances sometimes leach from LANDFILLS and move into GROUNDWATER. In areas where MINING occurs, rainwater leaches through the deposits of waste materials and goes into groundwater and SURFACE WATER. Heavy metals and other HAZARDOUS SUBSTANCES get carried throughout the layers of soil by rainwater, creating health and environmental problems. Leaching can thus expose people and other organisms to hazardous substances. [*See also* WATER CYCLE.]

LEGUME

Any plant, such as peas and beans, that carries its fruit in seed pods. Many legumes are important human food crops. Others, such as alfalfa, and clover, are foods for livestock and other grazing animals. The seeds of some legumes are also used to make medicines and chemicals.

Farmers often use legumes as cover crops—that is, they plant them in fields whose nutrients have been used up by previous planting. The legumes take in NITROGEN from the air and change it into nitrogen compounds that can be used by plants to help them grow. Nitrogen is thus important for improving poor SOIL. Farmers plow under legumes and plant other crops in the improved soil. [*See also* NITROGEN CYCLE; NUTRIENT CYCLE.]

LICHEN

Small, ground-hugging plant without stems and leaves, often found in harsh environments where other plants cannot grow. A lichen is composed of two types of plants—ALGAE and FUNGI—living together in a relationship beneficial to both. This relationship is called SYM-BIOSIS. The alga (singular of algae) which contains **chlorophyll** makes food through PHOTOSYNTHESIS, which it shares with the fungus (singular of fungi). The fungus provides water and nutrients, which the alga takes in through its cell walls.

There are more than 20,000 types of lichens. They grow in crusty-looking patches or mats of green, gray, and orange on rocks, wood, and SOIL. Lichens are often found in cold, windswept subpolar areas and in severe mountain climates. Although they grow slowly—often less than one inch (2.54 cm) a year—lichens can expand over wide areas.

Lichens that grow on rocks are an agent of weathering, the breaking down of rock into SOIL. The plants produce acids that dissolve the rock on which they grow. As a result, lichens play an important role in the formation of new soil.

LIFE CYCLE

The series of stages through which an organism passes during its lifetime, sometimes called life history. The types of life cycles are as varied as the organisms that exist on earth. Humans, for example, undergo relatively little in the way of physical change—primarily varying only in size from birth to death. But the forms of some adult organisms may not even resemble their forms at the beginning of life. One example is the monarch butterfly: Adult monarch females lay their eggs on milkweed plants. Soon afterward, the adult butterflies die. Young caterpillars, called larvae, hatch from the eggs and spend most of their time feeding on the milkweed leaves. After they eat and grow for about three weeks, the caterpillars undergo a process called metamorphosis, which means to change form. This process takes about a month. A hard case, called a chrysalis, forms around each caterpillar. Inside, the caterpillar changes into an adult butterfly. Soon the chrysalis splits open and the adult emerges.

Most INSECTS that live in temperate regions have what is called a heterodynamic life cycle. The adults appear for a limited time during a particular season, and some form of their life stage passes the winter in dormancy. Many of the insects in the United States complete their life cycle in one year; a few require two or three years. The longest life cycle of any insect is probably that of the periodical cicada, which lasts 17 years. The insects in tropical regions have a homodynamic (a continuous succession of generations) life cycle. The life cycle of these insects is continuous and there is no dormant period.

Frogs also undergo metamorphosis during the course of their life cycle. The eggs of the frog are laid in water, where they hatch into tadpoles—aquatic fishlike animals that breathe oxygen in the water through gills. As the tadpoles mature into adult frogs, their bodies undergo change. They develop legs and reabsorb their heavy muscular tail. The gills also disappear, and the animals develop lungs and breathe oxygen from the air.

Most BIRDS and MAMMALS reproduce two or more times during their life cycle, and the adults may live for a number of years. Natural populations of these animals contain individuals of different ages. [*See also* ENERGY CYCLE; PHOTOSYNTHESIS; POLLINATION AND SEED DISPERSAL.]

LION

A member of the cat family. Lions are CARNIVORES that live on the SAVANNAS of AFRICA. Male lions have distinctive bushy manes around their head and shoulders. Females do not have manes and do most of the hunting. Lions are almost purely meat-eating. Though they are excellent hunters, sometimes they are SCAV-

The lion has long been known as the king of beasts.

ENGERS that feed on dead animals they find on the plains.

Lions are highly social animals. They live in groups called prides, with from 1 to 1 males, 5 to 15 adult females, and their cubs and juveniles. Male lions are 20 to 35 percent larger than females, weighing as much as 500 pounds (226 kg). Females have two to four cubs at a time. The cubs will stay with their pride for at least 18 months.

Lions play an important role in the FOOD CHAINS of the African plains. They are the top carnivores, eating the young, old, and weak among HERBIVORES, such as antelope, zebra, and giraffe. They will regularly kill prey of more than 550 pounds (249 kg). Lions use their golden coloring to hide in the golden-colored GRASSLANDS where they live. They move slowly while watching a potential prey animal, remaining undetected, and then pounce at the last minute when they are quite close.

Like many large mammals in this century, lions are threatened by loss of HABITAT and the expansion of human populations into their environments. [See also MAMMALS; PREDATORS.]

LITHOSPHERE

Layer of land that forms the earth's surface. The lithosphere includes SOIL, rocks, and sand. The thickness of the lithosphere is between 6.25 and 125 miles (10 and 200 km). The outermost layer of the earth, the lithosphere contains the huge ☑ blocks of the earth's upper **mantle** and crust materials—known as tectonic plates—that hold up the continents.

Three main types of rocks form the lithosphere: igneous rock, sedimentary rock, and metamorphic rock. Igneous rocks, such as pumice and obsidian, are formed by volcanic action. Sedimentary rocks, such as sandstone and limestone, are formed when small particles of minerals in water sink to the bottom in layers and harden. Metamorphic rocks, such as marble, are formed when any kind of rock is heated and crushed beneath the earth's crust, changing its basic structure [See also CONTINENTAL DRIFT.]

LOGGING

The process of cutting down trees for timber. People have been logging for thousands of years, but when human populations were smaller, FORESTS could regrow over time. Logging occurs because people need wood for fuel, home-building, paper, furniture, and other wood-based products. As the world population has grown and become industrialized, people need increasing amounts of wood. Thus, the rate of logging has increased dramatically in the past 150 years.

Commercial logging, where trees are sold as timber to companies throughout the world, is a major cause of destruction of tropical RAIN FORESTS and HABITAT LOSS. In the United States, less than 10 percent of original forest cover remains due to past logging.

When logging is done poorly, it can completely destroy forest HABITATS. DEFORESTATION occurs when all the trees in an area are removed. One cause of deforestation is a logging technique known as CLEAR-CUTTING. With clear-cutting, the habitats of many animals are lost. Logging operations also build roads into forests, dividing up larger areas of habitat that may be important for animals. The loss of trees and their roots also affects the SOIL, leaving it more susceptible to EROSION.

"Sustainable yield" logging is much less destructive to forest HABITATS and provides longer-term profits for companies as well. In this type of logging, loggers cut trees selectively and rotate logged areas of forests in 20- to 50-year cycles, which allows the forest to regenerate itself. Many timber and paper companies are now trying to manage their forests carefully over the long term rather than cut everything at once. That way they can ensure long-term profits, jobs, and resources for everyone, as well as prevent large-scale loss of habitats. [See also FORESTRY; NATURAL RESOURCES; RENEWABLE AND NONRENEWABLE RESOURCES.]

M

MAMMALS

Warm-blooded animals whose females feed their young with milk produced by specialized organs called mammary glands. In addition to nursing their young, mammals share various other characteristics. They are VERTEBRATES, are partially or completely covered with hair, and have complex nervous systems with well-developed brains. As warm-blooded animals, they have a constant body temperature regardless of the temperatures around them. This constant temperature is maintained by internal regulation, and their body hair also helps to keep mammals warm.

Mammals are very diverse. They vary greatly in size—from tiny rodents to enormous WHALES—and live in many different ECOSYSTEMS around the world. Some mammals are CARNIVORES; others are HERBIVORES. There are approximately 4,000 different species of mammals. Some large mammals—such as TIGERS, GORILLAS, and RHINOCEROSES—are endangered species that have been hunted to the brink of extinction. Others are threatened because the disruption of their habitats.

Endangered Species: Giant Armadillo

The giant armadillo is a large mammal with hard, bony plates running from its nose to the tip of its tail. It measures about 4 feet (1.2 m) long, and eats termites, ants, and occasionally snakes. When attacked, the armadillo rolls into a ball and the bony plates protect it. Once abundant in tropical forests from Venezuala to Argentina, the giant armadillo is now rare because of hunting and habitat loss.

MANATEE

A rare and strange-looking MARINE MAMMAL.

Manatees can only live in warm-water environments.

There are three species of manatee found in oceans, rivers, and ESTUARIES along the coasts of tropical and subtropical NORTH AMERICA, SOUTH AMERICA, AFRICA, ASIA, and AUSTRALIA. Manatees are all highly ENDANGERED SPECIES. They live in brackish (mixed salt and fresh) water in lagoons and the mouths of rivers, where they play an important role of controlling acquatic weeds. They prevent clogging of river mouths and canals by eating huge quantities of weeds and grasses, from which they gained the nickname sea cows.

Manatees have few natural PREDATORS other than humans, who have sometimes killed them for their meat. But the animals' rate of reproduction cannot keep up with increased HUNTING, destruction of their HABITATS, and accidental capture by fishing nets. All manatees are now protected by international law, but these regulations are hard to enforce. The future of these creatures remains uncertain. [*See also* AQUATIC HABITATS.]

MANGROVES

Mangroves are specially adapted to their watery environment.

Unusual-looking species of tree, uniquely adapted to growing near oceans, the mouths of rivers, and saltwater MARSHES in tropical and subtropical areas. To adapt to soil with little or no OXYGEN, mangroves have roots that stick up straight into the air instead of growing into the ground. The mangroves balance the salt in the water all around them by producing their own salts. This allows them to absorb only freshwater and avoid drying out. Mangroves grow quite tall and put out branches and leaves only at their very tops. This ADAPTATION allows them to survive in the often crowded conditions in which they grow. It also produces their distinctive look.

Mangroves play an important role in their environments, stabilizing the soil, purifying the water, and providing root habitats for many birds, mammals, crustaceans, and fish. However, mangrove forests throughout the world are threatened by ocean pollution and by the conversion of coastal areas to agriculture. [*See also* AQUATIC HABITATS; MARINE ECOSYSTEMS.]

MARINE ECOSYSTEMS

Ecosystems characterized by the plants, animals and natural cycles of saltwater communities. Marine ecosystems include coral reefs, coast-lines, and salt marshes. Animals typical of marine ecosystems include fish, marine mammals, sharks, and many crustaceans, such as shrimp, lobsters, and crabs.

Marine ecosystems throughout the world are threatened by pollution and destruction of HABITATS caused by humans. Many have been overexploited through extensive fishing, or destroyed by too much tourism. Like all ecosystems, marine ecosystems are often quite sensitive to changes that take place too rapidly. [*See also* AQUATIC HABITATS.]

MARINE MAMMALS

MAMMALS that make their homes in the oceans. Mammals are warm-blooded animals that feed their young with milk produced in special glands. Marine mammals include WHALES, dolphins, sea lions, seals, and walruses. Marine mammals are very well adapted to life in the water. They have streamlined shapes and flippered limbs to ease their swimming, thick layers of fat to keep them warm, and oily skins to make them sleek.

All marine mammals must breathe air, just like land-based mammals. But their blood is specially adapted to hold more OXYGEN, so they need to breathe less frequently. This allows them to stay underwater for quite long periods of time. Marine mammals are all excellent swimmers and highly intelligent. Many marine mammals are also highly social, living in large groups that feed together.

Many marine mammals are threatened or endangered by WATER POLLUTION and commercial fishing practices, which often catch these animals in nets meant for fish. They are protected by law under the Marine Mammal Protection Act of 1972, which prohibits their capture and provides for protection of their HABITATS. [*See also* MARINE ECOSYSTEMS.]

MARINE SANCTUARIES

Protected areas where oceanic organisms live. Similar to NATIONAL PARKS, marine sanctuaries were first created by the U.S. government in 1972. The government recognized at that time that most efforts at protecting special places for wildlife had focused on national parkland. Because marine life is very sensitive to rapid environmental changes, the government felt that it was important to protect marine HABITATS as well. [*See also* AQUATIC HABITATS; MARINE ECOSYSTEMS.]

MARSHES

Marshes support a variety of plant species.

WETLANDS with flat, open areas and few trees. There are both freshwater and saltwater marshes. Freshwater marshes have mineral-rich SOIL and many plants. They can be found on the shores of LAKES, rivers, and in the middle of PRAIRIES. Those in prairies are known as prairie potholes and provide important HABITATS for migratory birds. Other animals typical of freshwater marshes include frogs, muskrats, and beavers.

Salt marshes can be found at the mouths of rivers, in coastal areas of ISLANDS, along seacoasts, or in ESTUARIES where salt water and fresh water mix. Ducks, crabs, and FISH can be found in salt marshes.

Marsh plants are well adapted to having water constantly at their roots. Some marsh plants, such as cattails, grow with their roots in the water for all of their lives. Other plants, such as water lilies, have leaves that float on the water's surface, while their roots go down through the water. Still other plants have their stems, leaves, and roots all underwater. Such plants are very sensitive to light, so they can gather sunlight even in murky water. [*See also* AQUATIC HABITATS; MARINE ECOSYSTEMS.]

MASS EXTINCTION

The disappearance of a species or many species due to a particularly rapid or extensive change in the environment. The most famous mass extinction is that of the dinosaurs about 65 million years ago. Nearly half of all the living species disappeared at that time. Scientists have found evidence of mass extinctions in the fossil record as far back as about three billion years ago, when life first arose on earth. Indeed, five mass extinctions like the one that occurred at the end of the age of the dinosaurs have occurred in the past 600 million years.

The worst known mass extinction occurred about 250 million years ago. In what scientists call the "mother of mass extinctions," about 90 percent of the species living in the oceans disappeared. On land, more than two-thirds of the species of REPTILES and AMPHIBIANS vanished. Thirty percent of all INSECTS ceased to exist. After the mass extinction, marine forms such as the relatives of our modern-day fish, squid, and crabs were able to expand their NICHES and multiply their numbers. As a result, many new species were formed.

Scientists can see the evidence of mass extinctions in the fossil record, but they are not sure what caused these events. One popular theory behind the extinction of the dinosaurs is that a huge asteroid struck the earth. Other scientists, however, think that the dinosaurs had been declining for a long time before the end, and that their disappearance was gradual rather than catastrophic, perhaps the result of climate change. [*See also* ADAPTATION; ENDANGERED SPECIES; EXTINCTION; NATURAL SELECTION; SPECIES LOSS.]

MEDICAL WASTE

Any undesirable product of medical activities. Medical wastes include old medicines, lab equipment, lab specimens, and medicine containers. Many types of discarded tools used in the medical field or in a laboratory can become a medical waste, including used syringes, blood vials, tissue samples, and used bandages. Accidental contact with many old or used medical tools and equipment has the potential for harm. Some may be toxic, while others may carry disease. Medical wastes can be dangerous when not disposed of properly. Most medical waste is incinerated or burned, and some types of waste are disposed of in LANDFILLS or discharged through sewage systems. [*See also* HAZARDOUS WASTE; SEWAGE AND SEWAGE TREATMENT.]

METEOROLOGY

The science of weather. Meteorology focuses on the forces and processes that cause weather to happen. The scientists who study meteorology are called meterologists. They study the ATMOSPHERE to gain greater knowledge about CLIMATE AND WEATHER. Meteorology allows scientists to predict future weather patterns and make day-to-day weather forecasts.

Temperature and PRECIPITATION are two very important weather factors in meteorology. By studying cloud patterns, air pressure, and humidity, meteorologists are able to make predictions about temperatures and precipitation up to a week in advance. The ability to make predictions about the weather has saved many people's lives by allowing communities to prepare for major storms before they hit.

METHANE

A colorless and odorless gas produced by the DECOMPOSITION of organic matter by BACTERIA. Methane is lighter than air and burns easily. The gas is produced naturally in many ways, including in the digestive process of cattle and in the decomposition of organic matter in MARSHES and WETLANDS. Methane is also released by various industrial processes such as MINING and drilling for FOSSIL FUELS. It is also produced by the decomposition of waste materials in LANDFILLS. Methane is a greenhouse gas—a gas that scientists worry may be contributing to global warming. Its concentration in the atmosphere has risen steadily since industrialization began in the late 1700s.

Several methods exist for trapping methane and using it as an energy source. In a process called biogasification, methane is collected from landfills and used to produce methane fuel for cooking, heating, generating electricity, and serving as a gasoline substitute. [*See also* ALTERNATIVE ENERGY SOURCES; GLOBAL CLIMATE CHANGE.]

MICROORGANISMS

Tiny living things that generally can be seen clearly only through a microscope. Some microorganisms, such as amoebas and BACTERIA, may be seen with the naked eye, although not clearly. Others, including viruses, are so small that they can be seen only with special microscopes.

Most microorganisms are single-celled organisms that live everywhere. Microorganisms can be found in SOIL, air, water, food, hair, skin, and nearly anywhere else. They are necessary for larger life-forms to exist. Through the process of DECOMPOSITION, microorganisms such as bacteria help make soil fertile by breaking down dead matter into nutrients that can be used by plants and animals. Microorganisms also help break down toxic substances and chemicals in SOLID WASTE. They clean up lakes, rivers, and beaches by decomposing wastes and pollution. But mircoorganisms are sometimes harmful. They can cause diseases or cause food

☼ Fast Facts

Methanogens, a certain type of bacteria, release the gas methane in swamps and marshes where the water contains no oxygen. Methanogens also live in the digestive tracts of many mammals, and they help break down plant material that would not be digested otherwise. The methane released by these microorganisms contributes to digestive gas.

M

to spoil. They can also attack nonliving material by corroding iron pipes or spoiling leather or wood.[*See also* ANAEROBES; BIODEGRADABLE MATERIAL; COMPOSTING; EUTROPHICATION; NUTRIENT CYCLE.]

Profile: René Dubos

Microbiologist René Dubos (1901–1982) was also an educator, writer, and environmentalist. One of the first scientists to call attention to the effects of environmental hazards on children, he did extensive research on microbes and soil that led to the first commercially produced antibiotic. His research also contributed to the development of penicillin, and he understood the relationship between people's environment and their health.

MIMICRY

A situation in which an animal has evolved characteristics that resemble another animal. Mimicry is a type of natural ADAPTATION that helps animals survive in their environment. A poisonous animal, for example, has a particular outer appearance that warns other animals not to eat it. Some nonpoisonous animals have evolved features that mimic the appearance of that poisonous animals. Another type of mimicry is an animal that closely resembles a tree bark or a leaf on which it spends a lot of time. Since the animal blends in with its immediate surroundings, it can remain hidden and avoid PREDATORS.

This insect resembles a leaf, helping it survive predators. Some animal species can mimic bark or branches.

MINERALS

Inorganic, naturally occurring, solid materials that make up the rocks in the LITHOSPHERE. Minerals are either elements—substances made up of one type of atom—or compounds—substances made up of two or more elements.

MINERAL	RESERVE BASE	
ALUMINUM	28,000	MILLION METRIC TONS
COPPER	630	MILLION METRIC TONS
GOLD	74,000	METRIC TONS
IRON ORE	270,000	MILLION METRIC TONS
SILVER	420,000	METRIC TONS

The earth has limited supplies of minerals.

Some minerals are hardened from molten rock. Others are deposited from solutions (mixture in which one substance is dissolved in another substance) or from gases. There are five categories of minerals. Mineral fuels include FOSSIL FUELS such as coal, oil, natural gas, as well as radioactive materials such as uranium. Ferrous metals are mineral substances that contain iron. Nonferrous metals include copper, aluminum, lead, zinc, tin, and mercury. Precious metals are valuable metals such as gold, silver, and platinum. Nonmetallic minerals include substances such as sulfur, quartz, mica, asbestos, calcium, phosphorus, and potassium. [*See also* MINING.]

MINING

Method by which MINERALS are extracted from the earth. The way minerals are mined depends on the location of the minerals. Minerals at or near the earth's surface are extracted by surface mining. Subsurface mining extracts minerals deep below the surface. Dredging is the extraction of minerals from water.

Surface mining is also known as open-pit mining. In this type of mining, layers of rock, SOIL, and vegetation are removed from the earth's surface, and large machines dig **ore** from huge holes or pits in the ground. Deposits of discarded materials called tailings are often left in piles near the mines. This can be hazardous because the piles often contain heavy metals that are poisonous to living things. The open-pit mines can also fill with water, which becomes polluted with heavy metals if the area is not restored. GROUNDWATER pollution can then occur due to RUNOFFS from the mine pits.

Quarries are another form of surface mining. Quarry mining moves very small amounts of rock and thus produces relatively little environmental damage. Quarries generally are mined to remove sandstone, limestone, marble, clay, gravel, and sand. The pits are small and fill up with water or vegetation when the mining is finished.

Subsurface mining involves digging shafts into the earth to extract minerals from deep beneath the surface. A long tunnel is dug into the ground, and other chambers and tunnels are dug outward from it. Explosives are used to expose the minerals, and machines bring the mineral deposits to the surface through the shaft. Subsurface mining is not as damaging to the environment as surface mining. However,

it is more dangerous for the workers. Inhaling dust particles produced during subsurface mining can contribute to lung disease. Miners also face the danger of natural gas and dust explosions caused by the mining activities. Subsurface miners can be trapped underground by collapsing walls, ceilings, and underground chambers.

Dredging is another method of extracting minerals. In this mining process, minerals are scraped or vacuumed from ocean floors, lake bottoms, and streambeds. Dredging can also be used to get sand and gravel for use in construction. This method of mining raises environmental issues because nutrients and organisms are removed in the process of scraping up minerals. Many people believe that this may disturb aquatic FOOD WEBS and possibly affect water currents, CORAL REEFS, and beaches [*See also* HEAVY-METAL POLLUTION].

MOLLUSKS

Soft-bodied animals, usually with a hard external shell. The mollusks are INVERTEBRATES. They include a variety of familiar creatures, such as snails, clams, mussels, octopuses, and slugs. They all have one feature in common, a shell at some stage in their life cycle. Most mollusks have a shell as adults. But the octopus, squid, and some deep-sea forms have only a small shell-like structure, called a shell gland, during their early stages of development.

Mollusks make up the second largest group of organisms in the animal kingdom, after the ARTHROPODS (which include INSECTS, spiders, and crustaceans such as shrimp and lobsters). There are an estimated 50,000 mollusk species. The first mollusk fossils appear in early Cambrian period rock and are about 600 million years old.

The mollusk shell is secreted by a tissue called the mantle, and it is made up of layers of

M

The giant squid is the largest invertebrate in the world. It can weigh as much as 1,980 pounds (900 kg). The largest giant squid ever recorded was captured in 1878. One of its "arms" measured 35 feet (12 m) long. The American Museum of Natural History in New York City has a male giant squid that has a 10-foot-long (3-meter-long) body and tentacles that extend another 15 feet (4.5 m). Giant squids live at depths of up to 3,000 feet (915 m). No one has ever seen one alive in its natural habitat.

calcium minerals. Some mollusks have multiple shells. Others, such as clams, have a pair of shells.

Most mollusks have separate sexes. The female and male release eggs and sperm into the water, where fertilization and early development occur. In most mollusks, a larval stage follows. After a period of time, the larvae settle to the bottom and mature. In some mollusks, fertilization is internal. Snails often evolve into hermaphrodites (having characteristics of both male and female).

Many mollusks are HERBIVORES, grazing on algae and other plant material. Most bivalves (mollusks with a pair of shells) filter suspended materials from the water, and some mollusks feed off the ocean floor. [*See also* MARINE ECOSYSTEMS.]

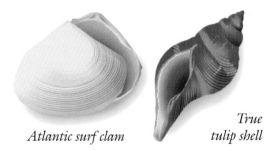

Atlantic surf clam　　　*True tulip shell*

MONOCULTURE

The cultivation of a single product to the exclusion of other uses of the land. The term monoculture is usually used to refer to a farming practice, such as the continual planting of corn to the exclusion of other crops. This practice can be financially profitable. But because monoculture crops are genetically identical, they can place a crop at risk of destruction from INSECTS and diseases. Monoculture also depletes the soil of **nutrients** that are required by that particular crop. Eventually, the soil will not be able to sustain the plant. Many farmers resort to using chemicals to solve these problems, spraying monoculture crops to ward off insects and diseases and adding artificial nutrients through FERTILIZERS to the SOIL. These chemicals can be harmful to the environment if they run off into rivers and streams or seep into the GROUNDWATER supplies.

The term monoculture has also been applied to FORESTRY practices to refer to a forest dominated by a single species of tree. Monoculture should not always be viewed in a negative context. There are natural forests that are technically monocultures. A mature Douglas fir forest, for example, may be called a monoculture. Pioneer tree species, such as lodgepole pine and some of the spruces, also often form natural monocultures after wildfires have burned lands. These monoculture forests have significant BIOLOGICAL DIVERSITY and are home to various shrubs, MOSSES, FERNS, BIRDS, MAMMALS, and other species.

MOSSES

A class of plants that have a small leafy stem bearing sex organs at the tip. Mosses belong to a group of plants called bryophytes, which typically grow in moist areas on soil , tree trunks, and rocks. Mosses are nonvascular plants, which means that they depend on direct contact with surface waters, as opposed to trees, which can draw in water and nutrients through their roots (a type of vascular system). Mosses lack

Many plants called mosses are, in fact, not even related to mosses. Club mosses are related to ferns. Spanish moss is a flowering plant that grows on tree trunks in the southern United States and on islands of the West Indies.

Mosses often cover the trunks of trees in damp climates.

true roots. Instead, they have a central plant body resembling a stem with tiny leaves and rootlike support structures called rhizoids.

After the FLOWERING PLANTS and the FERNS, mosses are the most diverse group of plants. There are more than 10,000 species of mosses. Some of the better-known mosses are peat moss and sphagnum moss. Mosses are extremely important in their ecological NICHES. They reduce EROSION along streams, help cycle water and nutrients in tropical FORESTS , and, along with LICHEN, help to decompose and break up rocks.

MOUNTAINS

Areas of the earth's surface that rise high above the surrounding land. Mountains are landmasses that usually reach at least 3,000 feet (915 m) in height. The formation of mountains can be explained by the idea of CONTINENTAL DRIFT, also known as plate tectonics. According to continental drift, the continents and ocean basins ride around on huge pieces of the earth's crust called tectonic plates. When the plates pull apart or grind against one another, the movement produces EARTHQUAKES. Mountains are also created when the plates collide.

Mountains can be divided into several types, based on the composition and arragement of rocks. Folded mountains are formed when tectonic plates collide head-on, causing rock to crumple and fold. The Alps in Europe and Appalachians in the United States are examples of folded mountains. Fault-block mountains are formed when an area between two parallel **faults** is lifted up as a result of tectonic plate movement. The Sierra Nevada in California and Andes in South America are fault-block mountains. VOLCANOES are another type of mountains. Volcanoes are formed when molten lava and other material from deep within the earth rise to the surface. Dissected mountains, sometimes called erosioned mountains, are not formed as a result of plate tectonics. These types of mountains are formed when plains or plateaus are eroded by natural processes.

SOME OF THE WORLD'S HIGHEST PEAKS

Name	Location	Height	
Everest	Nepal-Tibet	29,028 ft.	(8,848 m)
Aconcagua	Argentina	22,834 ft.	(6,960 m)
McKinley	Alaska	20,320 ft.	(6,194 m)
Logan	Yukon	19,850 ft.	(6,050 m)
Kilimanjaro	Tanzania	19,340 ft.	(5,895 m)
Citlaltepec	Mexico	18,700 ft.	(5,700 m)
Vinson Massif	Antarctica	16,864 ft.	(5,140 m)
Mont Blanc	France	15,771 ft.	(4,807 m)
Cook	New Zealand	12,349 ft.	(3,764 m)

MULTIPLE USE

The management of public lands and resources for more than one use—such as GRAZING, MINING, LOGGING, and recreation. The practice of multiple use arose out the belief that land and other natural resources can be used for many different purposes. This idea first emerged in the late 1800s when the United States government began to set aside and protect PUBLIC LANDS for future generations.

Multiple use has sometimes been a controversial issue in the United States. Managing any area for multiple use involves various factors, some of which conflict. Logging in public forests, for example, requires building logging roads. The logging and road building damages plant and animal HABITATS and can create problems with EROSION. It may also conflict with the recreational activities of hikers, campers, and wildlife observers. Managing multiple use successfully requires balancing the needs and purposes of many different groups. When done properly, multiple use helps to ensure that public lands are available to these groups and that resources are used wisely.

The multiple use of public lands in the United States is primarily the responsibility of various agencies within the U.S. Department of the Interior and the Department of Agriculture—such as the NATIONAL PARK SERVICE, the U.S. FOREST SERVICE, and the FISH AND WILDLIFE SERVICE.

MUSK DEER

A shy, primitive deer, standing about 20 inches (50 cm) at the shoulder, with large rounded ears and no visible tail. However, the upper canine teeth develop into short tusks. There are five species of musk deer, and they range from the Himalayas through Central Asia to Siberia.

Mature males develop a musk gland in the abdomen that secretes a waxlike substance used in the manufacture of perfumes, soaps, and medicines. Because only a small amount of musk can be obtained from each animal, the substance is very expensive. Female and young musk deer do not produce the substance, but they are often caught in traps set for the males. Because of excessive HUNTING for the musk glands and destruction of

Unlike other deer, the musk deer does not have antlers.

their forest HABITATS, musk deer have seriously declined in numbers.

MUTATION

A change in a cell's genes or chromosomes. Mutations cause sudden changes in the form or function of living things. If a mutation occurs in sex cells—sperm or egg cells—the mutation can be passed along to offspring. There are several sources of mutations. Certain types of radiation, such as X-rays, can cause mutations. Chemicals can also cause mutations. There are other sources of mutations as well, such as viruses.

Some mutations are so slight that they do not have much effect on the form or function of an organism. Other mutations can actually be helpful. For example, a plant that produces more seeds than normal would have a better chance to survive. However, great changes in genes or parts of chromosomes can cause mutations that can be harmful. In these cases, the changes that harmful mutations can cause decrease an organism's chance of survival. These harmful changes can also cause its death. For example, a bird with a mutation that deforms its wings so that it cannot fly would not survive. [*See also* ADAPTATION.]

MUTUALISM

A relationship in which two or more species depend on one another and usually cannot live outside the association. Mutualism is one of three types of SYMBIOSIS, and it refers to an interdependent relationship in which all the parties involved benefit. LICHEN is an example of mutualism. Lichen is composed of certain types of ALGAE and FUNGI that coexist. The algae carry out PHOTOSYNTHESIS and produce food for the fungi. The fungi provide physical support, and protection for the algae. Neither species could survive by itself. [*See also* PARASITES.]

NATIONAL FORESTS

Units of land under the direction of the U.S FOREST SERVICE. Millions of acres of national forests are among the public lands owned and managed by the U.S. government. There are 156 national forests in the United States. Combined with the 20 NATIONAL GRASSLANDS, the national forests cover 191 million acres (773 million hectares).

About 22 percent of the United States' commercial forest acreage is within the boundaries of the national forests. National forests are managed for multiple use, which includes LOGGING, GRAZING, and MINING as well as recreational use and protection of wildlife and NATURAL RESOURCES. [*See also* INTERIOR, DEPARTMENT OF THE.]

NATIONAL GRASSLANDS

Part of the public lands owned and managed by the United States government. National grasslands are units of land dominated by grass that, along with the NATIONAL FORESTS, are under the direction of the U.S FOREST SERVICE. The grasslands of the American Midwest are extensive and provide the seeds for many grain crops, such as corn, wheat, and oats, that provide food for people and livestock. Many exotic species of grasses have been introduced into the grasslands, replacing the NATIVE SPECIES. There are 20 national grasslands in the United States, including the Badlands National Grassland in South Dakota and the Wichita Mountains Wildlife Refuge of Oklahoma. In addition to many varieties of grasses and wildflowers, wildlife such as black-tailed prairie dogs, pronghorn, bison, coyote and mule deer thrive in grassland HABITATS. [*See also* INTERIOR, DEPARTMENT OF THE; NATIONAL PARK SERVICE.]

NATIONAL PARK SERVICE

Bureau of the U.S. Department of the Interior oversees public lands. Established in 1916, the National Park Service is the primary agency responsible for conserving the country's natural scenery, wildlife, and historic sites and with providing for the public enjoyment of these areas while leaving them "unimpaired" for future generations.

The more than 370 units managed by the service are called the National Park System, and they fall under three main categories for administrative purposes: natural areas, historical areas, and recreational areas. Areas set aside for preservation of nature include the NATIONAL PARKS, NATIONAL GRASSLANDS, national rivers, and many of the national monuments. Area preserved for historic reasons encompass national monuments and national historic sites, the national military parks, and the national battlefields. Recreation areas include the NATIONAL SEASHORES and lakeshores, and the national recreation areas. The National Park System encompasses about 80.7 million acres (32.7 million hectares). [*See also* INTERIOR, DEPARTMENT OF THE.]

NATIONAL PARKS

Areas set aside by the U.S. government in order to preserve them for the future. National parks in the United States are part of the National Park System, which is managed by the NATIONAL PARK SERVICE. The first national parks were selected because they had remarkable physical features, such as spectacular scenery.

Yellowstone National Park became the nation's first national park in 1872. Today, there are more than 50 national parks. Most are preserved for the beauty of their natural features. Mesa Verde National Park (1906), though, is set aside for historical reasons. It is the site of

N

SELECTED U.S. NATIONAL PARKS

Crater Lake

Yellowstone

Acadia

Redwood

Yosemite

Mammoth Cave

Bryce Canyon

Grand Canyon

Great Smoky Mountains

Kenai Fjords

Hawaii Volcanoes

Everglades

the best-preserved prehistoric Indian cliff dwellings in the United States. Other national parks have features of scientific importance, such as the Channel Islands (1980), which are rich in MARINE MAMMALS, seabirds, ENDANGERED SPECIES, and archaeological sites.

To keep national parks in their natural condition, officials try to maintain the balance of nature. That means interfering as little as possible with plant and animal life. Some national parks allow recreational uses, such as camping and fishing. There may be limits on other activities. Public interest in using national parks has increased in recent years. The number of visitors has grown so much that it has resulted in overcrowding during peak seasons. The parks' popularity has the potential of ruining the very qualities that make them so popular. Too much automobile traffic, for example, causes AIR POLLUTION that can damage plants and affect animal life as well. The National Park Service is trying to balance the needs of the public and the laws requiring it to protect the parks. In some

parks, for example, visitors now must use public transportation instead of taking their cars into the most sensitive areas. The Park Service has also put restrictions on the number of campers permitted.

NATIONAL SEASHORES

Coastal lands set aside by the U.S. government. Administered by the NATIONAL PARK SERVICE,

This lighthouse, at Cape Hatteras National Seashore, is located on an island.

the national seashores consist of ten seashores located on the Atlantic, Pacific, and Gulf coasts. They are administered as recreational areas. Some national seashores are developed and some are relatively primitive.

The Outer Banks of North Carolina became the first national seashore in 1953. Today it is called Cape Hatteras National Seashore. It protects over 70 miles (11.3 km) of barrier islands that provide a variety of plant and animal HABITATS, such as MARSHES, woodlands, and sand dunes. In particular, the seashore is a valuable wintering area for migrating waterfowl. It also provides crucial protection for the mainland beaches from erosion by crashing surf and storms.

NATIONAL WILDLIFE REFUGES

A network of WILDLIFE REFUGES has been set aside for the CONSERVATION of FISH, wildlife, and plants. The National Wildlife Refuge Sys-

tem, which consists of diverse public lands and waters, was begun in 1903, with the establishment of Pelican Island in Florida. This first wildlife refuge was created by President Theodore Roosevelt to protect nesting birds from hunters. Today, there are more than 500 national wildlife refuges, at least one in every state, covering 92 million acres (41 million hectares). They are managed by the U.S. FISH AND WILDLIFE SERVICE.

The national wildlife refuges protect wildlife HABITATS and natural ECOSYSTEMS, such as WETLANDS and FORESTS, and more than

Profile: Theodore Roosevelt

The twenty-sixth president of the United States, Teddy Roosevelt spent much of his childhood collecting rocks, bones, and other natural objects. Roosevelt studied natural history at Harvard University, obtained a law degree from Columbia, and was elected to the New York state legislature in 1882. Five years later, he and George Bird Ginnell, editor of *Forest and Stream* magazine, founded the Boone and Crockett Club, which supported scientific forest management, clean water, and restricted use of natural resources. In 1900 Roosevelt was elected vice president of the United States, and after William McKinley was assassinated, was sworn in as president. Elected president four years later, he initiated a program that emphasized improving and preserving the environment, particularly forests and wildlfe. Roosevelt established the first national wildlife refuge, Pelican Island Bird Reservation, in 1903, and created 50 more refuges during his presidency.

Some national wildlife refuges support millions of birds.

240 threatened and ENDANGERED SPECIES. Most of the refuges are open to the public for viewing and photographing wildlife. A few of the refuges are closed to the public or closed seasonally in order to protect sensitive wildlife activities.

NATIVE SPECIES

An organism that occurs naturally in a particular area. A native, or indigenous, species is one that is born or raised in an ECOSYSTEM, as

N

opposed to an EXOTIC SPECIES, which is an organism that has been introduced into an area either by accident or on purpose by humans. A native species is a functioning member of the ecosystem and is essential to the biological well-being of the region. [*See also* SPECIES AND SUBSPECIES.]

NATURAL GAS

(*See* FOSSIL FUELS)

NATURAL RESOURCES

Materials that support life and are used by humans. Many natural resources support life because they can be used for food, fuel, and the raw materials for manufactured goods.

There are various types of natural resources. Mineral resources include FOSSIL FUELS such as coal, oil, and natural gas that are used as a source of energy. Other mineral resources include metallic elements such as iron ore, gold, and copper, as well as stone, sand, and precious gems. Biological resources are a very important resource because they are the source of food for all living things. Biological resources include both plants and animals. The health of all biological resources depends, in turn, on other natural resources, such as SOIL, water, sunshine, and fresh air.

The CONSERVATION of natural resources is an important environmental issue because so much of life and the things that support it depends on them. The challenge is to find the right balance between the needs of today and conservation of the future. [*See also* ENDANGERED SPECIES; HABITAT LOSS AND CONSERVATION; RENEWABLE AND NON-RENEWABLE RESOURCES; SOIL CONSERVATION; WETLANDS; WILDERNESS.]

NATURAL SELECTION

The process by which certain species rather than others survive and reproduce. Natural selection is part of the process of EVOLUTION.

All plants and animals have ADAPTATIONS to the environment in which they live. As these adaptations are passed on from generation to generation, certain characteristics or traits will prove to help the organism more than others. If one organism survives to produce more offspring than another, that organism's traits, passed on through the GENES, will become more widespread in the population. Those organisms with less helpful traits will die out if those traits are not advantageous to the organism during changes in its environment. This is the process of evolution by natural selection. [*See also* GENETICS AND GENETIC ENGINEERING; MUTATION.]

NICHE

An organism's role within its ECOSYSTEM. Activities such as feeding habits, hunting behavior, methods of reproduction, and ways of producing shelter are all part of an organism's niche.

In an ecosystem, several organisms can share the same HABITAT, the place where an organism lives. But only one organism fills each niche when the ecosystem is in balance. If two organisms temporarily fill the same niche, they will compete for food and space. The organism that fits the niche best will survive and the other organism will be displaced.

Consider two species of BIRDS that share

A niche is a specialized ecosystem for various plant and animal species.

the same habitat. One bird might nest in the high branches of trees and hunt small rodents such as mice. The other bird might nest in holes in the tree trunk and eat insects. The two birds occupy separate niches because they have different feeding habits and make their homes in different places within their habitat. They do not directly compete for the same resources. [*See also* BIOLOGICAL COMMUNITY.]

NIMBY SYNDROME

People's efforts to keep environmental harms as far away from their homes and lives as possible. NIMBY is an acronym—a series of letters that stands for something else—for "Not In My Back Yard." The NIMBY syndrome developed as a result of years of observing the harmful effects that various activities have on the environment. For example, in 1979 the Three Mile Island nuclear power plant in Pennsylvania had a potentially dangerous situation that frightened an entire community about the potential effects of a nuclear accident. Other communities have been the victims of toxic chemical spills or high doses of radiation that may have contributed to increases in genetic defects or higher rates of cancer.

The NIMBY syndrome is most often seen when government or industry attempts to build a new power plant, incinerator, sewage treatment plant, LANDFILL, or other potentially harmful facility in a particular community. When plans for such facilities are made public, citizens' groups often respond by protesting in an effort to have the facility moved elsewhere. People generally desire the benefits of the facility, but they do not want to have it—and any potentially harmful environmental or health effects it may cause—near their homes and families. The problem lies, however, in the fact that if something is "not in my backyard," it will have to be in someone else's.

NITROGEN

An element essential to all life. Nitrogen plays an important role in the BIOGEOCHEMICAL CYCLES of earth and in the internal processes of organisms.

The NITROGEN CYCLE involves the movement of nitrogen moving from the earth,

☑ **Keywords**

Nutrients. Substances such as food, water, oxygen, and minerals that are critical for growth and sustaining life.

through plants, animals, and the ATMOSPHERE. BACTERIA convert nitrogen in the SOIL into a usable form for plants. Plants use this nitrogen to grow and build the protein they need to survive. Other bacteria break apart nitrogen compounds on land and release nitrogen as a gas into the atmosphere, where it may mix with water vapor and come back to the earth in rain.

Although nitrogen is essential for life, too much nitrogen can be harmful. Since nitrogen is a part of animal waste products and decay, too much waste in one place can lead to an excess of nitrogen. This can lead to an imbalance of **nutrients** in the cycle, causing excess bacteria and a process called EUTROPHICATION. In eutrophication, bacteria and ALGAE use up too much OXYGEN in water, leaving little for organisms that need it and making the body of water unhabitable for various species. [*See also* DECOMPOSITION; ENERGY CYCLE; FERTILIZERS; NUTRIENT CYCLE.]

NITROGEN CYCLE

Circulation of NITROGEN between the ATMOSPHERE and living things. Nitrogen is needed by all organisms for building the proteins needed for survival. However, most organisms cannot use nitrogen gas, the form in which nitrogen occurs in the atmosphere.

The nitrogen cycle begins when certain types of BACTERIA convert nitrogen gas from the atmosphere into a form that plants can use. These bacteria, known as nitrogen-fixing bacteria, live on the roots of LEGUMES and other plants and use the sugars provided by the plants to produce ammonia. Ammonia is a form of nitrogen that the plant can use for growth. Any extra nitrogen converted into ammonia by the bacteria goes into the SOIL. This is how plants without nitrogen-fixing bacteria get their nitrogen. Nitrogen-fixing bacteria can also live directly in the soil.

Other organisms get nitrogen by eating plants or animals. When bacteria and FUNGI

N

break down human and animal wastes, the nitrogen in the wastes goes back to the soil in the form of ammonia. The ammonia is then transformed into nitrogen gas by other bacteria, and the gas returns to the atmosphere to start the nitrogen cycle all over again.

NOISE POLLUTION

Sounds and noises that interfere with hearing or cause other psychological or bodily harm to humans. There are many types of noise pollution. Airplanes, cars, heavy machinery, appliances, loud music, lawn mowers, and firearms are some of the things that people use that create noise pollution. Many of these activities can damage the human ear through very loud noise. Noise pollution is especially a problem

COMMON NOISE LEVELS (in decibels)

100	jet plane at takeoff
90	heavy traffic, thunder
80	rock music, subway
70	normal traffic, quiet train
60	noisy office
50	loud conversation
40	light traffic
30	normal conversation
20	quiet conversation
10	a soft whisper

for people living in cities and near industrial and commercial sites.

The intensity or sound level of noise is measured in units called decibels (dB). The decibel scale increases in increments of power of ten, so a sound measuring one dB produces ten times more energy than a sound measuring o dB. A 110 dB noise like an explosion is deafening. Such loud noises can cause short-term or long-term hearing damage, depending on the length of exposure and the intensity of the sound. The Noise Control Act of 1972 was enacted to control noise pollution in the United States. It identifies noises requiring some type of control and sets standards for limiting them. Individuals can protect their ears by

wearing earplugs when necessary and by avoiding noisy environments.

NORTH AMERICA

The third largest continent, consisting of the nations of the United States, Canada, and Mexico. North America contains various ECOSYSTEMS, including DESERTS, GRASSLANDS, FORESTS, MOUNTAINS, and WETLANDS. It has a wide variety of climates and is home to thousands of different plant and animal species.

As in many areas of the world, North America's natural environment has been altered by human activities. LOGGING has removed many forested areas, the expansion of agricultural land has altered natural grasslands and other BIOMES, and industrial activities have contributed to AIR POLLUTION and WATER POLLUTION.

NUCLEAR POWER

Energy created by the process of nuclear fission or nuclear fusion. Nuclear fission is a process in which the nucleus of an atom is split into smaller nuclei (plural of nucleus), releasing a great amount of energy. Nuclear fusion occurs when smaller nuclei fuse, or join together, to form a larger nucleus. Scientist have not yet been able to develop a workable method for harnessing nuclear fusion to generate commercial nuclear power.

Nuclear power is created when the energy released by nuclear fission is converted into steam. Such nuclear reactions occur in nuclear power plants, where the energy is released slowly. The heat generated by these reactions is used to change liquid water into steam. This

☼ Fast Facts

No long-term facility exists for used fuel rods from nuclear power plants, which remain radioactive for millions of years. Many people believe that the rods are stored safely in a deep underground facility in the West. But all fuel rods are stored temporarily at the nation's 103 active nuclear plants.

Nuclear power plants are found in a number of countries, including the United States.

steam is then used to power electric generators. The steam is changed back into liquid water after it is used. Nuclear power plants use cooling towers to condense the steam from a gaseous to liquid form.

There are various advantages and disadvantages to using nuclear power. Nuclear power can generate electricity using less fuel than power plants that burn FOSSIL FUELS. Moreover, since nuclear energy does not release gases like CARBON DIOXIDE, it creates much less AIR POLLUTION than fossil fuels plants.

There are also disadvantages to using nuclear power. Radioactive wastes are produced from the processes used in nuclear power plants. The United States has no facilities for the permanent disposal of nuclear wastes at this time. These wastes, which can remain radioactive for tens of thousands of years, can cause health problems for different organisms, including humans. Such problems include birth defects and cancer. Nuclear power plants are also expensive to build. The use of nuclear power has slowed down throughout the world because of the costs of building and maintaining these plants. Environmental disasters, such as the accident at the Three Mile Island power plant in Pennsylvania in 1979, have also contributed to the slowdown in developmnent of nuclear energy. [*See also* ALTERNATIVE ENERGY SOURCES; HAZARDOUS WASTE.]

NUTRIENT CYCLE

The flow of nutrients through the environment. The nutrient cycle is the process by which organisms absorb or utilize food substances from their surroundings for the purposes of survival and growth. The nutrient cycle is part of other basic natural cycles, including the BIOCHEMICAL CYCLE, NITROGEN CYCLE, OXYGEN CYCLE, and WATER CYCLE. It involves natural processes such as EROSION, PHOTOSYNTHESIS, and DECOMPOSITION, and is an important part of FOOD CHAINS and FOOD WEBS.

OCEAN CURRENTS

Movements of water along regular patterns or paths in the ocean. The water in the world's oceans is constantly moving. Surface movements are caused primarily by winds and TIDES. There are also currents of water, like enormous rivers, that move along regular paths beneath the ocean surface. These ocean currents vary in size and strength. Some are composed of warmer water than others. These currents are also caused by tides and winds, as well as by differences in water density, water temperature, and the rotational movement of the earth on its axis.

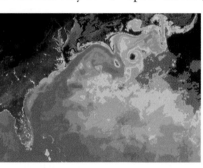

These currents in the Atlantic Ocean are made visible through special photography.

Ocean currents play an important role in CLIMATE AND WEATHER, creating conditions that produce certain types of climate and weather patterns. For example, one of the largest and most famous currents on earth is the Gulf Stream, which carries warm water toward Europe and helps warm the climate there. Ocean currents carry FISH and nutrients such as PLANKTON, which play an important role in the earth's FOOD CHAINS and FOOD WEBS. They also carry pollution caused by human activities and disperse it around the oceans. This has raised concern about the long-term effects of OCEAN POLLUTION.

OCEAN POLLUTION

Contamination of the oceans by adding harmful substances or changing the water temperature. People once believed that because the oceans are so large, they could absorb all matter of toxic chemicals and waste products dumped into them without harm. In recent years, however, scientists have discovered that the oceans are delicately balanced ECOSYSTEMS and that human actvities are polluting them.

Pollutants reach the seas from shorelines, ships, and oil spills. Oil spills kill life in tidal pools, and oil coats the feathers and fur of BIRDS and MAMMALS, causing the animals to drown or die of exposure. Animals can also become ill and die when they groom themselves and swallow the oil. Not only do oil spills kill fish, but toxic substances in the oil settle into the sediment on the ocean bottom. For a long time afterward, these toxins seep out and are carried by currents, killing marine animals and plants and collecting in the tissues of creatures such as shellfish.

Oil isn't the only toxic substance that pollutes the ocean. Chemicals such as DDT and FERTILIZERS used by farmers and gardeners can wash off the land into the sea and travel up the food chain. As different species in the food chain eat each other, the toxic substances build up in fatty tissues, becoming increasingly dangerous to animals higher in the chain.

Ocean pollution can also be caused by other types of pollution. SULFUR DIOXIDE enters the ATMOSPHERE from power plants, and the polluted air mixes with moisture to form sulfuric acid, which falls to earth as ACID RAIN. The acid rain enters rivers and is carried to the sea, changing the chemical balance of the oceans and harming many sensitive plants and animals that live in these ECOSYSTEMS.

For centuries, people have been dumping wastes in the oceans. But today, there is so much sewage and garbage that ocean dumping is endangering the marine environment. The United States passed the Ocean Dumping Ban Act in 1988, and the United Nations Law of the Sea Convention, adopted in 1982, contains rules to limit ocean dumping around the world. Still, ocean pollution remains a considerable threat.

OCEANS

(*See* ARCTIC OCEAN; ATLANTIC OCEAN; INDIAN OCEAN; PACIFIC OCEAN)

OIL SPILLS

When oil is leaked onto land or water. Because most areas where oil is found are far from places that use a lot of oil, it has to be transported—often by pipelines or ships. Oil spills can occur when pipelines rupture or when tankers have accidents at sea.

Oil spills can cause long-lasting harm to the environment.

Oil spills can cause great environmental damage, especially if they occur near CORAL REEFS, MARSHES, or other sensitive HABITATS. Oil that covers aquatic animals may prevent their bodies from keeping them warm and dry. If animals swallow significant quantities of oil, it can kill them. Oil spills can cause problems for humans as well, discouraging tourism and destroying fishing in the area of the spill.

After an oil spill occurs, it is difficult to clean up the residue. Some of the oil may evaporate and dissolve in the water naturally. Workers try to clean up the rest, often using machines that resemble giant vacuum cleaners or hoses. Petroleum HYDROCARBONS from oil can be detected in high concentrations in sediments even decades after an oil spill.

In 1989 the tanker *Exxon Valdez* ran aground in Prince William Sound in Alaska, spilling millions of gallons of oil. This spill killed thousands of MARINE MAMMALS, BIRDS,

and FISH, and oil from the spill still coats area beaches despite extensive cleanup efforts. Since the *Exxon Valdez* spill, new regulations require oil tankers to have double-hulls with two layers of metal protecting their cargo rather than just one. Regulations also encourage tankers to use shipping lanes where they are less likely to have accidents that will endanger ecological areas. [*See also* FOSSIL FUELS; OCEAN POLLUTION; WATER POLLUTION.]

OLD-GROWTH FORESTS

FORESTS that are hundreds or thousands of years old that have not been harvested by humans. The presence of large, mature TREES does not in itself constitute an old-growth forest. An ancient or old-growth forest has trees of varying size, shape, age, and, in some cases, SPECIES and subspecies. In addition to large, mature trees, the old-growth forest has lots of dead and dying trees that are very important to this ECOSYSTEM. For example, decaying trees that are still standing, called snags, provide sites for owls to sit during the day. Snags are full of insects that provide food for woodpeckers. Raccoons and other mammals may use holes in the snags for their burrows. Trees that die and fall down become nursery logs, rotting slowly on the forest floor and releasing their nutrients, which increase SOIL fertility and provide food for other organisms.

In the United States, most old-growth forest is in the Pacific Northwest, primarily in the Cascade Range of northern California, western

☀ Fast Facts

A seabird called the marbled murrelet makes its nest high in the canopy of old-growth forest along the coast of the Pacific Northwest. The murrelet goes out to sea each day to find fish to eat, but then returns to its nesting site in the trees. It depends on large, tall trees with massive branches high up in the canopy. If people continue to cut down old-growth forests for lumber, the murrelet species will not survive.

Oregon and Washington, and southeast Alaska. The species found in these forests include the majestic coastal redwood and giant sequoia in California and the great Sitka spruce in Alaska. Unfortunately, nine-tenths of the ancient woodland in this area has been cut down; only about five percent survives intact. Numerous wildlife species and ecosystems depend on the old-growth forests. Heavy cutting of timber in old-growth forests threatens dozens of species. In some areas, cutting of trees along rivers has created soil EROSION that suffocates SALMON as they try to return upstream to breed and lay their eggs.

In the eastern United States less than one percent of the old-growth forest has been saved, about a million acres (404,700 ha) in all. Most of it is found in the Great Smoky Mountains of North Carolina and Tennessee and in the Adirondack Mountains of northern New York State.

Old-growth forests are usually recognizable by the size of their trees.

OMNIVORES

Animals that eat both plants and other animals. Omnivores include bears, raccoons, coyotes, and some FISH. Humans are also omnivores. Like CARNIVORES, omnivores are often PREDATORS that hunt and kill other animals for food.

Omnivores will take advantage of any opportunity for food. The brown bear is a good example. In the spring, when salmon swim upstream to spawn, brown bears wade into streams to catch fish as they leap out of the water. But when fish are not available, the bears eat fruits and berries. Because omnivores have flexibility in the choice of food, they are a resilient link in food chains. Food shortages that might decrease the populations of species that depend on just one type of food source do not have as marked an effect on omnivores. [*See also* ECOSYSTEMS; WILDLIFE MANAGEMENT.]

ORGANIC AND NONORGANIC WASTE

A distinction made between waste products that are easily broken down and returned to the environment and those that take time to decompose, or biodegrade. Generally, this is the difference between living and nonliving materials, although the natural world also contains substances like glass that do not decompose.

Organic waste, such as food scraps, is called "biodegradable" because it breaks down into simpler substances through biological action in the environment. For example, a banana peel quickly returns to earth through the action of INSECTS, FUNGI, and BACTERIA. This is the same natural RECYCLING process we observe when we see a piece of candy on the ground covered by a swarm of ants. Everything in the natural system of plants and animals is organic and therefore recyclable, although some things take longer to decompose than others. A deer antler will not decompose as quickly as a banana peel, but it will be gnawed on by forest animals as a source of calcium until it, too, disappears.

Nonorganic waste is mostly manufactured. It includes metals like iron and steel, most plastics, many building materials like insulation, and chemical compounds, including some toxic substances like PCBS (polychlorinated biphenyls) and CHLOROFLUOROCARBONS (CFCs). All human waste must be disposed of or it creates health hazards. SOLID WASTE consumes valuable space in areas now referred to as LANDFILLS

☀ Fast Facts

Although construction waste is the largest single component of landfills, the average American family throws away over one ton of garbage per year. Paper and cardboard make up 30 percent of this total, kitchen waste 23 percent, metals and plastics 14 percent, and cloth 10 percent.

once called dumps. Many coastal cities tow their garbage out to sea and dump it, which contributes to OCEAN POLLUTION. RECYCLING is the attempt to reuse products rather than throw them away. [*See also* BIODEGRADABLE MATERIAL; DECOMPOSITION SEWAGE AND SEWAGE TREATMENT.]

OVERGRAZING

(*See* GRAZING)

OVERHARVESTING

Overfishing and use of FISH and other marine life. As the world's human population increases, so, too, does the number of fish that are harvested in the oceans. Overfishing affects many different species of fish, and such species as bluefin TUNA , cod, and flounder have declined drastically in number. Many fish species are caught and killed directly. Others are killed inadvertently when they are caught in fishing nets intended for other fish. OCEAN POLLUTION and the destruction of marine HABITATS has also contributed to a decline in fish populations.

Various regulations and laws have been established in the United States to combat the overexploitation of fish. The Magnuson Act of 1976, for example, established quotas that increase control over commercial fishing to limit the amount of commercial fish that can be used or sold. Regulations against overfishing may help to stabilize and repopulate the ocean's fish. [*See also* HUNTING.]

OWL, NORTHERN SPOTTED

Large, dark brown bird found in dense OLD-GROWTH FORESTS of the coastal ranges of British Columbia, Washington, and Oregon to central California. The northern spotted owl is one of three subspecies of the spotted owl. The two sexes of this species look similar, except the female is larger than the male.

Northern spotted owls have large home ranges—a single pair of birds may require 100 acres (hectares) of mature redwoods, firs, or hemlocks. Spotted owls spend a great deal of

The northern spotted owl is found primarily in the western United States.

the day sitting quietly in shady trees, sticking close to the tree trunks in cold and wet weather. The birds feed on flying squirrels and other small MAMMALS, BIRDS, and REPTILES. They often nest in cavities in old-growth trees or in stick platforms on tree limbs.

In 1990, the U.S. FISH AND WILDLIFE SERVICE listed the northern spotted owl as a threatened species and limited the legal sale of timber from areas where it is known to nest. Because the mature redwoods and other trees are worth a great deal of money to the logging industry, this action caused conflict among conservationists, loggers, and local residents of areas affected, many of whom depended on the logging industry for their livelihoods. The controversy over the northern spotted owl and the logging of old-growth forests has continued.

☀ Fast Facts

The male spotted owl defends its territory by giving loud, deep calls that sound something like the barking of a dog and can echo for great distances. The male feeds the female as she sits on her nest.

OXYGEN

A gaseous chemical element essential to life on earth. Most living things need oxygen to survive. Oxygen combines easily with other elements to form compounds called oxides. One example of an oxygen compound is CARBON DIOXIDE. About one-fifth of the ATMOSPHERE is made up of oxygen. Oxygen has a number of different forms. One form, a gas called ozone, is found primarily in the OZONE LAYER of the atmosphere.

Different species of animals get oxygen from the air through the process of respiration, or breathing. Most aquatic animals get oxygen from water, absorbing it through special organs such as gills. After an animal takes in oxygen, its bloodstream carries it to the body's cells. Plant cells produce oxygen in a process called PHOTOSYNTHESIS. [*See also* OXYGEN CYCLE.]

OXYGEN CYCLE

Circulation of OXYGEN between organisms, land, water, and air. Oxygen is an essential element for the survival of plants and animals and for many processes within an ECOSYSTEM. Oxygen can be found in many different forms as it moves from the land, water, and air. It interacts with other elements to form such compounds as water, carbon monoxide, CARBON DIOXIDE, SULFUR DIOXIDE, and nitrate. Oxygen can also be found in minerals and ores.

The oxygen cycle begins when plants and TREES produce oxygen during PHOTOSYNTHESIS, in which water is broken down into hydrogen and oxygen and released into the air. Humans take in oxygen during respiration from the air and exhale carbon dioxide, which is then used by trees and plants during photosynthesis. Some of the carbon dioxide dissolves in water. Water that evaporates also releases oxygen gases back into the ATMOSPHERE.

OZONE HOLE

A thinning of the protective layer of ozone gas in the earth's upper ATMOSPHERE. Ozone is a rare form of OXYGEN formed when sunlight strikes oxygen or when lightning passes through air. In its pure form, ozone is a bluish, bitter-smelling gas. In the upper atmosphere the OZONE LAYER has the ability to reflect more than 95 percent of the sun's ULTRAVIOLET RADIATION, radiation which is known to cause skin cancer when humans are overexposed to it. Ozone loss is caused by man-made chemicals called CHLOROFLUOROCARBONS (CFCs), which once were used in aerosol cans and are still used in refrigerators and air conditioners. CFC molecules and ozone molecules combine in a way that destroys the ozone in the atmosphere and allows greater amounts of ultraviolet radiation to reach earth. Ozone "holes" have been detected over both the North and South Poles since the early 1980s, although the problem is worse in the south where evidence of the death of phytoplankton has been found. Phytoplankton are tiny floating plants which form the basis of all ocean food chains.

The ozone problem is so serious that scientists have persuaded the United States and over 100 other national governments to ban production of CFCs by the year 2000. However CFCs already in the atmosphere may be active for up to 100 years. [*See also* AIR POLLUTION; OZONE POLLUTION.]

OZONE LAYER

A layer of the ATMOSPHERE that lies about 12 to 15 miles (10 to 25 km) above the earth's surface. Ozone is a form of OXYGEN present in the atmosphere in small amounts. It is concentrated mostly in the upper atmosphere.

The ozone layer is very important to life on earth. It serves as a shield that makes life possible. It does so by absorbing, or soaking up, almost all ULTRAVIOLET RADIATION from the sun's rays. If this radiation reached the earth's surface, it could harm all forms of life. Overexposure to the sun's ultraviolet rays can, for example, cause skin cancer.

In the 1970s, scientists detected that ozone concentrations in the upper atmosphere were declining. Most of the decline had occurred over the polar regions. Scientists were able to link most ozone loss directly to the use of CHLOROFLUOROCARBONS (CFCs) a group of chemical compounds widely used in such manufactured goods as aerosol cans, refrigeration, plastic packaging, and cleaning fluids. When CFCs are released, they rise into the atmosphere, where they react with the ozone, con-

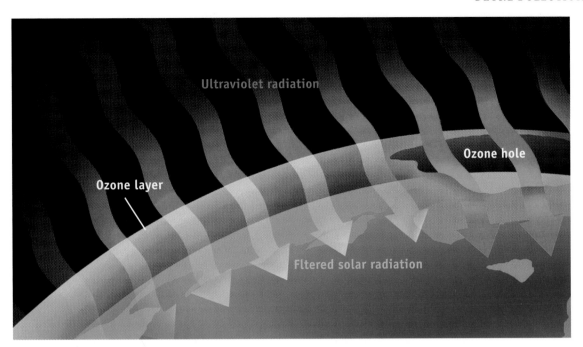

The ozone layer of the atmosphere is vital to life on earth.

verting it to ordinary oxygen. This chemical reaction depletes the ozone layer by reducing the concentration of ozone.

In 1978, the United States banned the use of CFCs in aerosol cans. However, CFCs were still used in other things, such as insulation and refrigeration. An international agreement called the Montreal Protocol was signed in 1987, calling for a worldwide reduction in the use of CFCs. In 1989, a number of nations agreed to phase out CFC production and aid poorer nations to do the same. Then, in 1990, the agreement was further strengthened to require a total phasing out of CFCs by the year 2000. The agreements appear to be working, though replacement chemicals for CFCs have proved to be expensive.

OZONE POLLUTION

Increased amounts of ozone near the surface of the earth. Ozone is a special form of oxygen gas that contains three atoms of oxygen. A natural compound, it is also formed when human activities form pollutants, such as nitrous oxide and hydrocarbons, which combine in the environment.

Ozone pollution is often referred to as ground-level ozone because the gas accumulates near to the ground. Ground-level ozone has very different effects on organisms than atmospheric ozone, which refers to the OZONE LAYER found in the upper ATMOSPHERE. The pollution effects of atmospheric ozone include the OZONE HOLE that forms over certain parts of the earth. Ground-level ozone pollution is created by industrial emissions, the burning of FOSSIL FUELS, paints, and pesticides.

Too much ground-level ozone can be toxic for many organisms. It can cause irritation and inflammation of the respiratory tract, leading to coughing, throat irritation, and breathing problems. It can irritate eyes and damage lung tissue, leading to heart and lung diseases. Ground-level ozone pollution can also have negative effects on FORESTS and crops, causing reduced crop yields and slower growth rates for trees. Ozone sensitive plants are used as indicators for AIR POLLUTION in many ECOSYSTEMS.

Amendments made to the Clean Air Act by Congress in 1990 were aimed at reducing ozone pollution. These amendments created regulations to control pollution emission levels in nearly 100 cities in the United States. The new amendments also established new controls on pollution emitted by motor vehicles.

P-Q

PACIFIC OCEAN

Large body of water extending from the ARCTIC region to ANTARCTICA, from western North and South AMERICA to eastern ASIA and AUSTRALIA. The name Pacific, meaning *peaceful*, was bestowed by the Portuguese explorer Ferdinand Magellan in 1520. The largest of the earth's four oceans, the Pacific covers 69,375,000 square miles (179,681,000 square km)—more than a third of the planet's surface—and contains more than half of its free water. The greatest known depth in the oceans occurs in the Pacific's Mariana Trench off Guam, at 36,198 feet (11,033 m).

The Pacific Ocean contains more than 30,000 islands, the largest of which include Japan, New Guinea, Indonesia, and New Zealand.

Much of the plant and animal life in the Pacific Ocean is concentrated along the coasts, occupying CORAL REEFS, seaweed forests, and MANGROVES. The open ocean has less variety, but it is still home to many kinds of FISH and MARINE MAMMALS. Scientists are just beginning to explore the bottom of the ocean and they are finding new SPECIES that can exist in the limited light that can reach these depths.

The Pacific Ocean is the largest and deepest of the world's oceans. It borders many different terrestrial ecosystems, from temperate and tropical rain forests to deserts and tundra.

⚔ Profile: Jacques Cousteau

French oceanographer Jacques Cousteau coinvented the Aqua-Lung, which replaced the heavy diving helmet and allowed humans to breathe under water. He also developed a one-person, jet-propelled submarine, and helped start the first manned undersea research station. Cousteau is probably best known for his many film documentaries about the world's marine ecosystems. In 1952, he took his ship *Calypso*, a converted mine-sweeper, to the Red Sea and shot the first color footage ever taken at a depth of 150 feet (46 m). His documentary film *The Silent World*, won various film awards. After Cousteau's 1972 expedition to Antarctica, the world saw the first pictures of ice formations under the sea. Cousteau spent 60 years exploring and helping to protect the world's oceans and marine life.

PANDA, GIANT

A large bear with distinctive black and white coloring found in bamboo FORESTS in western China. Giant Pandas eat mainly bamboo leaves, shoots, and stems, which they grasp with an enlarged wrist bone that functions as a thumb. Bamboo is not very nutritious, so giant pandas must eat a lot of it. Some species of bamboo flower all at once and then die, which can lead to starvation among the pandas.

Giant pandas are considered ENDANGERED SPECIES. Only about 1,000 giant pandas survive in isolated populations, and their forest HABITATS are being destroyed for agriculture and development. There are 13 panda reserves in

Giant pandas look and behave quite differently from other bear species.

China, and 14 more have been planned. The most famous of the existing reserves is Wolong Reserve in Sichuan Province. There are more than 20 captive giant pandas at the China Conservation and Research Centre for the Giant Panda in Wolong. Giant pandas do not reproduce well in captivity. Since 1991, natural mating has resulted in only eight births at the center. About 100 giant pandas live in zoos in China, and another 15 or so in other countries.

☀ Fast Facts

Giant pandas live for 18 to 20 years in the wild. The black and white pelt of the panda could cost $100,000 on the black market. Some people in Asia believe that if you sleep on the pelt you will be able to predict the future and keep ghosts away.

PARASITES

Organisms that benefit from feeding on the tissues or body fluids of another organism. Parasites are harmful to their hosts, the organisms that they feed on. Parasites feed on nutrients in their host, which weakens the host and makes it vulnerable to diseases and PREDATORS. Most parasites do not kill their hosts, however. Some examples of parasites include fleas, ticks, lice, worms, and protists (organisms like ALGAE, slime molds, and kelp). Parasites are dependent on their hosts for survival and cannot function well without a host. Parasites exist in many different species of organisms.

PCBs

Synthetic chemical compounds that cause environmental and human health problems. Before the 1970s, many products that people used, including paints, inks, plastics, and coatings for paper, wood, metals, and concrete, contained polychlorinated biphenyls (PCBs). However, PCBs were banned in the United States in the late 1970s, and many laws have been passed in different nations to control the use, production, and disposal of these chemicals.

Although PCBs have been banned in the United States, they are still released from industrial equipment made before the ban. PCBs are very toxic chemicals that do not break down very easily nor quickly. It is not known exactly how PCBs get into the ATMOSPHERE, but they can be carried to different places through the air. Sewage, leaking LANDFILLS, and waste dumping are among the most common ways in which PCBs enter the environment.

PCBs are most harmful when they enter rivers, LAKES, and oceans. The PCBs dissolve in the water and get absorbed into the bloodstreams of aquatic animals. As these animals eat each other, the PCBs are passed along to the other organisms in the FOOD WEB and the level of PCBs increases. As a result of BIOACCUMULATION, the PCBs get stored in the body tissues of organisms, and each step up in the food chain means an increase in the concentration of the PCBs, leading to the contamination of fish and other animals. A high concentration of PCBs can cause cancer and damage to the liver and reproductive systems.

P
Q

PELICAN, BROWN

Seabird with broad wings, a large bill, and a pouch that extends down from the bill. The brown pelican inhabits coastal waters from the southern United States to Brazil and Chile.

Brown pelicans feed almost entirely on FISH. Unlike other pelican species, which swim along the surface looking for food, the brown pelican hunts by plunging headfirst into the water from as high as 60 feet (18 m). Brown pelicans often nest in colonies on islands.

From the 1940s to the 1970s, brown pelicans were affected by the use of chemical pesticides, such as DDT, which they absorbed from the fish and which caused their eggshells to break before the chicks could develop and hatch. After the banning of DDT in the U.S. in 1973, brown pelican populations began to recover. These birds have a habit, however, of following fishing boats and may get hooked by longlines and tangled in nets and drown.

The brown pelican is the state bird of Louisiana.

PEST CONTROL

Efforts to control harmful insects and pests. The most common way to control pests in the 1900s has been through the use of chemicals. Pests include INSECTS that attack agricultural crops, and also weeds, rodents, and FUNGI. The general term for such chemicals is PESTICIDES. Different pesticides are used for different kinds of pests. They include insecticides, HERBICIDES, fungicides, and rodenticides.

Early pesticides were made of a mix of poisonous plants and chemicals. The production and application of stronger pesticides grew quickly from the 1940s to 1980s. The more they were used, the more evidence accumulated that pesticides were destroying wildlife and also endangering humans. Opposition to such pesticides grew, leading to restrictions or the outright banning of long-lasting pesticides, such as DDT.

In recent years, scientists have been searching for safer ways of controlling pests, especially in agriculture. The late 1900s saw new interest in organic gardening and farming—raising crops and farm animals without chemical pesticides and FERTILIZERS. Organic growers concentrate on safer methods of pest controls. These include taking advantage of the natural enemies of pests; using organic fertilizer to grow healthier, pest-resistant plants; planting varieties of crops that are insect-resistant; and mulching to cut down weed growth. A mulch is a protective covering that is spread on the ground between plants. It is made from small pieces of natural materials such as plant and grass clippings, sawdust, paper.

Another natural method of pest control is the rotating of crops from one year to the next. This helps discourage the buildup of insects that attack particular crops. Farmers have also worked to control pests by removing crop remains from fields, thus eliminating potential breeding grounds for insects. Another method of natural pest control is to plant short-season crops that mature before the pest populations increase enough to cause damage.

Farmers today often can choose pesticides targeted to particular pests. Such pesticides are harmless to other insects, such as butterflies and honeybees, which are useful for pollinating plants. Some farmers use pheromones—the scents, or odors, that animals release—as a form of communication. When chemically reproduced pheromones of harmful insects are released into the air, insects become confused. They cannot find other members of their species with which to mate. This reduces the size of that species' population. Pheromones can also be used in insect traps.

PESTICIDES

Any chemical used to control or get rid of pests. Different pesticides are used for different kinds of pests. There are several general types of pesticides. Insecticides are a type of pesticide used against INSECTS that eat crops or carry diseases. HERBICIDES are used to keep weeds under control on farms and lawns and in lakes and ponds. Fungicides are used to control plant diseases caused by FUNGI. Disinfectants found in hospitals and homes usually contain a fungicide. Rodenticides are special pesticides used mainly against rats and mice.

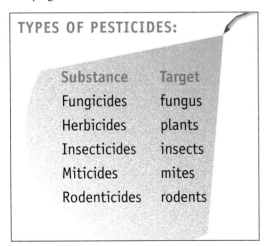

TYPES OF PESTICIDES:

Substance	Target
Fungicides	fungus
Herbicides	plants
Insecticides	insects
Miticides	mites
Rodenticides	rodents

Pesticides are dangerous to the environment because of their effects on the FOOD-CHAIN. A long-lasting pesticide may work its way up the food chain. For example, an herbicide is first absorbed by lower organisms in a pond. These organism are then eaten by FISH. The fish are then eaten by human beings. By the time the herbicide reaches higher organisms, such as humans, it is more concentrated and therefore more dangerous. This is why many long-lasting pesticides have been banned. Another problem with the use of pesticides is that some organisms develop a resistance to them. It takes more and more pesticide to control them, thus adding more poisons to the environment. [*See also* DDT; PEST CONTROL.]

PHOSPHATES

A chemical compound produced when PHOSPHORUS and OXYGEN combine with other chemicals. Plants and animals need phosphates to grow and function properly, which is why these chemical compounds are used as FERTILIZERS. Phosphates are also used in cleaning detergents because they are effective at removing dirt and softening hard water.

The use of phosphates can be harmful to the environment. Phosphates carried along by wastewater or in RUNOFF from fertilized fields contribute to WATER POLLUTION. Small, plant-like organisms called ALGAE live in streams and other bodies of water. They feed on the phosphates and multiply causing an algal "bloom" which can suffocate FISH. When algae die, their decaying also causes pollution of the water. In the 1970s, many communities were forced to ban the use of phosphate detergents because of their potential dangers to the environment.

PHOSPHORUS

A natural element that is vital to the life processes of all living things. Phosphorus is removed from the SOIL by plants and eaten by humans and animals. As various forms of PHOSPHATE—chemical compounds containing this element—phosphorus is crucial to many life functions. Phosphate groups are a component of the DNA in the nucleus of living cells. A phosphate called adenosine triphosphate is the basis for energy, whether we use that energy for sports or for internal activities like making proteins for muscle tissue.

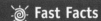

☀ Fast Facts

Phosphoric acid adds the sharp taste to cola and other soft drinks.

The phosphorus cycle describes the way an atom of phosphorus spends part of its time in inorganic substances like apatite (phosphate rock) and part of its time as a compound in the tissue of plants and animals. In the life and death of some short-lived forms of ALGAE, for example, an atom of phosphorus may complete the cycle from inorganic to organic and back more than a hundred times in a day.

PHOTODEGRADABLE MATERIAL

Any plastic material that degrades, or breaks down, when exposed to sunlight for a period of time. (The prefix photo- means "light.") Scientists developed BIODEGRADABLE MATERIAL and photodegradable plastics in the 1970s in response to concerns about the long life of such throwaway items as trash bags, foam cups, and plastic tableware. When photodegradable plastics break down, they do not change chemically. They only change physically, leaving small scraps of plastic behind. Because LANDFILLS are packed tightly in layers of WASTE and SOIL even degradable materials take a long time to break down. Moreover, the additives used to make up the plastic photodegradable can be harmful to the environment, which makes them unfit for RECYCLING. [See also ORGANIC AND NONORGANIC WASTE.]

PHOTOSYNTHESIS

Process by which green plants, ALGAE, and some other organisms use the energy of sunlight to convert CARBON DIOXIDE and water into the simple sugar glucose. An important by-product of the process is OXYGEN, on which most of the earth's living organisms depend for their survival.

In green plants, photosynthesis occurs in specialized structures called chloroplasts that are located in the leaves and stems. A plant leaf or stem contains tens of thousands of cells, and each cell has 40 to 50

chloroplasts. Embedded in the chloroplasts are hundreds of molecules of chlorophyll, a pigment that traps the energy from sunlight.

During photosynthesis, green plants produce millions of glucose molecules each second. They use glucose, a carbohydrate, as an energy source to build leaves, flowers, fruits, and seeds. They also convert it to cellulose, which forms the walls of their cells. Plants store excess glucose in the form of starch in their roots, stems, and leaves and can draw on these reserves for extra energy. Plants that live in water get their carbon dioxide from the water rather than the air. In cacti, which lack leaves, photosynthesis is carried out solely in the stem. In some epiphytes—plants such as orchids that grow high in the branches of tropical TREES— the long, trailing aerial roots carry out photosynthesis. Some flowering parts of plants can carry out photosynthesis, too.

Photosynthesis is crucial to life on earth. Humans and other animals, like plants, need glucose for energy, but they cannot produce it themselves. So they rely on the glucose in plant parts, such as potatoes, which they eat. In addi-

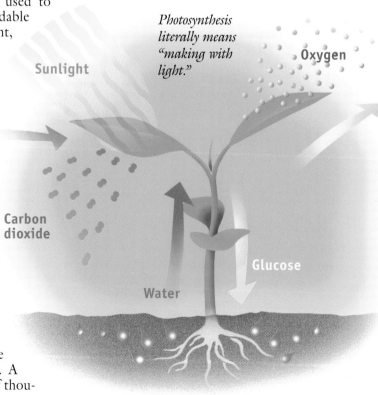

Photosynthesis literally means "making with light."

Oxygen

Sunlight

Carbon dioxide

Glucose

Water

tion, humans and other animals require the oxygen that is produced through photosynthesis. Photosynthesis also removes the carbon dioxide that is released into the air by natural processes and human activities. Carbon dioxide in the ATMOSPHERE helps regulate air temperatures on earth by trapping heat near the planet's surface. But many scientists believe that too much carbon dioxide in the atmosphere may cause global warming. As levels of carbon dioxide increase as a result of human activities such as burning of gas, coal, and other FOSSIL FUELS, plants can help remove some of the excess. [*See also* ENERGY CYCLE; FLOWERING PLANTS.]

PHYTOPLANKTON

(*See* PLANKTON)

PIPING PLOVER

A small, sandy-colored, migratory wading BIRD that lives in eastern North America. The bird is considered an ENDANGERED SPECIES in Canada and a threatened species in the United States. Dams built on rivers and coastal development have destroyed many of the plovers' HABITATS. Foot and vehicular traffic on beaches interrupts courting and nesting behav-

ior, destroys nests, and stresses young birds. Canada has developed the Piping Plover Guardian program, a largely volunteer effort to help protect the species' nesting areas. Various states in the United States have similar programs.

The name of the piping plover comes from its call, which resembles the sound of a flute.

☀ Fast Facts

Piping plovers are sometimes called ghost birds because they blend in so well with their background that people can hear them but not see them. The camouflage is critical to the survival of the adult birds, their eggs, and chicks on the open sand beaches where the species nests. Sometimes, however, the birds and their nests are run over by all-terrain vehicles, trucks, and boat trailers on the beaches.

PLANKTON

Small, often microscopic organisms that float on or near the surface of the ocean. These organisms form the foundation of ocean FOOD CHAINS and FOOD WEBS.

There are two types of plankton, phytoplankton and zooplankton. Phytoplankton are mainly green or yellow ALGAE that produce food through the process of PHOTOSYNTHESIS. Phytoplankton are the producers in ocean food chains. Zooplankton are tiny animals that occupy the next level of the ocean food chain. They feed on phytoplankton. Larger ocean organisms, such as FISH, consume both phytoplankton and zooplankton.

Phytoplankton produce large amounts of OXYGEN during photosynthesis and release it into the ocean. The oxygen is then released from the ocean into the ATMOSPHERE. Through this process, phytoplankton are responsible for producing most of the oxygen in the earth's atmosphere. [*See also* ECOSYSTEM, OXYGEN CYCLE, SEAS AND SEASHORES.]

PLATE TECTONICS

(*See* CONTINENTIAL DRIFT)

POLLINATION AND SEED DISPERSAL

Processes by which pollen is transferred from the male structure of a plant to the female structures, after which the seed separates from the parent plant. Pollination prepares plants for fertilization, which is the union of the male and female sex cells. Nearly all plants, from the tiniest wildflower to the tallest tree, must be pollinated and fertilized to produce seeds or fruits.

Various insect species play a vital role in pollination and seed dispersal.

In order for pollination to be successful, the pollen must be transferred between plants of the same species. Most plants have reproductive structures, such as cones or flowers, where the sex cells are produced. Pines, spruces, and other **gymnosperms** produce cones, which are either male or female and consist of spirally attached scales. In the pines, the male cones are produced in the spring on the tips of the plant's lower branches. Each scale on the male cones releases thousands of pollen grains. The female cones, which are longer than the male cones, usually develop on the upper branches of the same tree. The scales of the female cones open to catch drifting pollen and then close for a year or two to protect the developing seeds.

When the seeds are mature, the scales of some cones open and the seeds are dispersed by the wind. In other tree species, BIRDS and small MAMMALS break open the cones to get at the seeds. In the process, they may drop some seeds or take some away to bury or hide. This results in seed dispersal some distance from the parent plant. If the animals forget about the seeds and leave them where they have hidden them, the seeds are likely to germinate (sprout) and grow

into a new tree. This allows plants to spread to new areas.

In FLOWERING PLANTS, pollen is produced in the male part of the plant, called the stamen. The female sex cells, or eggs, are produced within the female part, the pistil, specifically in a part called the ovary. Fertilization occurs when a sperm cell unites with an egg. As the fertilized eggs begin to develop, the outer wall of the ovary hardens and forms a seed coat. Tissues of the ovary enlarge into a fruit, such as an apple, a grain of rice, or a nut. Unlike the seeds of pines and other **conifers**, which are exposed on the cones, the seeds of flowering plants are contained within a fruit.

☀ Fast Facts

Grains of pollen are tiny, microscopic in size. They range in diameter from less than 20 nanometers (about 0.0000008 inch) to a little over 250 nanometers (about 0.00001 inch).

Most plants pollinate in one of two ways: cross-pollination or self-pollination. Some plants are capable of both. In cross-pollination, pollen is transferred between different plants of the same species, ensuring that GENES from both plants are passed on to the next generation. To accomplish cross-pollination, some plants produce lightweight grains of pollen that are carried away by the wind. In other plants, eggs and pollen mature at different times. In self-pollination, pollen and eggs unite on a single plant. The genes of the new plant are identical to those of the parent. Many weeds reproduce this way. A whole patch of weeds may have origination from a single parent plant. This type of pollination is beneficial in areas where natural pollinators, such as bees, are scarce. But genetically identical plants are susceptible to disease and other natural disasters.

Seed dispersal occurs in a variety of ways. Milkweed plants, for example, produce seeds topped with a silky material that carries them on the wind. Pines and other conifers depend on squirrels and birds to break open cones and release the seeds. Other plants rely on pollinators—butterflies, BIRDS, bees, bats, even mice—to transport pollen. These plants must somehow attract the pollinators to them. For example, nectar attracts the hummingbird to a flower, and while the hummer is feeding at the blossom, it picks up pollen on its beak or body and transfers it to the next flower. [*See also* BIOLOGICAL DIVERSITY; FOOD CHAINS; FOOD WEBS.]

POLLUTION

(*See* AGRICULTURAL POLLUTION; AIR POLLUTION; HEAVY-METAL POLLUTION; NOISE POLLUTION; OCEAN POLLUTION; OZONE POLLUTION; THERMAL POLLUTION; WATER POLLUTION)

POLYCHLORINATED BIPHENYLS

(*See* PCBS)

POPULATION

(*See* HUMAN POPULATION GROWTH AND CONTROL)

PRAIRIES

Large areas of rolling land that, in their natural state, have deep fertile SOIL, a cover of tall coarse grasses, and few TREES. Prairies are also called GRASSLANDS. Grassland regions are found throughout the world, but they are called by different names: In Cental Asia they are called steppes; in South America, pampas and llanos; and in Africa, velds.

Prairies once made up much of the midwestern United States, covering all or parts of Iowa, Minnesota, Kansas, Nebraska, South Dakota, and North Dakota, and running north into Canada. The dominant grass plant of the tallgrass prairie is big bluestem, which can grow 6 feet (1.9 m) high. The most widespread tree is the bur oak, which has wide branches and thick dark green leaves.

Prairies depend on wildfires, which burn hot and move quickly, fueled by the dried dead grass. But the fires do not usually kill the green shoots and roots. The fires release nutrients in the dead plant material and warm the SOIL, encouraging regrowth of the grasses.

The early settlers plowed under the natural prairie vegetation and planted crops in the rich

Fast Facts

During the 1930s, the prairies in the central region of the United States experienced a severe drought. Because much of the original prairie grass had been damaged by farmers' planting crops and settlers' building houses, the rich topsoil had eroded away. High winds blew the dry soil into clouds, and the region was called the Dust Bowl.

True prairies–grasslands made up of tallgrass species–survive only in a few places today.

grows to 2 or 3 feet (.6 to .9 m). Mixed prairie is good HABITAT for bison.

Shortgrass prairie, also known as the Great Plains, extends from the mixed prairie to the Rocky Mountains. This region is drier, and the dominant grasses are blue grama and buffalo grass. Shortgrasses provide habitat for prairie dogs and pronghorn antelops. The shortgrass prairie has been altered less by man than the other two types of prairies.

PRECIPITATION

Any form of liquid or solid water particles that form in the ATMOSPHERE and then fall to earth's surface. Precipitation includes rain, snow, hail, sleet, and fog. It does not include frost and dew because they do not fall from the atmosphere but form on solid surfaces on or near the ground.

Rain is made up of drops of water. Raindrops are formed when water vapor (evaporated water) in the air cools. As the water vapor cools, it condenses around tiny particles of dust or other particles in the air to form CLOUDS. The water drops in the clouds grow, become heavy, and fall to the earth. Rain falls on nearly every part of the planet, but in different amounts. In a DESERT, there may be fewer than 3 inches (8 cm) of rain a year. But RAIN FORESTS may get as much as 400 inches (1,000 cm) of rain a year.

Snow consists of tiny ice crystals. These crystals form when water vapor freezes in cold clouds. The crystals stick together and form snowflakes. Snow acts as an insulator, protecting plant roots from the cold and helping to keep homes warmer, thus saving fuel. Melting

soil. By the turn of the twentieth century, most of the tallgrass prairie in the United States was gone, replaced by corn. With the planting of fields and building of houses and towns, wildfires became less frequent. In addition, settlers attempted to control the fires. Trees started to invade the remaining bits of true prairie and the tall grasses gave way to mature FORESTS through the process of SUCCESSION .

On its western edge, the tallgrass prairie region of the United States becomes an area known as mixed prairie, stretching through the Dakotas, Nebraska, Kansas, Oklahoma, and into central Texas. Soils there are not as rich and the grasses grow to medium heights. The common grass is the little bluestem, which

P
Q

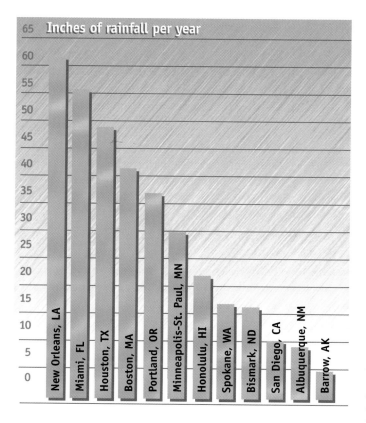

Inches of rainfall per year

65
60
55
50
45
40
35
30
25
20
15
10
5
0

New Orleans, LA
Miami, FL
Houston, TX
Boston, MA
Portland, OR
Minneapolis-St. Paul, MN
Honolulu, HI
Spokane, WA
Bismark, ND
San Diego, CA
Albuquerque, NM
Barrow, AK

and PEST CONTROL is administered by the U.S. FISH AND WILDLIFE SERVICE.

The range of predator species in need of "mangement" varies greatly. In Guam, for example, the introduction in the 1950s of the brown tree snake, which has no natural predators, virtually wiped out some NATIVE SPECIES of birds. Scientists and government agencies are studying the biology of the brown tree snake and ways to control its numbers in order to prevent other birds from becoming endangered and to prevent the snake from spreading to other islands.

Historically, predator control has usually referred to controlling the numbers of coyotes and WOLVES to minimize the damage to livestock and big-game animals such as elk. Many conservationists believe that ranchers and farmers have greatly exaggerated the damage that predators do to livestock, and that there is little justification for killing coyotes and wolves. They also point out that if too many coyotes and wolves are killed, the numbers of their prey animals, such as rodents and deer, may skyrocket, causing damage to crops and ornamental plants.

snow in the MOUNTAINS helps provide fresh water supplies for many communities.

Hail is precipitation in the form of lumps of ice called hailstones. Hail forms in thunderstorm clouds, beginning as frozen raindrops or hardened snow. Strong winds within the storm blow the hailstones up and down, allowing layers of ice to form. Sometimes this happens several times, forming larger and larger hailstones. Hailstones can get quite large and cause considerable damage to homes, vehicles, and crops.

Sleet is solid bits of clear ice. It is formed from freezing rain or partly melted snow. When sleet falls on roads and highway, it can cause very hazardous driving conditions.

A fog is like a cloud, except that it touches the earth's surface. It is made up of tiny drops of water suspended in the air. Fog can be quite dense and difficult to see through. [*See also* ACID RAIN; WATER CYCLE.]

PREDATOR CONTROL

Managing wild life species in order to reduce damage to agriculture and minimize threats to public safety. In the United States, PREDATOR

PREDATORS

Animals that hunt other animals for food. Among the world's largest predators are LIONS, bears, TIGERS, wolves, and sharks. The animals that predators hunt are called prey. Predators are also CARNIVORES. Carnivores are animals that eat other animals.

In a well-balanced ECOSYSTEM, there are more prey than predators. This ensures that the predators have a large enough food supply. It also ensures that the predators do not wipe out the population of prey. Animals begin to die if ecosystems get out of balance. If too many predators are killed, the population of prey will increase. If prey animals increase to the point where there is not enough food for them, they will begin to starve and die. On the other hand, if the population of predators increases too much, there will not be enough prey for them to

P
Q

eat. They will also begin to die. In either case, deaths will bring the populations in the ecosystem back into balance.

People can interfere with the natural balance of predator and prey in ecosystems by killing too many predators, such as wolves, through hunting. Good intentions can also throw ecosystems out of balance. By protecting populations of prey, such as deer, their numbers can increase too rapidly. In that case, the populations of deer could temporarily become too large for local food supplies. The starvation of some deer would then bring the ecosystem's population back into balance.

PRODUCER

Any organism in an ECOSYSTEM that can produce its own food. Most plants, except certain species of BACTERIA, are producers. Producers are the foundations of FOOD CHAINS. Living organisms could not exist on earth without plant producers.

Plants produce food through PHOTOSYNTHESIS, a process in which they convert the light energy from the sun into chemical energy that they store in their leaves. Plants are eaten by CONSUMERS, which are organisms that cannot produce their own food. When plant-eating consumers eat producer plants, they consume the energy stored in the plants. The consumers then utilize that energy to grow and reproduce. Farther up the food chain, the plant-eating consumers may be eaten by meat-eating consumers.

Producers also provide nutrients to other organisms in an ecosystem. Plants absorb nutrients such as potassium and NITROGEN from the soil. They store these nutrients in their leaves, stems, and roots. These nutrients are passed on to consumers when they eat plants. [*See also* BIOLOGICAL COMMUNITY; NITROGEN CYCLE; NUTRIENT CYCLE.]

PUBLIC LAND

Land owned primarily by a national or state government and held for the benefit of all its people. In the nineteenth century more than half the acreage in the United States was public land. Gradually, this land was distributed to railroads, companies and individuals. Today there are about 897 million acres (363 million

ha) of public land, with 742 million acres (300 million hectares) held by the federal government and 135 million acres (55 million hectares) held by state governments. About 20 million acres (8.1 million hectares) of federal land is managed without public access by agencies such as the U.S. Department of Defense.

Originally, public lands were managed for the benefit of mining companies, ranchers, and sportsmen. Today, however, recreational uses, such as skiing, camping and hiking are widely recognized. The view of public land has been changing since men like Henry David Thoreau and John Muir began to argue that land has wild and scenic beauty that benefits the spirit of people who go there.

The first NATIONAL PARK, Yellowstone, was established in 1871. President Theodore Roosevelt put his support behind the creation of an agency that would preserve areas of natural beauty, and in 1916 the NATIONAL PARK SERVICE was created. Today it manages about 75 million acres (30 million ha) of public land in all 50 states. The WILDERNESS movement argued for yet another kind of public land preserve. The Wilderness Act of 1964 stated that man should be "a visitor who does not remain" in these areas, which strictly limit roads and other human intrusions. The Gila Wilderness area in New Mexico, established in 1924, was the first national wilderness preserve. Today, more than 89 million public acres (36 million ha) in 44 states have a wilderness designation, and animals that were hunted off the land like the wolf and lynx are being selectively reintroduced. [*See also* NATURAL FORESTS; NATIONAL GRASSLANDS; NATIONAL SEASHORES; NATIONAL WILDLIFE REFUGES.]

PUPFISH, DEVIL'S HOLE

An ENDANGERED SPECIES of FISH found only in Devils Hole, Nevada. The Devil's Hole Pupfish is a small fish that grows to be about 8-10 inches (20-25 cm) long. They have whiskers and are cute, puffy-looking fish. During reproduction Devil's Hole pupfish lay about 12 eggs. They eat shrimp, small fishes and, tiny shrimp-like organisms called krill. Their existence is threatened due to habitat destruction, although they continue to survive in higher, inaccessible HABITATS. Their annual populations range from about 200 to 700.

R

RADIOACTIVE WASTE

(*See* NUCLEAR POWER)

RAIN FOREST

BIOME with a dense canopy of green, broadleaf trees supported by at least 79 inches (200 cm) of rain each year. There are tropical and temperate rain forests.

Tropical rain forests occur near the equator. They receive about 100 inches (250 cm) of rain per year and are always humid and warm. Due to their location near the equator, tropical rain forests get strong sunlight year-round. There are more diverse species of plants in tropical rain forests than in any other biome.

Temperate rain forests also receive large amounts of rainfall, but they are not as warm as tropical rain forests. The Pacific Northwest is home to North America's only temperate rain forest, which contains an abundance of forest plants.

Rain forests usually contain many different species of TREES. Among the trees found in tropical rain forests are cypress, balsa, teak, and mahogany. Temperate rain forests contain large evergreen trees such as Sitka spruce and Douglas fir. The trees in a rain forest often become very large. Many of the trees reach heights of more than 150 feet (46 m) and form a dense canopy. The canopy forms a type of "roof" high above the forest floor, or "understory," blocking most sunlight from reaching the ground. As a result, ground vegetation is usually sparse in the tropical rain forests. In temperate rainforests, the ground is often covered with FERNS.

Rain forests are among the richest ecosystems on earth in terms of the plant and animal species that live there.

Rain forests are the most diverse biomes on earth. They contain 70 to 90 percent of all the species on earth, and they hold 40 percent of the earth's land BIOMASS. Many species of plants and animals survive in the different zones of the rain forests. The understory does not have as much vegetation as the other layers, but MOSSES and ferns do thrive here. The diversity of plant life in rain forests provides good HABITATS for many animals.

The habitats in the rain forest vary from tree to tree and even from one part of a tree to another. The upper canopy supports a variety of INSECTS, BIRDS, and MAMMALS that spend their entire lives above the forest floor and use the trees for living areas and transportation. AMPHIBIANS and REPTILES live in the forest understory, where the moisture and warmth of the area are high. The streams and puddles of water on the forest floor are habitats and water resources for other animals.

Rain forests are also important for humans, providing various NATURAL RESOURCES. Their trees have become such valuable resources that rain forest ECOSYSTEMS are increasingly threatened by LOGGING and the expansion of agricultural lands. Some scientists believe that DEFORESTATION may affect global climate patterns and contribute to GLOBAL CLIMATE CHANGE. [See also BIOLOGICAL DIVERSITY; FORESTRY; FORESTS.]

Profile: Margaret Mee

An artist and environmental activist, Margaret Mee (1909–1988) was one of the first critics of rain forest destruction. She journeyed into the Brazilian rain forests many times, using her artistic skills to record and draw its plant life; she also discovered new species. Each time she went into the rain forest, she witnessed the disappearance of more habitat, and she protested against the forest policies of the Brazilian government.

RAPTORS

Powerful, usually large BIRDS that feed on flesh. Raptors have strong feet with sharp talons or claws, and large hooked beaks for grasping, killing, and carrying off their prey. There are two groups of raptors. One group

Raptors are also called birds of prey.

includes eagles, hawks, falcons, vultures, and other birds that hunt during the day. Night hunters, chiefly owls, make up the second group of raptors.

Raptors are at the top of their FOOD CHAINS, and they play an important role as KEYSTONE SPECIES in maintaining the balance of ECOSYSTEMS. For example, they keep rodent populations under control, and vultures feed on carrion, or the flesh of dead animals. Many raptor species are extinct or ENDANGERED SPECIES because of the use of PESTICIDES and the loss of their habitat. To save some endangered raptors, such as California condors, conservationists have begun programs to reintroduce the birds in protectected areas. [See also BALD EAGLE.]

RECYCLING

The process of saving materials and reusing them. Many products can be recycled, including those made from aluminum and steel, glass, paper, cardboard, and plastics. Some recycling programs reclaim used motor oil and tires.

Recycling has many advantages, both for individuals and the environment. It reduces the amount of waste material that must be disposed of in LANDFILLS. It also reduces the amount of AIR POLLUTION and WATER POLLUTION that might result from the disposal of these waste materials. Recycling reduces the cost of waste disposal to communities and individuals. Moreover, the recycled materials can be sold, earning money that can be applied to the costs of waste disposal.

Some NATURAL RESOURCES are not renewable, that is, they cannot be replaced when they are used up. They can be recycled, however. Recycling gives manufacturers the materials they need to continue making such products as packaging, books and newspapers, and some building materials, such as insulation, that are made from nonrenewable resources.

For recycling to really work, consumers have to make a deliberate choice to use recycled products. That may mean checking for the recycling symbol on a product's packaging. [*See also* COMPOSTING; CONSERVATION.]

RED TIDE

A mass of seawater containing toxins, or poisons. Red tides are natural events that occur in all oceans due to a huge multiplication—a "bloom"—of certain species of ALGAE and phytoplankton, or microscopic plantlike cells. The MICROORGANISMS clump together near the water's surface. Since some carry red pigments, the water takes on a reddish-brown color.

The phytoplankton in red tides produce powerful chemical substances that poison FISH by entering their bloodstream through their gills. Some shellfish, such as oysters, clams, and mussels, are contaminated by feeding on the phytoplankton. Dolphins and other MARINE MAMMALS are poisoned when toxins accumulate in their bodies.

Contaminated oysters, clams, mussels, and other MOLLUSKS are unsafe as human food because the toxins accumulate in the creature's soft body tissues. Fresh fish, shrimp, crab, scallops, and lobsters are safe since toxins do not accumulate in their meaty, muscle tissues. Rashes and throat irritation may result from contact with the red tides. Scientists are looking for ways to detect and monitor them to protect the MARINE ECOSYSTEM and human health.

Red tides occur periodically in certain parts of the world.

REFORESTATION

(*See* DEFORESTATION)

RENEWABLE AND NONRENEWABLE RESOURCES

A distinction made between resources that will not run out and those that will. SOLAR ENERGY and wind power are good examples of renewable energy resources. Scientists calculate that the sun's energy will not expire for several billion years, so from a human point of view it is

R

a limitless source of heat and power. FOSSIL FUELS, such as coal, oil and natural gas, are examples of nonrenewable resources because once used up, they are gone forever. Because they are constantly growing, TREES might seem to be a renewable source. But, just like fossil fuels, trees can be used up if people are not careful about the rate at which they cut them down. The same is true of water.

The United States consumes most of the world's energy and generates most of its waste. as a result, the wise use of resources is an issue of great concern in the U.S. RECYCLING is a way to create renewability through the reuse of limited resources. As current resources expire, other energy resources will need to be found as well. NUCLEAR POWER has been tried as a source of energy, but people around the world are concerned about the HAZARDOUS WASTE it generates. Truly renewable resources—including solar power, HYDROELECTRIC POWER, and WIND-GENERATED ENERGY—are constantly replenishing themselves, so it is likely that future power resources will depend on energy from the wind, the water, and the sun. [*See also* ALTERNATIVE ENERGY SOURCES.]

REPTILES

VERTEBRATES that have dry, scale-covered skin and breathe with their lungs. Reptiles—which include snakes, lizards, turtles, alligators, and crocodiles—are cold-blooded animals. That means that their body temperature stays about the same as that of its surroundings. Reptiles must thus avoid extreme temperatures that would make their bodies too hot or too cold. In moderate climates, reptiles are often active in the daytime, moving from one sunny spot to another. In a very hot climate, they are active mostly at night after the temperature cools. In colder climates, reptiles hibernate during the winter. In the tropics, some reptiles remain in a type of hibernation during dry summer months when food is scarce.

Destruction of HABITATS poses a threat to reptiles in different parts of the world. Many reptiles are also killed because humans fear them. This is especially true of snakes and crocodiles. Despite their fearsome reputation, reptiles are important members of FOOD WEBS, eating INSECTS, rats, mice, and other animals that can be harmful to crops and humans.

**Endangered Species:
African Dwarf Crocodile**

Native to central and western Africa, the African dwarf crocodile lives in swampy forests. It is a secretive animal and active mainly at night, so scientists know very little about this reptile. The dwarf crocodile has bony plates in its skin, which help it survive predators and also make the skin undesirable for people to use in making shoes, handbags, and other items.

RHINOCEROS

Large land mammal of AFRICA and ASIA. Rhinos have existed for over 50 million years. At one time there were many different kinds of rhinos. But only five species still survive, and their numbers are decreasing rapidly. These rhinos live in varied HABITATS, including FLOODPLAINS, GRASSLANDS, tropical RAIN FORESTS, and SAVANNAS, and mountain FORESTS. Poachers kill rhinos for their horns, which are used for medicinal or ornamental purposes in Asia and the Middle East.

The five species of rhinoceros are the black, white, Indian, Javan, and Sumatran. The black and white rhinos are found in Africa. Today, there are about 2,400 black rhinos and 8,000 white rinos in the wild. The Indian rhino is an Asian rhino, found in northern India and southern Nepal, whose numbers have risen from under 200 to over 2,000 within this cen-

**Endangered Species:
Javan Rhinoceros**

Originally, the Javan rhinoceros lived in the rain forests of Myanmar, Thailand, Indochina, Indonesia, and Northern India. Today, however, it survives only in two small reserves. Java has about 40 to 60 Javan rhinos in Ujung Kulon National Park. About 10 to 15 survive in the Cat Loc Nature Reserve in Vietnam.

Today, only about 13,000 rhinos survive in the wild, with another 1,000 in captivity.

tury. The Javan rhino is another Asian rhino found on the Indonesian island of Java and in Vietnam. It is the rarest of the rhino species with fewer than 100 animals surviving in the wild. The Sumatran, or hairy rhino (the other species are hairless), is an Asian rhino found primarily in Indonesia and Malaysia. Fewer than 400 of the animals still survive in the wild. Because of poaching. All five species of rhinos are at risk of EXTINCTION.

RIPARIAN RIGHTS

(*See* WATER RIGHTS)

RIVER SYSTEMS

Networks of streams that flow into each other, draining water from a large area known as "watershed," and growing larger as they approach the sea. All water flows downhill because of the force of gravity. It descends until it can go no lower. Water flows until it reaches the ocean, a point we call "sea level." Sometimes, though, a river will evaporate or flow into an inland sea like the Great Salt Lake in Utah, instead of flowing to the sea.

Water begins its journey as snow or rain falling in a particular watershed, the area from which a stream gets its water. The water gathers in narrow brooks or creeks draining a small area. These small streams, called **tributaries**, flow together and become larger, creating rivers which drain even larger watersheds. Very large rivers drain basins—watersheds covering as much as millions of square miles. For example, the Missouri River begins in Montana and flows southeast until it joins the Mississippi

---

☑ Keywords

Tributaries. Small streams or rivers that empty into larger ones.

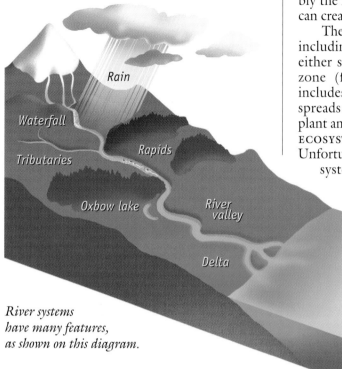

River systems have many features, as shown on this diagram.

Rain

Waterfall

Tributaries

Rapids

Oxbow lake

River valley

Delta

bly the most powerful example of what a river can create over time.

The corridor through which a river flows, including riverbanks and a narrow zone on either side of the river, is called a "riparian" zone (from the Latin word for river). It includes the wildlife and vegetation that spreads out along the sides of the river. Many plant and animal species depend on the narrow ECOSYSTEMS that the riparian zone provides. Unfortunately, dams can disrupt these riparian systems. Even though they provide recreation and HYDROELECTRIC POWER for people, the dams can create ecological stress for creatures that depend on the river for life. Glen Canyon Dam on the Colorado River destroyed valuable natural HABITATS and also flooded an area of great scenic beauty and archeological value. [*See also* AQUATIC HABITATS; DAMS AND DIKES; LAKES; MARSHES.]

RUNOFF

River in St. Louis. It drains an area known as the Missouri Basin. The Mississippi River drains the upper and lower Mississippi Basins, an area much larger than the Missouri Basin. The Mississippi rises in Minnesota and flows 2,350 miles (3,781 km) before it joins the ocean at New Orleans. In addition to the Missouri, dozens of smaller rivers like the Ohio, Tennesse, Des Moines, and Arkansas join as tributaries to make up the Mississippi river system, which drains the central United States.

Along their path to the sea, rivers ceaselessly carve their banks and pour over waterfalls, creating steep cliffs and canyons. This process of EROSION often creates spectacular beauty. The Grand Canyon in Arizona is proba-

The total of all water that flows over the surface of the land and empties into a body of water. Runoff is mostly rainfall, although it also consists of snow and ice that melt and flow from the land into RIVERS, LAKES, and oceans.

Runoff is part of the WATER CYCLE, the endless movement of water from the earth's surface to the ATMOSPHERE by evaporation, then from the atmosphere back to the earth's surface through condensation and PRECIPITATION. Most of the water that falls to earth in the water cycle becomes runoff that enters oceans to become precipitation again.

Runoff can be a carrier of pollution into bodies of water. This pollution comes from many sources. Water that runs off farm fields covered with FERTILIZERS and PESTICIDES carries those chemicals into nearby rivers and streams. Water from industrial sites, often contaminated with toxic chemicals, also runs off into nearby SURFACE WATERS. Erosion is the source of sediment that runs off into streams, rivers, and coastal areas. This sand and silt can smother underwater plants in coastal ESTUARIES or kill the living organisms that comprise CORAL REEFS, damaging coastal ECOSYSTEMS. [*See also* AGRICULTURAL POLLUTION; WATER POLLUTION.]

☼ Fast Facts

At 4,160 miles (6,693 km), the Nile River in Africa is the longest river in the world. But the Amazon River in South America carries the greatest volume of water of any river system on earth.

S

SALMON

A species of FISH that hatch in cold-water streams but spend most of their adult lives in the ocean. Salmon are CARNIVORES that eat smaller fish. When it is time to breed, salmon leave the ocean and swim upstream in rivers to return to the place where they originally hatched. There are many different species of salmon in NORTH AMERICA, EUROPE, and ASIA. The North American species are the Atlantic, coho, pink, chinook, chum, sockeye, and some species of trout. Salmon are fished for commercial and recreational uses. Overfishing and DAMS, which prevent salmon from swimming upstream to their breeding ground, have caused a decline in salmon numbers. DEFORESTATION causes EROSION, which damages salmon HABITATS. Federal and local governments are making efforts to protect salmon habitats to help ensure their survival. [*See also* FISHING; OVERHARVESTING.]

Coho salmon

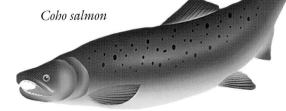

SAVANNA

Type of GRASSLAND that ranges from dry areas with scattered trees to wet, open woodlands. Found in ASIA, AFRICA, and SOUTH AMERICA, savannas receive rainfall only part of the year. A warm, wet season is generally followed by a cool, dry season and then a hot, dry season. The grasses, shrubs, and TREES of savannas are well adapted to the generally dry SOIL, having roots that stay alive and soak up water even when the stems and leaves die. These grasses can survive the frequent fires that sweep across grasslands, and they support the GRAZING of many animals. Among the animals that graze on savannas are zebras, antelopes, and gazelles as well as small animals like rodents and INSECTS. [*See also* BIOME.]

☀ Fast Facts

The savannas of Africa have a larger number of grazing mammal species than anywhere else in the world. Two large grazing animals in Africa are zebras and water buffalo.

SCAVENGERS

Animals that feed on the bodies of dead organisms. Scavengers, such as vultures and various types of INSECTS, feed on dead plants or the dead bodies of any type of animal that they find. They never actually hunt down a living organism. Scavengers start the process of returning nutrients to the environment by breaking down dead organisms into smaller pieces for the process of DECOMPOSITION by BACTERIA and FUNGI. The decomposers consume the dead organic matter, breaking it down into nutrients that go back into the soil where plants can use them to build new organic material. [*See also* COMPOSTING.]

SEAS AND SEASHORES

A network of large saltwater bodies that together create the earth's largest ECOSYSTEM. Oceans and seas cover 70 percent of the earth's surface. They provide HABITATS for many creatures from the darkest depths to sea level and the beaches and cliffs high above the waves.

Within these habitats live a rich variety of FISH, MARINE MAMMALS, and other animals, as well as many species of plants.

The earth has a number of oceans and seas, from the enormous Pacific Ocean to the smaller Atlantic and Indian Oceans, to small seas such as the Mediterranean Sea and Caribbean Sea. Each of these bodies of water has somewhat different characteristics, based on water temperatures, OCEAN CURRENTS, water depth, and other features. These characteristics create a variety of ecosystems, each with certain unique plant and animal species. For example, CORAL REEFS are very different from the undersea mountains and deep canyons found in certain places in the oceans.

There are two basic marine ecosystems. Within a few miles of shorelines lie the CONTINENTAL SHELVES, areas of shallower and warmer waters where the great majority of sea life is found. Farther out are the deep ocean zones. Light from the sun does not reach these great ocean depths, and the water is cold. A variety of fish and marine mammals live near the surface in these regions. But only a few species live in the great depths below.

Seashores are a traditional ecosystem blending the differences between water and land and sheltering a rich variety of life. Coastal bird life is concentrated along seashores, and living beneath the sand or clinging to tidal rocks are worms and clams, mussels and oysters. Crabs hunt in the tidal pools, and many types of seaweed cling like tidal forests to the deeper rocks. Sand is constantly being manufactured by the erosive action of waves on coastal rocks. The wind and surf shape it into dunes, and varieties of hardy shoreline vegetation help hold the dunes in place.

As the lowest areas of earth, the oceans collect water from all the world's RIVER SYSTEMS. Ocean water is salty because of evaporation, a process by which air absorbs water but not the solid matter dissolved in water. The minerals and salts rinsed out of the SOIL by rivers grow more and more concentrated as they are left behind, giving seawater its particular taste. Rivers can also carry pollutants—such as agricultural FERTILIZERS and chemicals. In addition, OIL SPILLS and various human activities also contribute to OCEAN POLLUTION. The United States and other nations have laws to help protect the world's seas and seashores, but much remains to be done to protect these important ecosystems. [*See also* AQUATIC HABITATS; ARCTIC OCEAN; ATLANTIC OCEAN; HYDROSPHERE; INDIAN OCEAN; MARINE ECOSYSTEMS; PACIFIC OCEAN.]

SEA LION, STELLER'S

A MARINE MAMMAL that is one of five species of sea lions. Steller's sea lion, also called the Northern sea lion, was first described by a German naturalist, Georg Steller, who explored the coast of Alaska in 1741. It is the largest sea lion: adult males can measure 11 feet (3.4 m) in length and weigh 2,200 pounds (1,000 kg). The smaller females range up to 8 feet (2.4 m) in length and 600 pounds (270 kg) in weight. Their HABITAT is the North Pacific Ocean.

These sea lions are good divers and swim-

Sea lions often bask on rocks between feedings in the ocean.

mers—propelling their sleek, torpedo-shaped bodies through the water by their foreflippers. They are agile on land, too, using all four flippers to move. The Steller's seal lion population has dropped severely since 1960, and they are now considered an ENDANGERED SPECIES. A shortage of the FISH they feed on—due to overfishing by commercial fisheries, entanglement in nets, WATER POLLUTION, and sport shooting—have reduced their numbers. Efforts to save the species include placing limits on the amount of fish that can be taken from their feeding grounds, a ban on shooting the animals, and protection for their breeding grounds.

SEA TURTLE, GREEN

Threatened species of turtle found throughout the world's oceans. Green sea turtles nest on beaches bordering the ATLANTIC, INDIAN, and PACIFIC OCEANS. Slow-growing REPTILES, they may not reach maturity until they are 40 years of age. Green turtles feed on marine grasses and other plants. Female turtles lay their eggs on sandy beaches. On land the eggs and young hatchlings are threatened by PREDATORS, such as seagulls and foxes, and in the ocean they face dangers from sharks and other MARINE MAMMALS that prey on them. Overexploitation of turtle eggs and meat as a source of food, commercial fishing operations, and disturbance of HABITATS have led to a decline in the numbers of these creatures.

The green sea turtle is one of the largest turtle species.

SEAFLOOR

Various regions of the ocean, including the CONTINENTAL SHELF, the shallow underwater extension of the continents; the continental slope, the steep cliff that drops from the continental shelf to the deepest part of the ocean; and the ocean basin, the deepest section in the middle of oceans. The seafloor and the rock formations under it are rich in mineral resources, such as petroleum, natural gas, and manganese.

The seafloor contains some of the world's most dramatic landforms. The world's longest mountain chain, the Mid-Ocean Ridge, winds for 40,000 miles (64,360 km) through the center of the Atlantic Ocean. The flattest places on earth are the abyssal plains that make up the bottom of the ocean basin. The seafloor also has the earth's deepest canyons.

Very few organisms live on the deepest parts of the seafloor. Because sunlight can only penetrate the upper few hundred meters of the ocean, PHOTOSYNTHESIS cannot occur on the seafloor. Therefore, plants that form the base of most food chains cannot live in the ocean depths. Recent deep-sea exploration, however, has uncovered unusual organisms living near undersea vents where earth's crustal plates are slowly pulling apart. The vents pour out hot water and hydrogen sulfide from deep inside the earth. BACTERIA and other organisms near the vents use the chemicals for food, making this the only ecosystem so far discovered that does not depend on plant producers that make food using sunlight. [See also OCEAN POLLUTION.]

SEDIMENT

Pieces of rock and soil carried by water, wind, and moving ice during the process of EROSION. Deposited sediment forms a number of common landforms, such as river deltas, sand dunes, and long ridges called moraines.

Sediment is created by weathering, the process that breaks down large chunks of rock into smaller rock pieces. When growing roots or freezing water expands inside crevices, it causes rock to weather, or erode. Chemical processes such as ACID RAIN also weather rock. Weathered rock can be carried away by flowing water, which jostles it and breaks it into smaller pieces. Winds can also chip and shatter rock by smashing it against hard surfaces. GLACIERS pick up rocks and grind them against the hard surface below them as they move.

Sediments also form sedimentary rock, one of the three main categories of rock. Sedimentary rock is formed when water or wind slow down and deposit layers of sediment. As new layers of sediment form, older layers underneath are compressed or squeezed tighter. As this happens, minerals in the sediment cement the particles together. Over millions of years, the sediments eventually become solid rock. [*See also* SOIL CONSERVATION.]

SEWAGE AND SEWAGE TREATMENT

Wastewater from homes and business, and treatment to make it less damaging to the environment. Wastewater contains liquid and semi-solid wastes that come from toilets, sinks, dishwashers, washing machines, and industrial equipment. It is collected in public sewer systems that move it along to sewage treatment plants. The water is then treated and released into rivers, LAKES or the oceans.

Sewage. The United States dumps enormous amounts of sewage into the ocean each year. Some of this is not treated before it is dumped, and much of the waste is from factories and contains toxic chemicals and metals. Sewage is generally more than 95 percent water, and it is classified according to amount, rate of flow, waste, and BACTERIA it contains. It can also be classified as sanitary, commercial, industrial, or surface runoff.

Sanitary sewage is waste from homes, hotels, apartment buildings, schools, hospitals, and prisons. The wastewater from these places contains human excrement, dirty water from washing and bathing, laundry and dishwashing water, animal and vegetable matter from food, and other wastes from day-to-day living. Commercial sewage is waste from businesses such as restaurants, stores, offices, and laundromats. It is a lot like sanitary sewage, although the amounts of wastes may vary. Industrial sewage is wastewater from factories. These wastes are often the same as commercial and sanitary wastes, but they also contain chemicals such as bleaches and paints. Surface runoff is rainwater that flows quickly over the land to gutters and storm drains. Waste matter in its natural condition that is not treated or change in any way and carried off by a sewer is called raw sewage.

Sewage treatment. Sewage is generally treated in three steps: primary, secondary, and tertiary. Primary treatment removes about 30 percent of the organic materials and bacteria from sewage. In this stage of treatment, sewage is passed through screens that filter out plastics, fabrics, and metallic objects. The water passing through the filters is sent into settling tanks, where the sewage is mixed with a clotting material to make clumps of organic matter float to the water's surface. These clumps are then skimmed off. Bacteria break down the material in the settling tank, and chlorine and other chemicals are used to sanitize and deodorize the treated water.

Secondary treatment is used to remove about 85 percent of the organic solids that remain after primary treatment. The waste flows from the settling tank into an aeration tank—where air is forced through the matter. The bacteria inside the tank decompose the organic substances to form less harmful matter. The liquid then flows into another tank, where SLUDGE is formed and digested by bacteria that break it down to produce METHANE.

Tertiary treatment results in even purer discharge. This treatment may use chemicals or radiation, or microscopic screens may be used to filter the liquid. The water from tertiary treatment is much safer than that released after primary or secondary treatment.

Environmental problems. Sewage produces methane, which can be used as an alternative energy source. But it often contains phosphates that increase the growth of ALGAE. Excess algae may cause OXYGEN depletion in the water. When the algae die, bacteria and other decay organisms absorb the oxygen from the water. Industrial sewage may also contain toxic and radioactive material that, if released into waterways, can have a harmful effect on human health and the environment.

SLUDGE

Thick liquid waste material containing BACTERIA, FUNGI, MINERALS, and other organic matter not completely broken down by bacterial action. Sludge is a concentrated suspension of solids in a liquid, usually water. Sludge often contains toxic substances and must be treated and disposed of carefully through sewage treatment systems. Sludge is formed during manufacturing processes and in sewage treatment plants. For many years sludge was disposed of in the ocean. Today, it is usually treated and disposed in LANDFILLS or used as a soil stabilizer. [*See also* SEWAGE AND SEWAGE TREATMENT.]

SMOG

A form of AIR POLLUTION caused by the combination of smoke and fog. The word "smog" was coined in 1905 to describe an irri-

tating haze that hung over London and other cities in England. The term later was applied to similar conditions in cities around the world.

Smog results when sunlight acts on air pollutants from vehicles and factories to form a thick atmospheric haze. A weather condition known as thermal inversion layer sometimes increases the incidence of smog. This weather condition results when a layer of warm air rests over a layer of cooler air near the ground. (The word "thermal" means "heated.") The warm air prevents the smog from rising and being dispersed. Surrounding MOUNTAINS can also hold polluted air in place.

Smog is a particular problem in industrialized cities with heavily traveled highways and factories. Fogs over a city are usually thicker than over the countryside because cities dis-

charge more moisture into the atmosphere. The moisture combines with auto exhaust, dust, and the smoke from factory chimneys. If the city lies in a valley, only very strong winds will blow the smog away.

The frequent presence of smog can cause various health problems. Smog can irritate the eyes and damage the body's respiratory system (which includes the nose, throat, and lungs). Smog can also affect animals and plant life. It can damage the exteriors of buildings. Smog carries droplets of sulfuric acid, which is very destructive to whatever surfaces it lands on.

A type of smog called photochemical smog is caused by the burning of gasoline and other petroleum products. Sunlight acts on the chemicals released into the atmosphere by that burning, producing gases called oxidants. One such oxidant is ozone, which can irritate, and even permanently damage, the respiratory systems of people and animals.

While some conditions—such as the location of the city—cannot be changed, there are some measures that can reduce smog. One is to enforce laws that call for cleaner exhausts from factories. Another is to cut down the amount of chemicals released into the air by the burning of petroleum products such as gasoline. Cleaner-burning cars, carpooling, and mass transportation can help in this effort.

SOIL

Thin layer of natural materials on the surface of the earth that provides a HABITAT for plants. Soil is classified according to its texture, and includes clay loams, sand, and silt. Soil contains various organic and inorganic materials that can support life, including MINERALS and particles such as decomposed materials from dead organisms. Water from rain makes up a liquid component of soil, and gases such as NITROGEN, OXYGEN, and CARBON DIOXIDE are found within the tiny network of pores that separate the mineral particles in soil.

Soil is usually formed by a process of EROSION known as weathering. Temperature and moisture changes cause the rock layer beneath

S

soil to crack and break apart, forming smaller and smaller particles of rock. When these combine with water, air, and decayed organic matter, soil is formed. The action of wind, water, ice expansion, plant-root growth, and DECOMPOSITION all add to the weathering of rocks.

Soil is structured into layers. The number of soil layers and characteristics of the layers may be different in various types of soils. The top layer of soil consists of surface litter, which includes fallen leaves and partially decomposed organic matter. The topsoil, the layer directly below the surface litter, is the loose surface layer of soil where most plant roots grow. It contains organic matter such as animal wastes and dead organisms in various stages of decay. Beneath the topsoil is a layer that contains dissolved or suspended materials moving downward through the process of LEACHING. The subsoil is the layer underneath the leaching zone. It contains larger rock particles as well as organic and inorganic matter leached down from the layer above. The bottom layer is the bedrock, a zone of solid rocks.

Soil is very important for plant and animal life. Most plants get nutrients from the soil through their roots. HERBIVORES eat these plants to get their nutrients. Some herbivores, such as beetles, snails, and slugs, actually live in the soil and depend on the nutrients in it. Just as animals and plants depend on soil, soil depends on dead organisms. When organisms die, BACTERIA and FUNGI provide nutrients to the soil through the process of DECOMPOSITION.

Soil can be worn away by many forces, including erosion and human activities such as farming. Erosion removes topsoil, taking away nutrients and materials needed to support plant life. It causes the soil to become much less dense, decreasing its capacity to hold water. Erosion also decreases the depth of the root

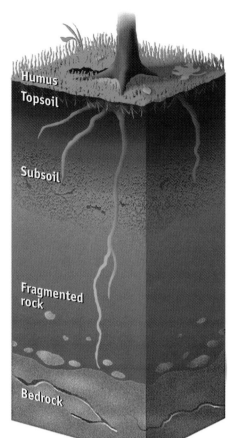

Humus
Topsoil
Subsoil
Fragmented rock
Bedrock

zone for plants. Human activities interfere with nutrient cycling in the soil. When humans grow crops, herbivores become dependent on them. Once the crops are harvested, they are no longer available for the herbivores, and the soil no longer receives the nutrients that the crops provided. [*See also* COMPOSTING.]

SOIL CONSERVATION

The practice of preventing soil loss caused by natural EROSION or human disturbances. In the 1920s and 1930s, farmers in the midwestern United States watched as wind stripped soil from their fields and blew it hundreds, even thousands, of miles away. Called the "dust bowl," this severe soil erosion came about as the result of an extended period of drought and unsound farming practices. Farmers in the region learned the hard way that soil was not a renewable resource but had to be saved and conserved.

In 1933 the federal government established the Soil Conservation Service to deal directly with the problem of soil erosion. Its activities include flood control projects, advising farmers about irrigation practices, and educating ranchers and others about overgrazing that exposes land to erosion. More recently the Soil Conservation Service has extended its authority to reclaiming abandoned coal mines, which are starting points for erosion and also pollution.

For their part, farmers can use various methods to help conserve soil. One method is crop rotation, in which crops are alternated each year on fields. This allows the soil to be replenished with nutrients, and crop rotation also helps to keep insect pests under control. Contour farming—plowing field along the natural contour of the land—also helps in soil conservation by reducing runoff and limiting erosion. Some farmers also practice no-till agriculture, in which plant debris is left on fields after harvesting to replenish the nutrients in the soil. No-till methods also protect against erosion.

SOLAR ENERGY

Energy from the sun. Solar energy provides more energy than all the FOSSIL FUELS on the earth. It is a clean form of energy that does not produce AIR POLLUTION or WATER POLLUTION. It is also a renewable energy source, one that is continually replenished.

Solar energy can be harnessed in four different ways. Passive solar heating is a simple and inexpensive way to heat homes and small buildings, using the sun's energy. Windows are placed on a building in positions that face the sun so that sunlight strikes against them. This warms the interior of the building. Insulation and heavy drapes help keep in the heat.

Active solar heating uses devices called solar collectors, which absorb energy from the sun and convert it into heat. The heat is then circulated through buildings by means of pipes, radiators and hot-water storage tanks. A third way of harnessing solar energy is with devices called photovoltaic cells, or solar cells. These specially designed cells capture the sun's energy and convert it directly into electricity. Photovoltaic cells are used to power solar cars, calculators, watches, and satellites. Some homes are also powered by electricity produced by photovoltaic cells. The problem with these cells is that they are expensive.

The last method of harnessing solar energy is the use of solar-thermal power plants. These specially designed power plants use large mirrors to reflect sunlight onto a series of solar collectors containing water or oil-filled tubes. The heat absorbed by the water or oil is used to generate electricity. The heated fluid in the tubes turns the blades of a turbine connected to a generator, and that produces electricity.

Only about one percent the world's energy comes from solar energy. But the use of solar energy is growing, and it may someday replace fossil fuels as the main source of electricity. [*See also* ALTERNATIVE ENERGY SOURCES.]

SOLID WASTE

Waste from human activities, generally disposed of in LANDFILLS. Solid wastes include old appliances, food, metal scraps, factory wastes, debris from lawns and gar-

dens, and wastes from the construction and destruction of buildings. MINING, and oil and gas production, agriculture, and industry produce most of the solid wastes in the United States, while sewage is responsible for a small percentage.

Many solid wastes are recyclable, such as bottles, cans, and paper. RECYCLING of these materials helps decrease the size of the nation's waste problem. Solid wastes can be dangerous because they may contain hazardous materials. The disposal of these substances can damage the environment by polluting air and water, and they can be harmful to human health.

The U.S. Congress passed several laws in the 1960s and 1970s to combat the growing solid waste problem. These laws established rules and regulations concerning the disposal of solid waste, and about the inspection and cleanup of waste sites. [*See also* SEWAGE AND SEWAGE TREATMENT.]

SOUTH AMERICA

The fourth largest continent, with most of its landmass in the Southern Hemisphere, South America contains the world's largest tropical RAIN FOREST. It also contains the Andes Mountains, a large mountain chain that runs down the western edge of the continent. Water from the Andes runs eastward into the enormous Amazon Basin, which contains tropical rain forests

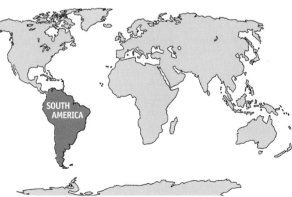

with lush vegetation and abundant animal life. Scientists estimate that the Amazon rain forests contain 75 percent of all plant and wildlife species on earth.

As South America's rain forest ECOSYSTEMS disappear under the pressures of population growth and economic development, so does a vast national treasury.

Endangered Species: Giant Otter

The giant otter lives in the tropical rain forests of the Amazon Basin of South America. These mammals have been hunted for their fur, so they have disappeared from many countries in their range. The largest of all the otters, the giant otter grows to about three feet (0.9 m) long and weighs about 50 pounds (23 kg). Giant otters live in groups, hunting, sleeping, and playing together.

SPECIATION

The process by which new species are formed. A major mode of speciation is geographic isolation. Suppose, for example, that an existing population of a species becomes isolated by some event such as climate change, the formation of a physical barrier (such as a mountain range), or the invasion of new HABITATS.

The isolated population exchanges GENES only among its members, without genetic input from the parent population or any other population. Over time, the isolated population becomes genetically different, either at random or by NATURAL SELECTION. The changed population thus constitutes a new species.

In some plants, speciation can be accomplished instantaneously by a mechanism called polyploidy, in which the normal number of genes is multiplied. This method produces offspring that usually cannot reproduce with offspring from the parent generation and, in effect, constitute a new species. Many of the FLOWERING PLANTS are polyploid. Very rarely does polyploidy occur among animals.

Random fluctuations of genes occurs within all populations. This is called genetic drift, and it is especially noticeable in small iso-

lated populations. The resulting offspring are not perfectly representative of the parental genes. Genetic drift is probably responsible for human diversity. [*See also* BIOLOGICAL DIVERSITY; EVOLUTION; SPECIES AND SUBSPECIES.]

SPECIES AND SUBSPECIES

Categories of scientific classification. Scientists classify, or arrange, organisms into related groups called taxonomic groupings. The science that deals with these classifications is called TAXONOMY.

Every organism can be classified according to various physical characteristics. The smallest classification groupings are species and subspecies. A subspecies is a population that is different from other members of the same species. Members of that population are a different variety of the main species.

Scientific classification. Seven basic taxonomic groupings make up the system of scientific classification: kingdom, phylum or division, class, order, family, genus, and species. The system of scientific classification begins with the largest group of living things that have certain shared features of form and structure. The smaller the group, the more features the individuals have in common. The division continues through ever-smaller groups until it arrives at a single unit, the species.

Kingdoms are the broadest taxonomic class. There are five kingdoms in all: (1) *Animalia*, the animal kingdom, had at least one million species. Animalia includes any living being that can be classified as an animal. (2) *Plantae*, or plants, includes more than 26,000 species, from the smallest wildflower to the largest tree. (3) *Fungi*, with more than 100,000 species, includes mushrooms, bread molds, and lichens. (4) *Protista*, with more than 100,000 species, includes single-celled organisms such as ALGAE. (5) *Monera*, which consist of bacteria, include more than 10,000 species.

The next largest animal classification is the phylum (in the plant kingdom, this classification is called a division instead). There are about 20 phyla (the plural of phylum) in the animal kingdom. All VERTEBRATES (animals with backbones) belong to the phylum *Chordata*. The other phyla are all INVERTEBRATES, and they make up about 95 percent of all known animal species. Among the invertebrates are

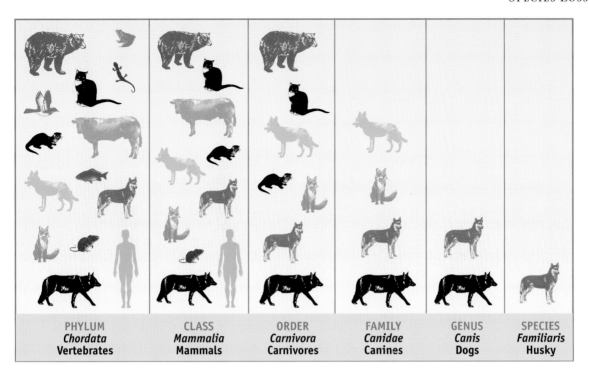

PHYLUM	CLASS	ORDER	FAMILY	GENUS	SPECIES
Chordata	*Mammalia*	*Carnivora*	*Canidae*	*Canis*	*Familiaris*
Vertebrates	Mammals	Carnivores	Canines	Dogs	Husky

Protozoa, which are one-celled animals; *Porifera*, the sponges; and *Coelenterata*, which include jellyfish, corals, and sea anemones.

The next taxonomic grouping is class, whose members have more characteristics in common than those in a phylum. Both mammals and birds are in the same phyllum, *Chordata*, but they are in different classes. Birds make up another class of *Chordata* called *Aves*.

Members of an order are even more alike than those in a class. For example in the class *Mammalia*, one order is *Carnivora*, or flesh-eating animals. Another is *Insectivora*, which are insect-eating animals.

Family is the next taxonomic category. Cats and dogs are both in the order *Carnivora*, but cats belong to the family *Felidae*, and dogs—along with wolves, jackals, foxes, and coyotes—belong to the family *Canidae*.

The taxonomic classification genus is made up of groups that are very similar but not enough so as to be able to breed with one another. (The plural of "genus" is "genera.") Members of a species are enough alike biologically that they can breed with one another, even if they are from different subspecies.

Scientific names. Species of animals and plants usually have common names, but these vary from language to language and sometimes differ from one region to another within the same country. But each species has only one scientific name, and that name is used by scientists in every part of the world. The languages of taxonomic classification are Latin and Greek. Each species name has two parts. For example, the common dandelion is *Taraxacum officinale*. A house sparrow is *Passer domesticus*. The first term identifies the genus and the second the species. [*See also* BIOLOGICAL DIVERSITY; EVOLUTION.]

SPECIES LOSS

A reduction in the total number of organisms in an ECOSYSTEM. The irreversible loss of BIOLOGICAL DIVERSITY has a serious impact on the ability of other organisms to survive. Humans, for example, depend on healthy ecosystems to provide food, clean air, water, and fertile SOIL. In a process called DESERTIFICATION, for example, a period of exceptionally dry weather can cause the natural plants in a region to die. With less vegetation cover, the temperature of the soil rises, increasing the speed at which organic matter breaks down and increasing evaporation of moisture. The soil may become hard, reducing its ability to absorb rainfall. This leaves the soil vulnerable to RUNOFF and EROSION by water and wind, respectively. Nutrients

S

in the soil are lost, leading to the loss of even more plant species, which in turn leads to further desertification. As the cycle continues, it may become catastrophic and lead to the deaths of animals and even humans from starvation.

Each species in an ecosystem plays a role. The relationships resemble a web of connections from one living thing to others. The removal or disturbance of one part, one species, may affect the functioning of many other components of the ecosystem. In many cases, scientists do not even know the extent of these relationships or how they function. Ecosystems that have greater variety in numbers of species usually show greater resilience in the face of natural disasters, such as floods, or diseases. When species are lost, the choices and opportunities for adapting to natural events become fewer.

Some scientists believe that more than 50 percent of the species that exist today may be lost in the next 100 years. Halting species loss depends in large part on halting loss of HABITATS due to human activity. [*See also* CLEAR-CUTTING; DEFORESTATION; ENDANGERED SPECIES; EXOTIC SPECIES; HABITAT LOSS AND CONSERVATION; KEYSTONE SPECIES; NATIVE SPECIES; SPECIES AND SUBSPECIES.]

Endangered Species: Hawaiian Goose

The state bird of Hawaii, the nene is also called the Hawaiian goose or lava goose. Its name comes from the bird's nasal bark, *nay, nay*. Unlike other geese, the nene does not need to live near water. It lives on the high, rocky volcanic slopes of the islands of Hawaii and Maui. Once abundant, the nene faced extinction in 1947 after the population had dropped to about 50 birds. A captive breeding and release program helped save the nene. Today, an estimated 800 birds exist in the wilds of Hawaii, but they remain vulnerable to predators and disease.

SPIDERS

(*See* ARTHROPODS)

STORK, WOOD

A large, long-legged wading bird that stands 4 feet (1.2 m) tall. The wood stork has a wing span of about 5 feet (1.5 m). The large bird has white plumage with black primary feathers on the wings and a short black tail. The neck is dark gray, and the bill is black.

The wood stork is widespread in Central and SOUTH AMERICAS, from Mexico to northern Argentina. In the United States, the species once inhabited much of the southeastern states and Texas. But today it is restricted to Florida, Georgia, and South Carolina. The U.S. population of wood storks, which is listed as an ENDANGERED SPECIES, began to decline in the 1930s due primarily to the destruction of the bird's native HABITATS. In south Florida, in particular, the construction of canals, drainage of WETLANDS, and other water-level management schemes have greatly damaged the storks' preferred nesting sites.

The wood stork is one of several species of stork in the Western Hemisphere.

STRATOSPHERE

Second innermost layer of the earth's ATMOSPHERE. The stratosphere is located above the TROPOSPHERE and extends from about 6 miles (10 km) to about 28 miles (45 km) above the earth. The air is very thin in the stratosphere, and this is the layer of the atmosphere that contains the OZONE LAYER. Airplanes travel in the lower part of the stratosphere, where strong winds called the jet stream blow steadily in the same direction.

STREAMS

(*See* RIVER SYSTEMS)

SUBSISTENCE FARMING

Growing only enough crops for one's own use, usually on small plots of lands. Throughout human history, many societies have been based primarily on subsidence farming. Farmers grew only enough to feed their own families, with perhaps a little left over. The growth of towns and cities made it necessary to provide surplus food to feed urban dwellers. As societies grew and became more advanced, subsistence farming gave way to commercial agriculture, in which farmers grow crops to sell in markets. Most wealthy nations today rely on commercial agriculture to feed their populations. In poorer countries, however, subsistence farming remains a significant part of the economy.

SUCCESSION

A natural change in the composition of an ECOSYSTEM, as competing organisms, especially plants, respond to and modify the environment. No plant community is completely stable. Over time, some organisms weaken and die. Younger organisms, which now have less competition, replace them. Or newly created openings in the environment may allow new species to establish themselves, gradually changing the character of the environment.

There are two kinds of succession. Primary succession begins on a bare area where no vegetation has grown before, such as on a fresh lava flow from a volcano, a beach, or even the surface of a concrete sidewalk. Such HABITATS are unsuitable for most plants, but pioneer species are more tolerant. Pioneer species, such as MOSSES, LICHENS, and BACTERIA, reproduce rapidly and can withstand harsh conditions. Most of these species are hardy but short-lived and poor competitors.

In secondary succession, a natural disaster or human activity interrupts a normal succession. A forest fire or lumbering will open up an area to succession. Secondary succession proceeds more quickly than primary succession. That is because the necessary soil for plants is already present. An extremely devastating forest fire or the eruption of a volcano, however, can destroy all the vegetation and the soil base.

In any event, as succession proceeds, the species of animals living in an area will change along with the vegetation. The biodiversity of the ecosystem increases, eventually arriving at a final point called the climax. Then, further changes take place very slowly, and the ecosystem remains generally the same for a long period of time. [*See also* BIOLOGICAL RESTORATION; EUTROPHICATION; HABITAT LOSS AND CONSERVATION; LOGGING.]

| 5 | 15 | 25 | 50 | 100 | 200 |

Over a period of 200 years, an abandoned field can grow into a forest as a result of succession.

S

SULFUR DIOXIDE

Chemical compound produced by burning FOS-SIL FUELS that contributes to AIR POLLUTION. Coal contains a great amount of sulfur, while oil and natural gas contain smaller amounts. Sulfur released into the atmosphere from burning fossil fuels combines with OXYGEN gas to form sulfur dioxide. When sulfur dioxide mixes with rainwater, it forms ACID RAIN, which can harm organisms and damage substances such as stone and rubber. Acid rain is very corrosive, and it can destroy tissues in the respiratory tracts of humans and animals.

One way to control sulfur dioxide pollution is to remove the sulfur from fossil fuels before they are burned. But this can be very expensive. Another option is to use fuel that contains less sulfur. Pollution-control devices in smokestacks can also reduce sulfur emissions, but they must be cleaned and maintained regularly, adding to the expense of fuel use.

SUPERFUND

Federal program to clean up the worst inactive HAZARDOUS WASTE sites in the United States. The Superfund program, established by the U.S. Congress in 1980, is administered by the ENVIRONMENTAL PROTECTION AGENCY (EPA). Superfund came about as a result of chemical pollution at a place called Love Canal in Niagara, New York. In the early 1900s, the Hooker Chemical company built a factory next to Love Canal and began dumping waste into the water. Eventually, in 1953, the town decided to fill the canal with dirt and build a school on top of the waste. During the 1970s, a series of rainstorms caused much of the chemical waste to rise up through the ground. The pollution was eventually carried into nearby creeks and streams. The polluted areas were fenced off, and the residents eventually moved to other areas. A giant cement cap was placed over the property to prevent the chemicals from coming to the surface.

There are currently more than 1,300 sites on the Superfund National Priorities List, an official list of hazardous waste sites that are eligible for extensive, long-term cleanup. These sites score high on the Hazard Ranking System used by the EPA to rank sites according to the danger they may pose to health and the environment.

SURFACE WATER

Water that flows on the earth's surface. Surface water can include rivers, lakes, streams, oceans, ponds, and reservoirs—any body of water that is above the ground. Surface water is a part of the WATER CYCLE, in which water falls to the earth as rain or snow, collects in rivers and lakes, and then evaporates into the air to begin the cycle again.

Surface water is rarely "pure" water. As water falls through the air and flows through riverbanks, other substances are dissolved into the water. For example, a high concentration of mineral in the SOILS of an area may dissolve into and change the area's water. Pollutants that can contaminate surface water include wastewater from sewage treatment plants and industries, polluted water runoff from streets and sidewalks, and ACID RAIN.

Because surface water often serves as a source of drinking water, as irrigation water for farms, and sites for recreation, the federal and state governments enforce laws to keep surface water clean. The primary law protecting surface water is the Clean Water Act passed in 1977. [See also GROUNDWATER.]

SUSTAINABLE DEVELOPMENT

(See CONSERVATION)

SWAMPS

A type of WETLAND—that is, an area of land that has a water level near or above the surface of the ground. Swamps are one type of wetland along with bogs and MARSHES. Sometimes these terms are used to mean the same thing. However, swamps are usually areas that are saturated with water and whose vegetation is mainly woody plants, such as trees and shrubs. Any plant that grows in a swamp must have the ability to survive with its roots underwater for long periods of time.

Swamps attract a variety of wildlife. Many MAMMALS, plants, BIRDS, AMPHIBIANS, REPTILES, and INSECTS can be found in swamps. Swamps in different regions often have distinct species of plants and animals. In the northeastern United States, for example, the red maple is

Swamps and other wetlands are transitional zones between aquatic and terrestrial ecosystems.

found that wetland plants can filter out pollutants from air and water. In the United States, government programs have been developed to preserve many wetlands. However, wetlands are still being destroyed by human activity. [*See also* GROUNDWATER; WATER TABLE.]

SYMBIOSIS

A relationship between two organisms that live with or around each other. There are several types of symbiosis or symbiotic relationship. MUTUALISM is a type of symbiosis in which both organisms benefit from the relationship. For example, LICHENS are organisms composed of FUNGI and ALGAE that exist together in a symbiotic relationship. An alga (singular of algae) is a green plantlike organism with the ability to make food. The alga in a lichen shares the food it produces with the fungus (singular of fungi), which cannot make its own food. The fungus can store water and create a moist environment, which, in turn, is needed by the alga.

Commensalism is a type of symbiosis in which one organism benefits while the other is neither helped nor harmed. An example of commensalism is the relationship between a squirrel and an oak tree. The squirrel gets shelter and food from the tree. The squirrel's presence in and around the tree neither helps nor harms it, although the squirrel may spread the tree's seeds.

Parasitism is a symbiotic relationship in which one organism is helped and the other is harmed. Mosquitoes have a parasitic relationship with many living things, including people. Mosquitoes bite people and benefit by using their blood for food. People can be harmed by mosquitoes that carry disease. [*See also* ECOSYSTEM, PARASITES.]

a common swamp tree. In the Southeast, bald cypress and gum trees are usually found in swamps. Waterbirds, such as wood ducks, like swamp environments because they can use the hollow trees for their nests. Other swamp animals include raccoons, beavers, muskrats, otters, frogs, salamanders, ALLIGATORS, snakes, and turtles. Many wildflowers also like the wet environment of swamps.

Since the 1970s, more and more people have become aware of the ecological value of swamps and other wetlands. These wetlands are important for flood control and water storage. They are also necessary to the survival of many plant and animal species. Scientists have even

TAIGA

A moist coniferous FOREST that begins where the TUNDRA ends and runs in a band across the Northern Hemisphere below the ARCTIC Circle. The taiga is also called the boreal forest. Temperatures in the taiga are very cold in the winter, which lasts for six to eight months of the year. Spring, summer, and fall are very short. During the summer there is sunlight nearly 24 hours a day.

Though it is cold in the taiga for much of the year, there is plenty of moisture and enough warmth for dense forests of conifers (cone-bearing evergreen trees) to grow. The dominant trees are pine, spruce, fir, and hemlock. Because the dense trees shade much of the forest floor, few plants grow on the ground. There are, however, some MOSSES, FERNS, small shrubs, and a few FLOWERING PLANTS. LICHENS often grow on the trunks of the conifers and on rocks. Many areas of the taiga are also covered with bogs and SWAMPS.

The taiga provides habitats for many owls, small rodents, lynx, wolverines, porcupines, wolves, black bears and grizzly bears, mule deer, and moose. Some animals, such as BALD EAGLES and shorebirds, migrate to and from the taiga seasonally.

TAXONOMY

The science of classifying plants and animals. Biologists arrange and name all living organisms in an orderly manner so that, no matter what language scientists speak, they can know precisely what organism is being discussed.

Plant and animal classification systems were first developed in ancient China and a number of early civilizations. Today's systems are based on the work of the Greek philosopher Aristotle, who established a taxonomy recognizing two kingdoms of living forms: *Plantae* (plants) and *Animalia* (animals).

In the Middle Ages, scholars translated the common names of plants and animals into Latin in order to unify the naming of the increasing numbers of organisms being identified. In the mid-1800s, Swedish botanist Carolus Linneaus developed a system of naming in which each organism is given a two-word name. The first word in a name is the genus, into which related organisms are grouped. The second word, the species, often describes the organism, its geographical location, or the person who discovered it.

Using scientific classification, scientists are able to arrange all the world's organisms into related groups. To date, more than 1.5 million organisms have been classified. Scientists estimate that from 5 million to more than 30 million different species of organisms exist on earth. [*See also* SPECIES AND SUBSPECIES.]

TERRESTRIAL ECOSYSTEMS

A community of plants, animals, and other organisms in a land environment. The various terrestrial ECOSYSTEMS are categorized by the earth's climate and vegetation regions, which are called BIOMES. The most northerly of these ecosystems is the the TUNDRA, characterized by patchworks of bogs and LAKES that attract a great many INSECTS, which in turn attract BIRDS during the short summer season. Small MAMMALS, such as foxes, eat the birds and their eggs. Caribou graze on the grasses, MOSSES, and LICHENS of the tundra.

South of the tundra is the TAIGA ecosystem. Here, FORESTS of conifers, such as pines and spruces, provide shelter for small mammals such as lynx, snowshoe hares, and rodents, and larger ones, including bears and deer. Still farther south, the temperate forest has a greater variety of seasons with differences in rainfall and temperature, which encourage more plant and animal diversity.

Even more diverse are the tropical RAIN FORESTS, which contain HABITATS for thousands of plant and animal species. Other types of terrestrial ecosystems are GRASSLANDS—with grasses, few trees, and grazing animals—and DESERTS—areas that receive little rainfall and have very high temperatures for most of the year. [*See also* BIOLOGICAL DIVERSITY; BIOREGION.]

THERMAL POLLUTION

Form of pollution caused by a rise in temperature in a body of water. Thermal pollution is usually a result of the disposal of heated industrial wastewater.

Some companies use large amounts of water to make or clean products. They pump cool water from lakes, rivers, and other bodies of water, use it, and then release it back into the environment. During its use, the water becomes heated, and it is this heated water that is released. According to U.S. water quality laws, companies can pour the water back into a river or stream if the water is clean enough. However, even if clean, the heated water can be damaging to the river's animal and plant life.

The temperature of water is very important to animals and plants that live in it. Even a slight rise in temperature can kill some kinds of animals. If the change in temperature is sudden, it could cause thermal shock or death to some aquatic animals. Even if the temperature change is gradual, it can disrupt the balance of the ECOSYSTEM and may kill some of the animals that are sensitive to heat.

Differences in water temperature also affect the amount of air that is present in water, called dissolved oxygen. Cold water has more dissolved oxygen than warm water. Since both aquatic animals and plants need oxygen to live, rivers with thermal pollution cannot support as many fish and other organisms.

THREATENED SPECIES

(*See* ENDANGERED SPECIES)

TIDAL ENERGY

Energy that is generated by the movement of tides. Because of their gravitational force, the sun and the moon raise and lower the levels of the earth's bodies of water. SURFACE WATER rising and falling creates tidal energy. People have discovered ways to use tidal energy to create electricity. One way to make electricity is to hold water behind a dam at high tide and then release it when the tide is low. Water rushing over the dam turns machinery that generates electricity. France was the first country to create electricity from tidal energy. Tidal energy plants are being planned in other areas. But, with current technology, few places in the world have a large enough difference between high and low tides to use tidal energy to create power. [*See also* ALTERNATIVE ENERGY SOURCES.]

TIDES

The periodic rise and fall of water along seacoasts. The rise and fall of the tides is due to the pull of the moon's gravity. The times of high tide—when the water level is highest—and low tide—when the water level is lowest—are predictable, so people know just when to expect them. The time between high tide and low tide, and vice versa, is about six hours. Thus high tide and low tide occur twice a day at any one spot on earth. The rise and fall of tides can be harnessed using tidal power plants to generate electricity. This is a form of HYDROELECTRIC POWER. [*See also* TIDAL ENERGY.]

TIDES OF NORTH AMERICAN CITIES		
Boston, MA	10' 4"	(315 cm)
Eastport, ME	19' 4"	(589 cm)
Galveston, TX	1' 5"	(43 cm)
Key West, FL	1' 10"	(56 cm)
New London, CT	3' 1"	(94 cm)
New York, NY	5' 1"	(155 cm)
Portland, ME	9' 11"	(302 cm)
Seattle, WA	11' 4"	(345 cm)
San Diego, CA	5' 9"	(175 cm)
Vancouver, BC	10' 6"	(320 cm)

TIGER

A large carnivorous mammal with a striped coat that lives in ASIA. The tiger is the largest member of the cat family. Tigers live in a variety of

T

HABITATS, from snowy mountains to monsoon rain forests. They usually avoid open spaces, preferring to remain camouflaged by their stripes in tall grass and trees. Tigers are PREDATORS that hunt deer, antelope, and wild cattle, and, in rare instances, may attack humans. Adult tigers are solidary, require large territories, and may travel up to 20 miles (32 km) in a day.

In the early 1900s there were more than 100,000 tigers in the wild. Today, there are fewer than 10,000. Human pressures from HUNTING and habitat destruction exterminated the Bali, Caspian, and Javan tigers, and the remaining tigers are considered ENDANGERED SPECIES. Though tigers are protected by international law, poaching still occurs. As human populations continue to grow, people compete more and more with tigers for land and food. Tigers are also killed for their bones and other parts, which are mixed into traditional medicines believed to cure various ailments. Although the Convention on International

☀ Fast Facts

It is very difficult to count tigers in their natural habitats because their stripes blend into the grass and trees. Scientists use camera "traps" to identify individual tigers by their snapshots. The scientists set up special camera-and-tiger systems along trails used by tigers and other animals. Each tiger has its own stripe patterns. By counting the number of tigers caught on film, the researchers can figure out how many of these big cats live in a particular region.

Trade in Endangered Species of Wild Fauna and Flora (CITES) banned the WILDLIFE TRADE in tiger parts in 1989, global sales of Asian medicines still pose a great threat to tiger populations.

Various conservation programs have been set up to help save tigers.

TOPOGRAPHY

Physical features of a region. Topography describes the surface features of an area, including MOUNTAINS, FORESTS, beaches, PRAIRIES, rivers, and LAKES. Topography plays an important role in ecological studies, environmental control, geological research, water-quality research, CONSERVATION, and reforestation. Topography is useful for showing the specific physical characteristics and climate of a particular area.

Scientists can use topography to help predict and monitor climate changes and weather patterns. Satellites in space gather information about OCEAN CURRENTS, rises in sea level, and changes in ocean temperature. This information is then used to analyze ocean processes and to determine the ocean's role in climate changes. ECOSYSTEMS and environmental changes can also be studied, using topographic charts, maps, and images. [*See also* GEOLOGY.]

TOPSOIL

(*See* SOIL)

TORTOISE, DESERT

A large, land-dwelling turtle with a domed, tan to black shell. The desert tortoise lives deserts of California, southern Nevada, Arizona, southwestern Utah, and Mexico. These REPTILES feed on grasses in the early morning and late afternoon. They spend the hottest part of the day in shallow burrows.

Desert tortoise populations are rapidly declining in their natural HABITATS because of vandalism, the hatchlings being eaten by ravens and coyotes, disease, their being collected for pets, and the loss or destruction of their habitat to development, highways, mining, and off-road vehicles.

The desert tortoise is an endangered species.

TOXIC WASTE

(*See* HAZARDOUS WASTE)

TOXICS RELEASE INVENTORY

A federal government list of the releases of certain toxic chemicals into the air, water, or soil. The list is compiled yearly by the U.S. ENVIRONMENTAL PROTECTION AGENCY (EPA). The Toxics Release Inventory (TRI) was established under the Emergency Planning and Community Right-to-Know Act of 1986. The purpose was to provide information about the presence and release of toxic and hazardous chemicals in their communities. The information also helps local fire, police, and health authorities plan for handling emergencies involving these chemicals. [*See also* AIR POLLUTION; HAZARDOUS WASTE; WATER POLLUTION.]

TREES

Woody plants, usually with a single distinct stem, or trunk. Trees are distinguished from shrubs by their height and trunk; shrubs are normally shorter and have many stems. Trees are perennials, plants that live for at least three years. (Many plants are annuals, which

☀ Fast Facts

Desert tortoise hatchlings are about the size of silver dollars. Female tortoises do not provide motherly care for their young; the females simply leave after they have laid their eggs. Only 1 to 5 out of every 100 hatchlings will survive to adulthood.

T

die each year.) Some tree species grow to lit-tle more than 10 feet (3 m), while the tallest trees can top 350 feet (106 m). The tallest trees are not necessarily the oldest. Bristlecone pines in the White Mountains of California grow to only 30 feet (9 m) but are up to 4,600 years old.

A mature tree's trunk supports the plant. Its inner core consists of vertical calls made of cellulose (a material made of glucose that forms the chief part of cell walls) and packed in parallel rows—providing the support column for the tree. Surrounding the trunk and branches is bark, which protects the plant and contains the tree's circulatory system. The trunk and branches must be strong yet flexible enough to blend with wind. The leaves grow

Maple

Elm

Oak

Fir

Pine

Five tree species common to North America

on the branches, where they gather sunlight and air to carry out PHOTOSYNTHESIS. The root system anchors the tree in the ground and absorbs water and other nutrients from the SOIL. Some species of trees, such as pines, have a strongly developed taproot or main root. In other trees, such as maples, there is no central taproot, and other roots grow in large numbers near the surface

There are two types of trees: angiosperms and gymnosperms. Angiosperms are plants that produce flowers. They are further divided into dicots, which have two cotyledons (seed leaf structures), and monocots, which have one cotyledon. Dicots includes maples, oaks, and other broadleaf trees. Monocots include palm trees. Gymnosperms do not produce flowers.

Their seeds are contained in structures such as cones. There are two major types of gymnosperms: conifers and ginkgoes.

There are about 40,000 species of trees in the world. They grow in all kinds of climates, from tropical RAIN FORESTS to ARCTIC regions, and in all kinds of conditions, from rich soils of temperate FORESTS to cracks in city sidewalks. In nature, trees often grow in stands rather than singly. In North America, a typical forest would include only a few species, whereas a Brazilian rain forest may contain hundreds of species.

Trees are extremely important. They protect the land against EROSION. They act as reservoirs, their leaves releasing their water reserves into the air in times of drought. Trees provide HABITATS for many plants and animals, and they play an important part in regulating the ATMOSPHERE by absorbing CARBON DIOXIDE and producing OXYGEN through photosynthesis. In addition, trees provide endless products that are used by people: lumber, fruits and nuts, rubber, medicines, and cork—to name just a few.

TROPHIC LEVEL

A level of nutrition in FOOD WEBS. The food web of each ECOSYSTEM consists of a series of trophic levels, or energy levels, which show the flow of energy through the cycle of PREDATORS and prey. Green plants belong to the first trophic level and are called primary producers. HERBIVORES, which eat green plants, belong to the second trophic level. The third trophic level contains CARNIVORES, which eat herbivores. OMNIVORES, which eat both plants and animals, belong to the second and third levels. At the fourth trophic level, secondary predators feed on other predators. Even the energy of secondary predators will continue through the trophic cycle. When predators die, BACTERIA, FUNGI, and other animals will use the energy to live, continuing the cycle of life. [*See also* ENERGY CYCLE; FOOD CHAIN.]

TROPOSPHERE

Layer of the ATMOSPHERE closest to the earth. The least dense layer of the atmosphere, the troposphere extends from the earth's surface to an altitude of about 6 miles (10 km). It contains nearly 90 percent of the atmosphere's gases, including the OXYGEN needed by all living things. The temperature of the troposphere decreases as the altitude increases. The troposphere is also where the earth's weather occurs. Movements of air in the troposphere cause the winds felt on earth, and these winds play an important role in weather. The movement of air in the troposphere influences the way AIR POLLUTION is carried from place to place. [*See also* STRATOSPHERE.]

TUNDRA

A treeless area in arctic and subarctic regions. One of the main features of tundra is permafrost, or permanently frozen SOIL. The upper layers of soil on the tundra alternately freeze and thaw with the changing seasons.

The tundra has long, cold winters and short, cool summers. It has many lakes, bogs, and streams and dark, wet, rocky soil. The vegetation of the tundra consists of MOSSES, LICHENS, and small shrubs. Animals that live on the tundra include musk oxen, polar bears, and caribou. Many BIRDS nest on the tundra

Although the tundra looks barren, it supports various plant and animal species.

during the summer, migrating south in the fall to avoid the harsh winter. These include ducks, Canada geese, and plovers.

The term "tundra" is also sometimes applied to regions in mountainous areas above the treeline, called Alpine tundra. Alpine tundra does not usually have permafrost. It may also have more precipitation than the tundra found in arctic and subarctic regions. [*See also* CLIMATE AND WEATHER.]

U-V

ULTRAVIOLET RADIATION

A type of radiation given off by high-temperature objects, such as the sun. Radiation is a form of energy that travels through space in waves. Ultraviolet radiation from the sun is important for human health because it causes skin cells to produce vitamin D, which is necessary for healthy bones and teeth. Ultraviolet radiation also activates pigments in the skin that cause skin to tan. Tanning is the body's way of defending the skin from sunlight. But too much exposure to ultraviolet rays can cause sunburns and skin cancer.

Ultraviolet radiation can be harmful in other ways as well. Microscopic organisms can be killed by overexposure to ultraviolet light, and this can cause disruptions in the FOOD CHAINS that sustain all life. Too much ultraviolet radiation can also kill plants, contributing to reduced levels of OXYGEN and a buildup of CARBON DIOXIDE.

The earth is protected from overexposure to ultraviolet radiation by the OZONE LAYER in the STRATOSPHERE. The ozone layer absorbs the ultraviolet rays, acting as a natural sunscreen for the inhabitants of earth.

The diagram below shows the types of radiation and their location in the frequency spectrum.

URBAN PLANNING

Process of organizing the growth and design of a community in order to protect the health and welfare of its citizens. Urban planning provides structure and policy to make sure that citizens have such things as clean water, sewage treatment, fair living conditions, parks, public and private transportation, and reasonable land use. Urban planners must consider a complex combination of physical, social, economic, and political issues. Urban planning is one of the ways that cities can protect their environment. As cities grow, planners can make sure that air and water are kept as clean as possible and that NATURAL RESOURCES such as WETLANDS and historic sites are protected.

VERTEBRATES

Animals that have a backbone. Vertebrates include all AMPHIBIANS, BIRDS, FISH, REPTILES, and MAMMALS (including humans). They usually have a skeleton of cartilage or bone, a head, and a body with two pairs of limbs. Many land vertebrates also have a distinct neck. The left and right sides of vertebrates are generally symmetrical. All vertebrates have complex muscular nervous systems. Because of their highly

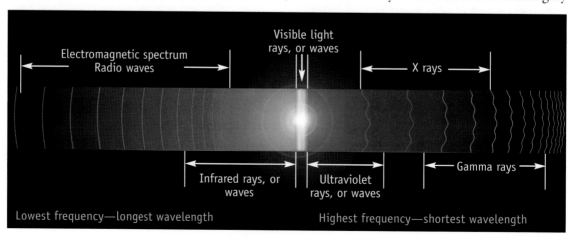

Electromagnetic spectrum
Radio waves

Visible light
rays, or waves

X rays

Infrared rays, or waves

Ultraviolet rays, or waves

Gamma rays

Lowest frequency—longest wavelength

Highest frequency—shortest wavelength

UV

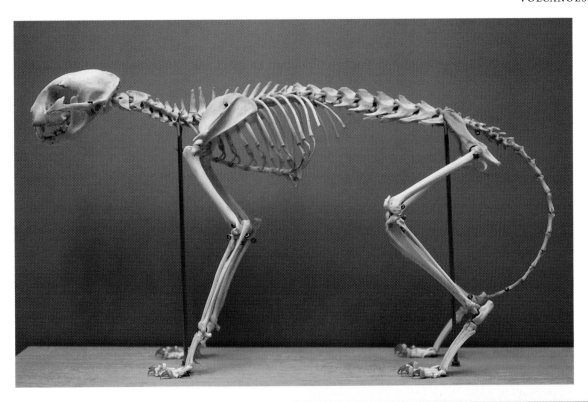

Vertebrates are easily identified by their bony skeletons.

developed muscular and nervous systems, many vertebrates engage in more complex behavior than other animals.

VOLCANOES

Mountains formed by molten rock (magma) that erupts from vents in the earth's surface. There are about 800 known active volcanoes in the world, most of which are located around the edges of the Pacific Ocean, an area called the "Ring of Fire." Others are found along ocean ridges and continental rifts, or splits, in the earth's crust. New islands may form from eruptions of oceanic volcanoes. The Hawaiian Islands were formed from repeated eruptions of volcanic material.

Volcanoes are formed as part of a geologic process called plate tectonics. Tectonic plates are large movable sections of the earth's crust. Molten rock from within the earth rises through cracks between the plates, and erupts on the surface. Repeated eruptions of this molten rock, or magma, slowly build up to

☼ Fast Facts

The biggest volcanic eruption in recorded history occurred on the Indonesian island of Sumbawa in 1815, when Tambora erupted. Ten thousand people died during the eruption, and another 82,000 people died of disease and starvation because of the disruption of their environment.

form a volcano. Movement of the tectonic plates is also responsible for EARTHQUAKES and the processes that form MOUNTAINS.

Volcanoes vary in formation and size. Some are formed from the ejection of rock debris from a central vent. Others form when molten rock spews out of cracks along fractures. Some volcanoes can be quite small, while the largest are tens of thousands of feet high.

☑ Keywords

Viscosity. The property of a liquid that describes how it flows.

U
V

Volcanoes have played a major role in the earth's geologic history.

When a volcano erupts, columns of magma and gases rise to the surface. The gas helps thrust the magma out of the volcano's vent. The nature of a volcanic eruption is determined by ☑ the **viscosity** of the magma, the amount of gas dissolved in the magma, the quantity of

 Endangered Species:
Mauna Loa Silversword

This yellow flower is found only on the slopes of the Mauna Loa volcano on the island of Hawaii. The erect, branched woody shrub has small flowers and small clumped leaves on opposite stems. It can be found at elevations ranging from 1,800-8,700 feet (600-2,900 m). The silversword survives in areas where it receives about 1.2-9 feet (40-300 cm) of annual precipitation.

groundwater near the vent area, and the pressure of the magma as it reaches the surface. Some volcanic eruptions are slow and steady, with lava gently flowing out of the volcano's vent. Other eruptions may be violent explosions of gases, magma, and other debris.

Volcanoes are characterized by their three main parts: the base; the cone, which rises from the base; and the crater, a depression often located at the top of the cone. All volcanoes are very different, and the frequency, vigor, and extent of their eruptions varies.

Volcano eruptions can cause great damage to the environment. Ash spewed from an eruption can kill TREES and other plants. It can also enter the ATMOSPHERE and cause temporary changes in climate. Violent eruptions can cause human and animal deaths. Towns and buildings can be destroyed, and crops killed. Yet volcanoes also produce long-term benefits to the environment, creating fertile soils that are excellent for growing crops. [*See also* CONTINENTAL DRIFT.]

WASTE

(*See* HAZARDOUS WASTE; ORGANIC AND NONORGANIC WASTE; SOLID WASTE; SEWAGE AND SEWAGE TREATMENT)

WATER

(*See* DRINKING WATER; GROUNDWATER; SURFACE WATER; WATER CYCLE; WATER POLLUTION; WATER QUALITY AND TREATMENT; WATER RIGHTS; WATER TABLE; WATERSHED)

WATER CYCLE

Series of stages through which water passes in its various states. The water cycle is also sometimes called the hydrologic cycle. It is a cycle because no matter how much water is used, the total amount of water on the earth never changes. The same water may appear in different states, but it is continuously recycled, never increasing or decreasing.

Water has three states: liquid, solid, and gas. Most of the earth's water is in the liquid state. It is found in the oceans, lakes, rivers, and underground reservoirs. About two percent of the earth's water is frozen, either in GLACIERS or the polar ice sheets. Snow and frost are also solid forms of water. A very small part of the earth's water is an invisible gas called water vapor. Water vapor is found in the lowest layer of the ATMOSPHERE, a region called the TROPOSPHERE. It plays an important part in the planet's weather.

Water is always evaporating from the oceans, seas, and lakes, as well as the surfaces of plants. The process of evaporation is caused by the sun. As water evaporates, it becomes water vapor. The amount of water vapor in the atmosphere at a particular place and time is called humidity. Air can hold only a certain amount of water vapor. When the air cannot hold any more, it becomes saturated. As saturated air cools, the water vapor in it condenses into droplets. That is, the water vapor changes to a liquid state. The droplets condense around tiny particles, which can be made up of microscopic bits of dust or other matter. The condensed water then forms clouds. The water droplets inside the clouds join to form bigger drops. When the drops grow large enough, they fall back to earth as rain or snow. Eventually, that water ends up in the oceans, rivers, lakes, or reservoirs. Then the water cycle starts all over again.

Precipitation

Evaporation

Groundwater

WATER POLLUTION

Water that is contaminated by some substances such as sewage, toxic chemicals, oil, and PESTICIDES. Water pollution can affect SURFACE WATER and GROUNDWATER. Polluted water can seep into wells that homes and businesses rely on for their water supply. Pollution can also seep into reservoirs that provide drinking water for towns and cities. Polluted water carries BACTERIA and viruses that can cause illness and even death.

Healthy water contains organisms that digest wastes. This keeps the water clean and recycles nutrients that are in the waste. Water pollution results when people put so much waste into the water that the natural cleaning process cannot keep up. The pollutants then work their way up the aquatic FOOD CHAIN. Plants and fish are harmed by the pollutants, as are any animals that use the water or eat anything that was in it. Chemical FERTILIZER, animal manure, and detergents can add so many nutrients to water that ALGAE living in it multiply too quickly. When the algae die, they are eaten by bacteria. The bacteria use up a lot of the oxygen in the water as they consume the algae. The fall in the oxygen level of the water causes many aquatic plants and animals to die. As they decay, they use up even more oxygen. The body of water is dying.

Industrial waste is a major source of water pollution. Many industries discharge, or release, pollutants directly into rivers and streams. This may include dangerous chemicals. ACID RAIN can carry pollutants from air pollution. In running water, such as streams and rivers, the pollutants can be carried a long way, so that toxic substances discharged in an industrial area might find their way to a distant river and finally the ocean.

Thermal pollution is another problem. Some industries use water to cool equipment, which causes the water to become warmer. When that water is discharged into a river or stream, it can be harmful to aquatic plants and animals that are adapted to certain temperatures. Sewage is another pollutant. In most towns and cities in the United States, sewage is treated before being discharged into rivers. In rural areas, however, sewage is sometimes still

Shipping and industry are major sources of water pollution.

discharged into septic systems in the ground, which have to be cleaned out periodically to prevent overflow. Agricultural pollutants, including chemical fertilizers, pesticides, and animal wastes, may be carried into streams and rivers by rain and melting snow.

There are three main ways of dealing with water pollution: pretreatment of industrial wastes, sewage treatment, and government standards for water quality. Pretreating industrial wastes means that companies remove the harmful chemicals before they discharge any water into a stream or river. Sewage treatment by waste-treatment plants can be very effective in removing pollution, though some chemicals may remain. Government standards set limits on how many of these chemicals can be in the water. In 1974, the U.S. government passed the Safe Drinking Water Act, which gave the ENVIRONMENTAL PROTECTION AGENCY (EPA) authority to set standards for public water systems in the United States.

☀ Fast Facts

Throwing trash into waterways not only pollutes water but can also harm animals. Plastic bags can kill fish and other aquatic animals that swallow them accidentally or because they think they are food. Birds and other animals can also get entangled in the plastic holders used with six-packs of canned soda, causing them to starve to death or drown.

WATER QUALITY AND TREATMENT

Process to improve the quality of water. Good water quality is essential to the health of all plant and animal ECOSYSTEMS. Water quality and treatment is thus a vital environmental issue. Water officials determine water quality by testing it regularly. In most cases, water must be treated in some way before it can be consumed by humans. Sewage, or wastewater, must also be treated so it does not contaminate DRINKING WATER or the environment.

All water naturally has various organic and inorganic materials dissolved in it. To make it fit for drinking, water must go through a series of processes before it is released into the water supply for communities. First, the water is drawn from a source and pumped to a treatment plant. There it flows into tanks where heavy particles called "sediment" settle to the bottom. Fine particles may not settle out of the water, thus leaving the water cloudy. These fine particles are cleaned out by adding a chemical called a "coagulant." The coagulant forms a jellylike substance that picks up the particles and causes them to settle out.

Other elements and chemicals may be added to water to remove a bad taste or odor. Chlorine is usually added to disinfect water by killing harmful organisms. Sometimes chemical softeners are added to "hard" water that has a high mineral content. Fluoride is often added to water because it prevents cavities in teeth. The treated water finally passes through a filter made up of sand, gravel, and carbon that removes any remaining particles.

Wastewater, or sewage, must also be treated. In the United States and other developed countries, wastewater treatment is a major factor in reducing diseases such as cholera, typhoid, and dysentery. Elsewhere, however, contaminated water causes deadly sickness of epidemic proportions. Poorly treated water can contaminate reservoirs and GROUNDWATER, which provide drinking water. Untreated sewage can also seep into the ground and contaminate groundwater.

Scientists and engineers have designed and built sewage treatment plants that remove harmful wastes from used water, and some communities are trying to reuse sewage water that has been treated. In a process called "aeration," purification plants spray water through the air so that oxygen will remove bad odors from it. Sunlight and heat are used to destroy harmful BACTERIA. Then the water goes through the usual purification processes.

Water containing chemicals from factories also must be treated. Before the Clean Water Act was passed in the United States in 1972, industries often dumped chemical waste directly into nearby rivers and lakes. The law stated that water quality was to be improved, regardless of what it cost. Every city in the United States was required to build a wastewater treatment plant. Today, industries must build water-treatment systems before dumping water into the environment.

Another form of water treatment is "desalination," or removing salt from water. Ninety-seven percent of all water on earth is in the oceans. Seawater is undrinkable and cannot be used to irrigate crops or in factories. Scientists have developed ways to desalt the water so it can be used by humans. This is especially useful in areas where natural sources of freshwater are scarce or do not exist. Desalination is also carried out in water-treatment facilities on ships.

WATER RIGHTS

Legal rights to use water from a river, LAKE, reservoir, or other water supply. Water rights govern how water is used, who may use it, and how much may be taken from the supply. The legal system of water rights controls the use of water so that all people and animals can share water resources. Water rights are especially important in the arid parts of the southwestern United States, where there are few sources of surface water.

Under water right laws, landowners are sometimes not allowed to use water flowing on their land if other landowners have need for it as well. Water rights have generally been of most concern in agricultural areas where farmers divert water to irrigate their fields. As population increased and more farmers, industries, and individuals began to need water, more complex rules were developed to decide how the water would be used.

Traditionally, farmers were allowed to divert water to irrigate their fields and then return the water that had not been absorbed back to the river. When farmers began to use more FERTILIZERS, water returning to streams from farmers' fields contained a high level of pollutants. Now other laws and regulations govern how clean water must be before it can be returned to a river, stream, or other water supply.

In some areas, growing populations have reduced water supplies to dangerous levels. When a river no longer has water, the plants, fish, or other animals living in it die. In addition, when very little water flows in a stream or lake, even small amounts of WATER POLLUTION can cause high concentrations of toxic chemicals. Such problems are also a concern of modern water rights laws.

W
X
Y
Z

WATER TABLE

The upper limit of GROUNDWATER within the earth's crust. The water table can change over time. If the water table drops, it means that water that has been drawn out of the ground has not been replaced by natural processes. Sometimes land will crack and sink if the water table drops too low. This can cause buildings, roads, and underground pipes to shift and break. Near the ocean, missing freshwater may be replaced by saltwater, harming supplies of DRINKING WATER. Some municipalities try to find ways to replace groundwater with water from other places in order to ensure an adequate supply of drinking water.

WATERSHED

An area of land drained by a river, stream, or LAKE. When rain and other forms of PRECIPITATION fall over land, some of the water soaks into the ground and replenishes supplies of GROUNDWATER. The rest, called SURFACE WATER, flows across the surface of the land and enters small streams. These streams flow into larger streams and rivers, which eventually empty into the oceans. A watershed is the total area of land drained by a single system of interconnecting streams and rivers, called a RIVER SYSTEM. A watershed can be quite small or very large. The watershed of the Amazon River, for example, covers much of SOUTH AMERICA.

In most watersheds, water moves slowly into the ground. Sometimes, however, it remains in ponds and lakes, where it helps to sustain plant and animal life. When rain falls in a watershed, some of the water returns to the ☑ ATMOSPHERE through the process of **evaporation**. The rest soaks into the ground through tiny channels in the SOIL and is absorbed by plant roots.

The soil in a healthy ECOSYSTEM is filled with many holes and spaces that absorb water. This water contributes to the WATER TABLE. The amount of water in the water table varies with the seasons and depends upon the amount of precipitation that falls. During heavy rains, the ground sometimes cannot soak up all the water, and much of it flows into streams.

Humans can disturb watersheds when they clear FORESTS for agriculture or allow grazing animals to eat away grasses. Such activities decrease soil quality by removing important ☑ **nutrients** and contributing to EROSION. In unhealthy ecosystems, mud may clog the channels in the soil, causing the water to soak more slowly into the ground. On flat land, excess surface water collects in pools. In sloped areas, it races downhill. This moving water can uproot grasses and small plants and carry away rich soil.

The chances of flooding are increased when a watershed is disturbed because more water remains on the surface. This water flows into streams and rivers, causing them to overflow their banks. The water table is also changed because water is prevented from fully soaking into the ground. To prevent such problems, humans have adopted techniques to manage watershed. Watershed management is also essential for protecting the health of ecosystems, maintaining the quality of soils, and preserving supplies of fresh DRINKING WATER. [See also SOIL CONSERVATION; WATER CYCLE; WATER QUALITY AND TREATMENT.]

WEATHER

(See CLIMATE AND WEATHER)

WETLANDS

Areas of land that have a water level near or above the surface of the ground. There are three main types of wetlands: SWAMP, MARSHES, and bogs. The differences among the three are not exact. Sometimes different terms are used to describe the same place.

Generally, wetlands are defined by the types of SOIL found there and the kinds of vegetation they support. Some wetlands are coastal—that is, they are located near the sea. Others lie inland. The different kinds of wet-

---

☑ **Keywords**

Evaporation. Process by which a liquid, such as water, changes to a gas.

Nutrients. Substances such as food, water, oxygen, and nitrogen that are necessary for life.

lands provide HABITATS for a wide variety of plants and animals including various species of BIRDS, MAMMALS, AMPHIBIANS, REPTILES, and INSECTS. Many wildflowers also like the wet environment of wetlands.

Swamps are areas that are usually saturated (drenched) with water and whose vegetation (plant life) is mainly woody plants, such as trees and shrubs. Any plant that grows in a swamp must have the ability to survive with its roots underwater for long periods of time. One such plant is the MANGROVE. In a mangrove swamp, which is a coastal wetland, the trees or shrubs send out many roots to form a dense mass. This not only helps the plants to stay upright, but it also keeps the coastline from eroding.

A marsh is similar to a swamp, but its vegetation is mainly grasses or sedges. A bog may appear fairly dry, with only shallow areas of water, but its surface is spongy and wet to the touch. A plant commonly found in bogs is sphagnum moss. Other kinds of wetland include salt marshes, which are flatlands that are flooded periodically by saltwater, and ESTUARIES which are areas where saltwater from the ocean meets the freshwater from a river flowing into the sea.

Wetlands are necessary to the survival of many plant and animal species. They are also important for flood control and water storage. Wetlands act as natural storage areas for rainfall. They hold excess water, gradually releasing

		1780s	1980s
	Alaska	45%	45%
	Florida	54%	30%
	Georgia	18%	14%
	Louisiana	52%	28%
	Maine	30%	24%
State Area	Michigan	30%	15%
Covered by	Minnesota	28%	16%
Wetlands	North Carolina	33%	17%
(in percentages)	Texas	9%	4%
	Wisconsin	27%	14%

it into nearby streams and rivers and allowing it to seep slowly into the ground.

Many wetlands in the United States have been lost because they were filled in for use as farmland, commercial sites, and residential areas. Government programs are being developed to preserve the remaining wetlands. However, many wetlands are still being lost to agriculture and commercial development. There has also been increasing interest in using wetlands for the treatment of human wastes since scientists discovered that some plants can filter out pollutants. Wetland restoration may someday make up for some of the loss of wetlands over the years.

WHALES

Large MARINE MAMMALS, some species of which are the largest of all the marine creatures. Superficially, whales resemble FISH. But whales are actually warm-blooded mammals that breathe air through lungs, nurse their young on milk, and move their tails up and down instead of side to side when they swim. There are about 75 SPECIES AND SUBSPECIES of whales, and they include dolphins and porpoises. All are called cetaceans, and they are divided into two groups: the toothed whales and the baleen whales. Instead of teeth, the baleen whales have a system of horny plates called baleen that they use to filter PLANKTON and other small organisms from the water.

The vast majority of cetaceans are toothed whales, which vary in size from 6-foot (1.8-m) harbor porpoises to sperm whales that can grow to 55 feet (16.7 m) in length and weigh nearly 45 tons (41 metric tons). Among the more unusual toothed whales are two Arctic species: the narwhal, which has a single ivory tusk that grows

Profile: Marjory Stoneman Douglas

Marjorie Stoneman Douglas led the fight to preserve the Florida Everglades. In 1947 she helped get nearly 1,6 million acres (648,000 hectares) designated as Everglades National Park. That same year Douglas published the book *The Everglades: River of Grass*, a history of this huge wetlands ecosystem. Until then the Everglades region had been considered a wasteland that should be drained and converted into farm land. Douglas explained in the book that the Everglades is really a wide river of shallow water that flows slowly southward and is an important habitat for many species of wildlife. Douglas continued working to protect the Everglades until her death in 1998, at the age of 108.

WXYZ

Many species of whale have the ability to leap far out of the water.

almost eight feet (2.4 m) straight out from its head, and the beluga, a white whale with a large rounded forehead. Belugas that live in the St. Lawrence region of eastern Canada have been found to have high levels of toxic chemicals in their bodies, and scientists believe that OCEAN POLLUTION has harmed many of these whales. Toothed whales actively hunt fish, squid, and other prey. The familiar black-and-white killer whales, also called orcas, hunt animals as big as sea lions and penguins.

There are about ten species of baleen whales. Although they feed only on relatively small organisms, some baleen whales grow quite large, such as the endangered blue whale. The baleen plates are made up of a material called keratin—the same substance that is in human hair and fingernails and a rhinoceros's horn. These flexible baleen plates hang down from the inside of the whales' upper lip, filtering plankton as the whales swim slowly through the water with their mouth open.

Whales are found in all the world's oceans and even in a few rivers. The pink river dolphin, for example, lives in the Amazon and other rivers of South America. Many whales live and migrate in well-organized social groups, called pods. Some species, such as the gray whale, migrate thousands of miles each year from feeding grounds in the Northern Hemisphere to breeding and calving grounds in the Southern

Endangered Species: Blue Whale

The largest species of whale and the largest creature ever to inhabit the earth, the blue whale can grow to 100 feet (30 m) in length and weigh as much as 300,000 pounds (136,000 kg). Blue whales live in all the earth's oceans. Most populations of blue whales migrate from the tropics in the winter to the edges of ice in the northern and southern hemispheres in the summer. Blue whales were nearly hunted to extinction for their oil, meat, and other products. Although protected by law, they are still a threatened species.

Hemisphere. Whales have excellent hearing, and they can produce sounds underwater. Humpback whales produce sounds in a certain order, much like a song, which they repeat. These "songs" can last 20 minutes, and they are usually sung in the winter mating grounds. All of the whales in a migrating group sing almost the same song, which changes progressively from year to year.

Humans have hunted whales for centuries. In the 1800s, a huge whaling industry killed whales to provide oil for lamps and spermaceti, a thick liquid that was used to make fine candles. Though most large whales are now scarce and many species are protected by law, whales are still killed for their meat by Native Americans and by several nations.

WILDERNESS

An area where the earth and its ECOSYSTEMS are undisturbed by man. It is difficult to find a place that has not been changed in some way by humans. Even the barren ICE of the ARCTIC and ANTARCTICA bears evidence of humans. Today, there probably is no true wilderness left anywhere on the planet.

Wilderness areas provide HABITATS for wild animals and plants and protect the country's natural resources, such as water and soil. Henry David Thoreau's famous words, "in wildness is the preservation of the world," express the tremendous emotional, intellectual, and spiritual value of wild lands.

WILDLIFE MANAGEMENT

Managing and protecting the health, population, and environment of wild animals and their ECOSYSTEMS. In the United States, the U.S. FISH AND WILDLIFE SERVICE and similar state agencies govern wildlife management. These agencies enforce national, state, and local laws that concern wildlife.

During the 1960s, CONSERVATION an important focus of wildlife management. In 1964, the U.S. Congress passed two laws—the Wilderness Act and the Water Conservation Fund Act—to protect the forest lands where many wild animals and plants live. The Endangered Species Act, passed in 1973, was also aimed at stopping the rapid loss of plant and animal life. In addition to government agencies, many other organizations help to manage the nation's wildlife by teaching about wildlife issues, threats to particular animals or areas of wilderness, and how they can live in harmony with wildlife. [*See also* WILDLIFE REFUGES.]

WILDLIFE REFUGES

Areas of land set aside for the protection and preservation of wild animals. In 1908 President Theodore Roosevelt realized the importance of protecting wildlife and set up the nation's system of NATIONAL PARKS, NATIONAL FORESTS, and wildlife refuges or reserves. Though

W X Y Z

National Parks and National Forests protect wildlife inside their boundaries, wildlife refuges are specifically designed to provide protected habitat for animals.

In 1997, President Bill Clinton signed the National Wildlife Refuge System Act. This law builds on the National Wildlife Refuge System Administration Act of 1966, and other past wildlife refuge laws.

The National Wildlife Refuge System has been managed by the U.S. FISH AND WILDLIFE SERVICE for more than a century. The system has 503 refuges nationwide, with more than 93 million acres (37,665,000 hectares) of land for big game (such as BISON, bighorn sheep, and elk); small game; waterfowl; and nongame birds such as pelicans, terns, and gulls. The refuges are home to millions of migratory BIRDS and hundreds of ENDANGERED SPECIES.

Wildlife refuges have also been established by individuals and conservation organizations such as the Nature Conservancy. Other countries also maintain parks, refuges, and game preserves. [*See also* WILDLIFE MANAGEMENT.]

WILDLIFE TRADE, INTERNATIONAL

The business of buying and selling wild animals, their parts, and their products on the world market. People have always traded wild animals for food and other purposes. Many species have been driven to EXTINCTION by commercial interests.

WIND-GENERATED ENERGY

Energy created by the force of the wind. The wind's energy has been used for hundreds of years to propel ships, pump water, grind grain, and other activities.

Today, wind is becoming an increasingly important source of electric energy. Electricity is created when wind moves the wheel of a wind turbine, which runs a generator to covert the force into electricity. Electricity made this way creates no pollution and is a renewable energy source, compared to the tra-

ditional way of creating electricity by burning coal. Coal-burning power plants are the largest source of AIR POLLUTION in the United States, contributing to global warming, ACID RAIN, and smog.

Using wind turbines to create energy is most common in areas that are less populated and have strong consistent winds. In the United States, 90 percent of the electricity produced by wind comes from three large wind farms in California. Wind farms must be placed carefully, since they can disrupt the flight of birds migrating through the area. [*See also* ALTERNATIVE ENERGY SOURCES.]

WOLF, GRAY

A large, powerful canine, or member of the dog family. The gray wolf was once the most spread mammal (except for humans) outside the tropics and was greatly feared. Now the gray wolf is at risk, as human persecution and destruction of HABITATS have reduced its numbers. Today the gray wolf lives in Eastern European forests, mountain refuges in the Mediterranean region, mountains and semi-deserts in the Middle East, and wilderness areas of Asia and North America.

The gray wolf is an intelligent, social animal. Wolves live in packs, or family groups, of 7 to 20 animals. Pack size depends on the prey available—larger packs are seen where the prey is moose, and smaller packs are found in deer

Wolves typically roam in packs, which allows them to overpower many types of prey.

country. Where prey is scarce, a lone wolf may travel alone. The highly organized wolf pack hunts as a unit, cooperating to run down its prey. Wolves also eat smaller animals and plants, and may attack livestock.

Gray wolves mate for life. They breed in winter and produce four to seven pups. The pack cares for the pups until they can travel with the adults. In the wild, wolves live up to 16 years; in captivity they may live 20 years.

Most people today know wolves do not hunt humans, but the animals are still threatened by ranchers, herders, and others who fear attacks on their livestock or want to expand into the wolves' territories. Despite objections from such groups, gray wolf populations have been reestablished in areas such as Yellowstone National Park, to ensure their survival.

WOODPECKER, RED-COCKADED

Small, sharp-beaked, black and white bird. The adult male red-cockaded woodpecker has a rarely seen red spot or streak (the cockade) on each side of its black head. While other woodpeckers roost in dead or decaying trees, the red-cockaded woodpecker makes its home in living pine trees. It pecks out or excavates a cavity in the trunk where a family group—a male, a female, chicks, and some young adult helpers—roosts.

The red-cockaded woodpecker was once found from New Jersey to Florida, and westward through Kentucky, Tennessee, Missouri, Oklahoma, and Texas. However, as a result of LOGGING and the spread of agriculture, the population of these birds has declined. They are now considered an ENDANGERED SPECIES. To help their recovery, conservationists are using varied strategies, including providing protected HABITATS in National Forests, resettling groups of birds, creating artificial nesting cavities, and working to preserve remaining habitats.

ZOOPLANKTON

(*See* PLANKTON)

ZOOS AND AQUARIUMS

Collections of living animals, usually for public display. Zoos or zoological parks, mainly exhibit terrestrial, or land-based, animals. Aquariums feature animals that live in MARINE ECOSYSTEMS and AQUATIC HABITATS.

Zoos and aquariums had their beginnings in ancient times. The rulers of ancient China gathered animals and put them in cages for viewing. The world's first formal zoo was built by Queen Hatshepsut of Egypt in the fifteenth century B.C. The first operating zoo in the United States was started in New York City's Central Park, about the year 1873.

During their early history, zoos kept animals in barred cages. But in 1907, a zoo in Stellingen, Germany, exhibited animals in mixed groups in open displays without cages. The animals and visitors were separated by deep moats. It was the first time wild animals were seen in HABITATS that resembled the areas in which they live in nature. This revolutionary idea of zoo design eventually spread throughout EUROPE, NORTH AMERICA, and elsewhere. Today, most zoological institutions have replaced barred cages with habitats that resemble tropical RAIN FORESTS, SAVANNAS, CORAL REEFS, and other ECOSYSTEMS.

The world s first aquarium was built in London in 1853. Others were soon built in Paris, France, and Berlin, Germany. Marineland, near St. Augustine, Florida, opened in 1938, and since then, most aquariums have been located on an ocean or bay and feature outdoor pools and aquatic environments. The Tennessee Aquarium, which opened in Chattanooga in 1992, is the first predominantly freshwater aquarium in the United States.

Beginning in the late 1960s, zoos and aquariums realized that many of the animals they were collecting for their exhibits were disappearing in the wild because of habitat destruction, overhunting for meat and trophies, and human population expansion. Zoo and aquarium biologists became active in forming captive breeding programs for rare and ENDANGERED SPECIES. Today, many North American zoos and aquariums have captive-breeding and conservation programs. Some species, such as the Mongolian wild horse, exist only in zoos and protected reserves.

W X Y Z

SELECTED BIBLIOGRAPHY

Abbey, Edward. *Desert Solitaire*. New York: McGraw-Hill, 1968.

——. *The Monkey Wrench Gang*. Philadelphia: Lippincott, 1975.

Allaby, Michael. *The Concise Oxford Dictionary of Ecology*. New York: Oxford University Press, 1994.

Attenborough, David. *Life on Earth: A Natural History*. Boston: Little, Brown and Co., 1979.

Audubon Nature Encyclopedia. Philadelphia: Curtis Books, 1965.

Behler, John, and Deborah Behler. *Alligators and Crocodiles*. Stillwater, Minn.: Voyageurs Press, 1998.

Beston, Henry. *The Outermost House*. New York: Rinehart, 1949.

Blashfield, Jean F. *Rescuing Endangered Species*. Chicago: Children's Press, 1994.

Botkin, Daniel B., and Edward Keller. *Environmental Science: Earth as a Living Planet*. New York: John Wiley and Sons, 1995.

Bowler, Peter J. *The Norton History of the Environmental Sciences*. New York: W. W. Norton, 1992.

Brewer, Richard. *Principles of Ecology*. Philadelphia: Saunders College Publishing, 1979.

Brown, Lauren. *Grasslands*. Audubon Society Nature Guide. New York: Alfred A. Knopf, 1985.

Brusca, Richard C., and Gary J. Brusca. *Invertebrates*. Sunderland, Mass.: Sinauer Associates, 1990.

Campbell, Neil A. *Biology*. Menlo Park, Calif.: Benjamin/Cummings Publishing, 1987.

Caras, Roger A. *North American Mammals*. New York: Meredith Press, 1967.

Carson, Rachel. *Silent Spring*. New York: Fawcett Crest, 1964.

——. *The Sea Around Us*. New York: Oxford University Press, 1961.

Corson, Walter H., ed. *Global Ecology Handbook*. Boston: Beacon Press, 1990.

Cousteau, Jacques-Yves, and Philippe Diole. *Life and Death in a Coral Sea*. New York: Doubleday, 1971.

——. *The Whale: Mighty Monarch of the Sea*. New York: Doubleday, 1972.

Cronon, William. *Changes in the Land*. New York: Hill and Wang, 1983.

Darwin, Charles. *On the Origin of Species*. London: John Murray, 1859.

Dashefsky, H. Steven. *Environmental Literacy*. New York: Random House, 1993.

Dubos, René. *Health and Disease*. New York: Time-Life Books, 1965.

Duedall, Iver W., et. al., eds. *Wastes in the Ocean*. New York: John Wiley and Sons, 1985.

Ehrlich, Paul R., and Jonathan Roughgarden. *The Science of Ecology*. New York: Macmillan, 1987.

Fleisher, Paul. *Ecology A to Z*. New York: Dillon Press, 1994.

Franck, Irene, and David Brownstone. *The Green Encyclopedia*. New York: Prentice-Hall, 1992.

Fricke, Hans W. *The Coral Seas*. New York: G.P. Putnam's Sons, 1973.

George, Uwe. *In the Deserts of This Earth*. New York: Harcourt Brace Jovanovich, 1977.

Gore, Albert, Jr. *Earth in the Balance*. New York: Plume, 1992.

Goudie, Andrew. *The Human Impact on the Natural Environment*. Cambridge, Mass.: The MIT Press, 1994.

Gross, Grant M. *Oceanography: A View of the Earth*. Englewood Cliffs, N.J.: Prentice-Hall, 1977.

Groves, Donald G. *Ocean World Encyclopedia*. New York: McGraw-Hill, 1980.

Gutnik, Martin J., and Natalie Browne-Gutnik. *Great Barrier Reef*. Austin: Raintree/Steck-Vaughn Publishers, 1995.

Hanik, Dr. V., and Dr. V. Mazak. *Illustrated Encyclopedia of Mammals*. Secaucus, N.J.: Chartwell Books, 1979.

Harms, Valerie, et. al. *Almanac of the Earth: The Ecology of Everyday Life*. National Audubon Society. New York: G. P. Putnam's Sons, 1994.

Hazen, Robert M., and James Trefil. *Science Matters: Achieving Scientific Literacy*. New York: Anchor Books, 1991.

Jonas, Gerald. *The Living Earth Book of North American Trees*. Pleasantville, N.Y.: Reader's Digest, 1993.

Jones, Gareth, Alan Robertson, Jean Forbes, and Graham Hollier. *Dictionary of Environmental Science*. New York: HarperCollins, 1993.

Kellert, Stephen R., ed. *Macmillan Encyclopedia of the Environment.* New York: Simon & Schuster Macmillan, 1997.

Krebs, Charles J. *The Message of Ecology.* New York: HarperCollins, 1988.

Leopold, Aldo. *A Sand County Almanac.* New York: Oxford University Press, 1949.

Ley, Willy. *The Drifting Continents.* New York: Weybright and Talley, Inc., 1969.

——. *The Poles.* New York: Time-Life Books, 1962.

Library of Pittsburgh, comp. *The Handy Science Answer Book.* Detroit: Visible Ink, 1994.

Little, Charles E. *The Dying of the Trees.* New York: Penguin Books, 1995.

Lovelock, J. E. *Gaia: A New Look at Life on Earth.* Oxford: Oxford University Press, 1979.

Lutgens, Frederick K., and Edward J. Tarbuck. *The Atmosphere.* 2d ed. Englewood Cliffs, N.J.: Prentice-Hall, 1982.

MacDonald, Dr. David. *Encyclopedia of Mammals.* New York: Facts on File, 1984.

Miller, G. Tyler, Jr. *Living in the Environment.* 8th ed. Belmont, Calif.: Wadsworth Publishing, 1994.

Miller, Kenton, and Laura Tangley. *Trees of Life.* Boston: Boston University Press, 1991.

Minasian, Stanley M., Kenneth C. Balcomb, III, and Larry Foster. *The World's Whales.* Washington, D.C.: Smithsonian Books, 1984.

Naar, Jon. *Design for a Livable Planet.* New York: Harper & Row, 1990.

Naar, Jon, and Alex J. Naar. *This Land is Your Land: A Guide to North America's Endangered Ecosystems.* New York: HarperCollins, 1993.

National Parks and Conservation Association. *Our Endangered Parks: What You Can Do to Protect Our National Heritage.* San Francisco: Foghorn Press, 1994.

Nebel, Bernard J., and Richard T. Wright. *Environmental Science: The Way the World Works.* 5th ed. Upper Saddle River, N.J.: Prentice-Hall, 1996.

Noss, Reed F., and Allen Y. Cooperrider. *Saving Nature's Legacy: Protecting and Restoring Biodiversity.* Washington, D.C.: Island Press, 1994.

Nowak, Richard M. *Walker's Mammals of the World.* 5th ed. Baltimore: The John Hopkins University Press, 1991.

Odum, Eugene. *Basic Ecology.* Philadelphia: Saunders College Publishing, 1983.

——. *Ecology and Our Endangered Life-Support Systems.* 2d ed. Sunderland, Mass.: Sinauer Associates, 1993.

Page, Jake. *Arid Lands.* Alexandria, Va.: Time-Life Books, 1984.

Patent, Dorothy Hinshaw. *Biodiversity.* New York: Clarion Books, 1996.

——. *The Challenge of Extinction.* Hillside, N.J.: Enslow Publishers, Inc., 1991.

Press, Frank, and Raymond Siever. *Understanding Earth.* 2d. ed. New York: W. H. Freeman and Company, 1998.

Schmidt-Nielsen, Knut. *How Animals Work.* Cambridge: Cambridge University Press, 1972.

Soule, Michael, and Bruce Wilcox, eds. *Conservation Biology.* Sunderland, Mass.: Sinauer Associates, 1980.

Steger, Will. *Saving the Earth: A Citizen's Guide to Environmental Action.* New York: Alfred A. Knopf, 1990.

Strahler, Arthur N., and Alan H. Strahler. *Elements of Physical Geography.* 3d ed. New York: John Wiley and Sons, 1984.

Talbot, Dr. Frank H., ed. *Under the Sea.* Alexandria, Va.: Time-Life Books, 1995.

Thoreau, Henry David. *Walden.* Boston: Ticknor and Fields, 1862.

Time-Life Books Editors. *Grasslands and Tundra.* Alexandria, Va.: Time-Life Books, 1985.

Tyning, T. F. *A Guide to Amphibians and Reptiles.* Boston: Little, Brown and Co., 1990.

Westman, Walter E. *Ecology, Impact Assessment, and Environmental Planning.* New York: John Wiley and Sons, 1985.

Whitfield, Dr. Philip. *Macmillan Illustrated Animal Encyclopedia.* New York: Macmillian, 1984.

Whitney, Stephen. *Western Forests.* Audubon Society Nature Guide. New York: Alfred A. Knopf, 1985.

Wilson, Edward O. *The Diversity of Life.* New York: W. W. Norton, 1992.

Wilson, Roberta, and James Q. Wilson. *Watching Fishes: Life and Behavior on Coral Reefs.* New York: Harper and Row, 1985.

ORGANIZATIONS AND AGENCIES

African Wildlife Foundation
1400 16th Street NW
Washington, DC 20036
(202) 939-3333
www.awf.org

Alliance to Save Energy
1200 18th Street NW, Suite 900
Washington, DC 20036
(202) 857-0666
www.ase.org

American Rivers
1025 Vermont Avenue NW, Suite 720
Washington, DC 20005
(202) 347-9224
www.amrivers.org

Americans for the Environment
1400 16th Street NW, Box 24
Washington, DC 20036
(202) 797-6665
www.afore.org

Bureau of Land Management
Department of the Interior
18th and C Streets NW
Washington, DC 20240
(202) 452-0330
www.blm.gov

Center For Environmental Information
55 Saint Paul Street
Rochester, NY 14604
(716) 262-2870
www.epa.gov/ceis

Center for Marine Conservation
1725 Desales Street NW, Suite 600
Washington, DC 20036
(202) 429-5609
www.cmc-ocean.org

Clean Water Action
4455 Connecticut Avenue NW
Washington, DC 20008
(202) 895-0420
www.cleanwateraction.org

Conservation International
2501 M Street NW, Suite 200
Washington, DC 20037
(202) 429-5660
www.conservation.org

Defenders of Wildlife
1101 14th Street NW, Suite 1400
Washington, DC 20005
(202) 682-9400
www.defenders.org

Earth Island Institute
300 Broadway, Suite 28
San Francisco, CA 94133
(415) 788-3666
www.earthisland.org

Earthwatch
680 Mount Auburn Street
P.O. Box 9104
Watertown, MA 02471-9104
(617) 926-8200
www.earthwatch.org

Environmental Defense Fund
257 Park Avenue South, 16th Floor
New York, NY 10010
(212) 505-2100
www.edf.org

Environmental Protection Agency
401 M Street SW
Washington, DC 20460
(202) 260-2090
www.epa.gov

Fish and Wildlife Service
Department of the Interior
Main Interior Building
1849 C Street NW
Washington, DC 20420
(202) 208-4131
www.fws.gov

Forest Service
Department for Agriculture
14th Street and Independence Avenue SW
P.O. Box 96090
Washington, DC 20090-6090
(202) 205-0957
www.fs.fed.us

Friends of the Earth
1025 Vermont Avenue NW, Suite 300
Washington, DC 20005
(202) 783-7400
www.foe.org

Greenpeace USA
1436 U Street NW
Washington, DC 20009
(202) 462-1177
www.greenpeaceusa.org

Humane Society of the United States
2100 L Street NW
Washington, DC 20037
(202) 452-1100
www.hsus.org

League of Conservation Voters
1707 L Street NW, Suite 750
Washington, DC 20036
(202) 785-8683
www.lcv.org

Marine Mammal Center
Marin Headlands
Golden Gate National Recreation Area
1065 Fort Cronkhite
Sausalito, CA 94965
(415) 289-7325
www.tmmc.org

National Audubon Society
700 Broadway
New York, NY 10003
(212) 979-3000
www.audubon.org

National Geographic Society
1145 17th Street NW
Washington, DC 20036
(212) 857-7000
www.nationalgeographic.com

National Oceanic and Atmospheric Administration
Department of Commerce
14th Street and Constitution Avenue NW
Washington, DC 20230
(202) 482-2291
www.noaa.gov

National Parks and Conservation Association
1776 Massachusetts Avenue NW
Washington, DC 20036
(800) 628-7275
www.npca.org

National Park Service
Department of the Interior
Main Interior Building
1849 C Street NW
Washington, DC 20240
(202) 208-3100
www.nps.gov

National Wildlife Federation
8925 Leesburg Pike
Vienna, VA 22184
(800) 822-9919
www.nwf.org

Nature Conservancy
4245 North Fairfax Drive, Suite 100
Arlington, VA 22203
(703) 841-5300
www.tnc.org

Population Action International
1120 19th Street NW, Suite 550
Washington, DC 20036
(202) 659-1833
www.populationaction.org

Rainforest Alliance
65 Bleecker Street, 6th Floor
New York, NY 10012-2420
(212) 677-1900
www.rainforest-alliance.org

Rocky Mountain Institute
1739 Snowmass Creek Road
Snowmass, Colorado 81654
(970) 927-3851
www.rmi.org

School for Field Studies
16 Broadway
Beverly, MA 01915
(978) 927-7777
www.fieldstudies.org

Sierra Club
85 Second Street
San Francisco, CA 94105
(415) 977-5500
www.sierraclub.org

Soil and Water Conservation Society
7515 Northeast Ankeny Road
Ankeny, IA 50021
(515) 289-2331
www.swcs.org

Student Conservation Association, Inc.
P.O. Box 550
Charlestown, NH 03603
(603) 543-1700
www.sca-inc.org

Wilderness Society
900 17th Street NW
Washington, DC 20006
(800) 843-9453
www.wilderness.org

Wildlife Conservation Society
2300 Southern Boulevard
Bronx, NY 10460
(718) 220-6891
www.wcs.org

Wildlife Society
5410 Grosvenor Lane
Bethesda, MD 20814
(301) 897-9770
www.wildlife.org

Worldwatch Institute
1776 Massachusetts Avenue NW
Washington, DC 20036
(202) 452-1999
www.worldwatch.org

World Resources Institute
10 G Street NW, Suite 800
Washington, DC 20002
(202) 729-7600
www.wri.org

World Wildlife Fund
1250 24th Street NW, Suite 400
Washington, DC 20037
(202) 293-4800
www.worldwildlife.org

INDEX

Page numbers that appear in boldface type indicate where main topics can be found. Those page numbers set in italics indicate the presence of a photograph or drawing for a topic. And names set in italics indicate a special feature box for a biographical profile or an endangered species.